MODERN HUMANITIES RESEARCH
CRITICAL TEXTS
VOLUME 67

APHRA BEHN'S *EMPEROR OF THE MOON*
AND ITS FRENCH SOURCE
ARLEQUIN, EMPEREUR DANS LA LUNE

Aphra Behn's
Emperor of the Moon
and its French Source
Arlequin, Empereur dans la lune

Edited and translated
with critical notes by
Judy A. Hayden *and* Daniel J. Worden

Modern Humanities Research Association
Critical Texts 67
2019

Published by

The Modern Humanities Research Association
Salisbury House
Station Road
Cambridge CB1 2LA
United Kingdom

First published 2019

ISBN 978-1-78188-885-8

CONTENTS

ILLUSTRATIONS

Cover: From *Arlequin, Empereur dans la lune*. Published in Tome I of Evaristo Gherardi's *Le Théâtre Italien de Gherardi, ou le Recueil général de toutes les comédies et scènes françaises jouées par les comédiens italiens du roi, pendant tout le temps qu'ils ont été au service* (Paris: J. B. Cusson et P. Witte, 1700). By permission of the Bibliothèque nationale de France.

1.1: Title page to Aphra Behn's *Emperor of the Moon* (1687). RB 112066. The Huntington Library, San Marino, California.

1.2: Title page to *Arlequin, Empereur dans la lune*, by Monsieur D***. From the Garnier edition published in Troyes. By permission of the Bibliothèque nationale de France.

ACKNOWLEDGMENTS

We would like to thank the staff of those libraries and archives who provided us with their learned expertise as we worked to bring this project to fruition, particularly the Huntington Library in San Marino, California, the Bibliothèque nationale de France, and the British Library in London.

Colleagues, friends and family have also been of particular support as this project of many years finally comes into being. Judy Hayden would like to thank the University of Tampa for a grant that assisted in the research for this book, and the Dean in the College of Arts and Letters at the University of Tampa, Dr David Gudelunas, who managed to find financial resources as she neared the end of this journey. Colleagues and friends were always willing to offer a supporting shoulder, but she would particularly like to recognise her colleague and friend, Professor Emma Rees at the University of Chester, who championed her through the lean periods as well as those productive ones. And finally, she would like to thank her family, Tamara and Barney, Alex, Ethel, Sebastian, and Mikaila, who encouraged her with each new find, who supported her in those twelve-hour days of writing and revising, and who ignored her when it was necessary, particularly through those hours of heavy sighs and groaning — and perhaps a whimper or two.

Daniel J. Worden would like to thank Kristin for her support at many stages of the project, from New Jersey to Oregon to South Carolina. At Reed College, his colleagues Professor Luc Monnin and Professor Hugh Hochman deserve many thanks for their guidance and camaraderie. He would like to recognize his former student at Furman University, Ashton Nicewonger, for her diligent assistance in working with the Garnier edition of *Arlequin, Empereur dans la lune*. The conversations with friends and family beneath the Moon, on the *terrain de pétanque*, and alongside the redwoods have made this work possible.

Lastly, we must admit that we have no cats to accuse of lying or walking on keyboards nor parrots nor cockatiels who, when we were absent from the room, pecked at keys and thus made unobserved additions or deletions to the text. Frankly, we have no one to charge for any errors in this text — except ourselves, for which we must take the unhappy credit and apologize profusely.

PERMISSIONS

Fatouville, Anne Mauduit de [Monsieur D***], *Arlequin, Empereur dans la lune* (Troyes: Garnier, n.d.), by permission of the Bibliothèque nationale de France.

Cover Image, from *Arlequin, Empereur dans la lune* in Tome 1 of Evaristo Gherardi's *Le Théâtre Italien de Gherardi*, by permission of the Bibliothèque nationale de France.

THE AUTHORS/EDITORS

Judy A. Hayden is Professor of English and Director of Women's and Gender Studies at the University of Tampa. She has written extensively on Aphra Behn, seventeenth-century drama, and on women's literature and culture in the seventeenth century. Her recent research explores the interconnection between Restoration science and literature. She has published her work in *English*, *Huntington Library Quarterly*, *Seventeenth Century*, *Philological Review*, and *Studies in English Literature*, for example. She has published *Of Love and War: The Political Voice in the Early Plays of Aphra Behn* (Rodopi, 2010) and has recently edited *Literature in the Age of Celestial Discovery: Copernicus to Flamsteed* (Palgrave, 2016), *Through the Eyes of the Beholder: The Holy Land 1517–1714* with Nabil Matar (Brill, 2013), *Travel Narratives, the New Science, and Literary Discourse 1600–1800* (Ashgate, 2012), and *The New Science and Women's Literary Discourse: Prefiguring Frankenstein* (Palgrave, 2011).

Daniel J. Worden is Assistant Professor of French at Furman University in Greenville, South Carolina. He obtained his PhD in French from Princeton University, having completed a doctoral dissertation on imposture and fiction in the work of Cyrano de Bergerac, Montfaucon de Villars, and Tyssot de Patot. His publications include articles on early modern fantastical travel narratives in French and neo-Baroque aesthetics in contemporary science fiction. He is currently completing essays on fairy tales by Marie-Catherine d'Aulnoy and on the representation of astronomy, poetry, and medicine in Fatouville's *Arlequin, Empereur dans la lune*.

INTRODUCTION

The French playwright Anne Mauduit de Fatouville's (d.1715) *Arlequin, Empereur dans la lune* (1684) proved such a 'highly entertaining comedy' that it attracted 'unusually large crowds', much to the ire of the French troupe in Paris, the *comédiens français*.[1] Aphra Behn's (c.1640–1689) adaptation, *The Emperor of the Moon* (1687), was so popular with audiences that it was restaged well into the eighteenth century, numbering over one hundred performances.[2] Both plays employ *commedia dell'arte*, a highly charged art form that owes its popularity, at least in part, to its engagement with social satire, politics, and polemical debate on numerous issues of contemporary significance. The French language scenes that enliven Fatouville's *Arlequin* are offered here in full in an English translation,[3] while Behn's *Emperor of the Moon* is provided in a comprehensive annotated transcription with a critical analysis. We present for the first time in one volume, then, both Behn's play and Fatouville's French language scenes, which we hope will contribute to further study on Aphra Behn and *commedia dell'arte*.[4]

Fatouville's *Arlequin, Empereur dans la lune* targets scientific language and pretensions as fodder for scatological jokes, bawdy pranks, and physical comedy. Behn reinterprets this material in *The Emperor of the Moon*, using *commedia* to overtly critique her contemporaries' notions of science, particularly astronomy, while covertly staging her political concerns for the state.

1. The Early Modern European Tradition of *Commedia dell'Arte*

From the mid-sixteenth to the late eighteenth centuries, troupes of performers

---

[1]   *French Theatre in the Neo-Classical Era, 1550–1789*, ed. by William D. Howarth and others (Cambridge: Cambridge University Press, 1997), Document 341, p. 323. Anne Mauduit de Fatouville, *Arlequin, Empereur dans la lune. Comédie* (A Troyes: Chez Garnier Imprimeur Libraire, rue du Temple, n.d.).
[2]   Aphra Behn, *The Emperor of the Moon: A Farce* (London: R. Holt for Joseph Knight and Francis Saunders, 1687).
[3]   To differentiate in our discussion of the Harlequin character from the original French scenes and Behn's English adaptation, we have used throughout our critical discussion 'Arlequin' in reference to the French scenes and 'Harlequin' in reference to the English farce. *Arlequin* italicised is a reference to the French text itself.
[4]   We refer in this edition to the French 'scenes' rather than French 'play' because in addition to the printed edition, improvisation was still an important aspect of these *commedia* performances. Improvisation involves unstructured, extemporaneous performance that adapts to unscripted individual movements and/or incidents on stage as well as to audience action and reaction.

speaking various dialects of the Italian peninsula took on stock character roles with familiar costumes which often included masks. These active improvisers played out scenes of buffoonery featuring physical gags, scatological and obscene gestures, and wild antics, entertaining audiences from Naples and Bologna, and eventually Paris and London, through an improvisational performance art form noted today as *commedia dell'arte*. This retrospective, historical term can be translated as a 'comedy of professional players',[5] but in its own era, the tradition was known as *'commedia degli zanni'* (theatre of the buffoons) or *'commedia all'improvviso'* (improvised theatre).[6]

Unlike the more widely known early modern theatre of Shakespeare (1564–1616), Lope de Vega (1562–1635), and Molière (1622–1673),[7] for example, which largely depended on scripted roles developed by the playwright, *commedia dell'arte*'s action was created spontaneously by the performers themselves, who in each performance set fixed character types (*tipi fissi*) against each other within the framework of a loose plot outline called a *canovaccio* (canvas).[8] The roles fell into recognisable performance categories resembling those present in the ancient comedies of Plautus and Terence, as well as in some contemporary Italian scripted theatre (*commedia erudita*).[9] Older characters (*vecchi*), many of whom wore half-masks, created obstacles to the lovers of the younger generation, the *innamorati*, who more often performed unmasked. Servants intervened subversively on behalf of the young lovers, and the *zanni* (buffoons) interrupted stage action with madcap and sometimes scatological interventions that often inspired complicity with the audience, further shaping the performance.[10]

One distinctive feature of *commedia dell'arte* is found in the readily integrated, zany comic routines called *lazzi*. As Mel Gordon notes, early modern writers defined the term *lazzo* in various ways.[11] While in 1699 Andrea Perrucci (1651–1704) rather vaguely described a *lazzo* as 'something foolish, witty or metaphorical in word or action', some thirty years later Luigi Riccoboni (1676–1753) specifically designated *lazzi* as interruptions of scenes by

---

[5]   Natalie Crohn Schmitt, '*Commedia dell'Arte*: Characters, Scenarios, and Rhetoric', *Text and Performance Quarterly*, 24.1 (2004), 55–73 (p. 56).
[6]   Virginia Scott, *The Commedia dell'Arte in Paris: 1644–1697* (Charlottesville: University Press of Virginia, 1990), p. 3.
[7]   Molière was the stage name of actor and playwright Jean-Baptiste Poquelin.
[8]   Scott, *The Commedia dell'Arte in Paris*, p. 5.
[9]   Paul Monaghan, 'Aristocratic Archaeology: Greco-Roman Roots', in *The Routledge Companion to Commedia dell'Arte*, ed. by Judith Chaffee and Olly Crick (New York: Routledge, 2015), pp. 195–206 (p. 195).
[10] Robert Henke, 'Form and Freedom: Between Scenario and Stage', in *The Routledge Companion to Commedia dell'Arte*, ed. by Chaffee and Crick, pp. 21–29 (pp. 25–26).
[11] Mel Gordon, 'Lazzi', in *The Routledge Companion to Commedia dell'Arte*, ed. by Chaffee and Crick, pp. 167–76 (p. 168).

masked characters who express fright or foolery.[12] Alongside the buffoons and their silly interruptions, other performers filled their notebooks (*zibaldoni*) with topical scenes, such as lovers' dialogues, tirades, and harangues, that they could readily insert into a wide variety of *canovacci*.[13]

2. Italian Players in Paris

Throughout the early modern period, *commedia dell'arte* troupes performed for Parisian theatregoers and were particularly in favour with the French court. As early as 1571, the queen of France, Catherine of Medici (1519–1589), invited Italian players to perform.[14] More than sixty years later, Louis XIII (1601–1643) called for a troupe led by Giuseppe Bianchi (c.1630–c.1670), who stayed from 1639 to 1644, and Cardinal Mazarin (1602–1661) sent for them again shortly thereafter.[15] In 1653, an Italian troupe, the *comédiens italiens*, settled in Paris and played in such venues as the *Hôtel du Petit-Bourbon* and the *Théâtre du Palais-Royal*; after 1673, they played regularly in the *Théâtre Guénégaud*, a space they shared with actors who had been part of the late Molière's troupe.[16] By 1680, a troupe of performers led by the famous Tiberio Fiorilli (1608–1694), playing Scaramouche, and Domenico Biancolelli (1636–1688), as the notorious trickster Arlequin, were earning a pension from Louis XIV (1638–1715) and performing regularly in the ageing theatre space called the *Théâtre de l'Hôtel de Bourgogne*.[17] One remarkable honour that Louis XIV bestowed on this troupe — designating the actor playing Arlequin, known as Dominique, the godfather of his first-born son — suggests just how much, at least in the early years of his reign, he appreciated their art.[18]

The character Arlequin, also known in Italian as Arlecchino and anglicised as Harlequin, had typically been a relatively minor buffoon, who specialised in wacky or scatological jokes, naiveté, and the foolishness of the *zanni*. Dominique's comic talent, however, brought the role to the fore and made him a major focus of audience interest as he revelled in puns, sly remarks, and multiple *lazzi*.[19] His contribution helped bring pre-written French language scenes into the standard, predominantly Italian shows, so that by the 1680s,

---

[12]   Gordon, p. 168.
[13]   Scott, *The Commedia dell'Arte in Paris*, p. 5.
[14]   'Fatouville', in *Théâtre du XVIIe siècle*, ed. by Jacques Sherer and others, 3 vols (Paris: Gallimard, 1975–1992), III, ed. by Jacques Truchet and André Blanc (1992), pp. 1112–16 (p. 1112).
[15]   Guy Boquet, 'Les comédiens italiens à Paris au temps de Louis XIV', *Revue d'histoire moderne et contemporaine*, 26.3 (1979), 422–38 (p. 427).
[16]   Truchet and Blanc, p. 1112.
[17]   Truchet and Blanc, p. 1112.
[18]   Boquet, p. 428.
[19]   Boquet, p. 429.

Parisian audiences would have witnessed fully scripted scenes in French integrated with the traditional improvised Italian ones.[20] To facilitate this transition to a more bilingual repertoire, the *comédiens italiens* recruited Anne Mauduit de Fatouville to help write French scenes.[21] Fatouville, who served as counsellor at the *Cour des Aides* in the city of Rouen, has been mistakenly referred to as 'Nolant', variously spelled, confusing him with someone else from a different Norman family.[22] In Appendix B of this text, we offer a brief biography of Fatouville.

3. *Commedia dell'Arte* in England

Continental *commedia* players visited England at least as early as January 1578, when Drusiano Martinelli (c.1557–1630) and his company 'were given permission by the Privy Council to perform in London',[23] in a move that was not particularly popular with the English literati. In *Pierce Penilesse* (1592), for example, Thomas Nashe (1567– c.1601) voices explicit distaste for these players:

> Our Players are not as the players beyond sea, a sort of squirting baudie Comedians, that haue whores and common Curtizans to play womens parts, and forebeare no immodest speach or vnchast action that may procure laughter, but our Sceane is more stately furnisht than euer it was in the time of *Roscius*, our representations honorable, and full of gallaunt resolution, not consisting like theirs of a Pantaloun, a Whore, and a Zanie, but of Emperours, Kings and Princes: whose true Tragedies (*Sophocleo cothurno*) they doo vaunt.[24]

Well into the seventeenth century, playwrights entertained little regard for these troupes. In the *Travailes of the Three English Brothers* (1607), for example, the character Kempe makes bawdy references to Harlakan's [*sic*] wife acting in a *commedia* performance: 'Your wife, why hearke you, wil your wife do tricks in publike', a reference not only to Kempe's dislike of *commedia* players but to women on the public stage as well.[25] After an extended jest, Kempe concludes that Harlakan is in the right way 'to Cuck-holds-hauen, Saint *Luke* bee your speede'.

In the second half of the seventeenth century, a number of *commedia* troops visited England regularly, since Charles II reportedly enjoyed them,

---

[20]   Scott, *The Commedia dell'Arte in Paris*, p. 251.
[21]   Truchet and Blanc, p. 1114; Scott, *The Commedia dell'Arte in Paris*, p. 281.
[22]   Truchet and Blanc, p. 1113.
[23]   Andrew Grewar, 'The Old Man's Spectacles: Commedia and Shakespeare', in *The Routledge Companion to Commedia dell'Arte*, ed. by Chaffee and Crick, pp. 300–11 (p. 302).
[24]   Thomas Nashe, *Pierce Penilesse his Supplication to the Diuell* (London: Richard Jhones, 1592), p. 27.
[25]   John Day [William Rowley and George Wilkins], *The Travailes of the three English Brothers* (London: for John Wright, 1607), unnumbered pages and lines, III.E3, III.F.

but playwrights and courtiers alike frequently demonstrated a decided lack of enthusiasm. John Dryden (1631–1700) complained in 1673 that the 'Italian Merry-Andrews' had 'quite Debauched the Stage with lewd Grimace',[26] while in the newsletters of Richard Bulstrode (1610–1711), a writer lodged a disparaging observation about a troupe of *commedia* players, who were given permission to perform at court in June 1675:

> There is arrived Scaramouchy, ye famous Italien comedian with his crew, to act againe, & are to have ye King's theatre in Whitehall for their use during their stay, and all people are allowed to come there & see them, paying as they doe at other houses, so y^t now a Papist may come to Court for halfe a crown. This is not so much lik'd by our other players, for it will half break both our houses.[27]

John Evelyn (1620–1706) also recorded having seen 'the *Italian* Comedie at the Court' in May 1673, and on 29 September 1675, Evelyn 'saw the Italian *Scaramucchio* act before the King at *White Hall*; People giving monye to come in, which was very Scandalous, & never so before at Court Diversions'.[28] Although Evelyn seems at first dismayed by the whole affair, he adds 'having seene him [Scaramucchio] act before in *Italy* many yeares past, I was not averse from seeing the most excellent of that kind of folly'. Andrew Marvell (1621–1678) described the means employed by the court to provide an opportunity in Whitehall for the common rabble to watch. In a letter to William Popple, Marvell observes that '*Scaramuccio* acting dayly in the Hall of *Whitehall*, and all Sorts of People flocking thither, and paying their Mony as at a common Playhouse; nay even a twelve-penny Gallery is builded for the convenience of his Majesty's poorer Subjects'.[29]

While the *commedia dell'arte* format was generally popular on the Continent, English playwrights engaged less widely in the art form. Although a number of scholars point out that the works of early playwrights, such as Shakespeare and Ben Jonson, were influenced by *commedia* characters,[30] significant

---

[26] John Dryden, 'Prologue and Epilogue to the University of Oxon (1673)', in *Works of John Dryden*, gen. eds Edward Niles Hooker, H. T. Swedenberg, Jr, and Vinton A. Dearing, 20 vols (Berkeley: University of California Press, 1956–2000), I: *Poems 1649–1680*, ed. by Hooker and Swedenberg, Jr (1956), pp. 147–48.

[27] Richard Bulstrode, *The Bulstrode Papers*, formed by Alfred Morrison, 1667–1675 (Printed for Private Circulation, 1897), I: *1667–1675*, p. 302. The entry is dated Monday 21 June 1675. Only one volume was published. Bulstrode lists several visits by their Royal Highnesses to see 'Scaramouchy'.

[28] John Evelyn, *Diary of John Evelyn*, ed. by E. S. De Beer, 6 vols (Oxford: Clarendon, 1955), IV: *Kalendarium 1673–1689*, pp. 12, 75.

[29] Andrew Marvell, *The Poems and Letters of Andrew Marvell*, ed. by H. M. Margoliouth, 2 vols, 3rd edn (Oxford: Clarendon, 1971), II: *The Letters*, p. 342. The letter is dated 24 July 1675.

[30] Artemis Preeshl, *Shakespeare and Commedia dell'Arte: Play by Play* (London: Routledge, 2017); Amy Matthews, *The Influence and Function of the Commedia Dell Arte in the*

development of *commedia dell'arte* on the English stage, even into the second half of the seventeenth century, was still limited. Aston Cokain (1608–1684) claimed his play *Trappolin suppos'd a Prince* (1658) was based on a *commedia dell'arte* performance, *Trappolino creduto principe*, that he had witnessed in Italy; the play was revived by Nahum Tate (1652–1715) as *A Duke and No Duke* and produced in August 1684.[31] Harlequin and Scaramouche had a limited role in Aphra Behn's *The Second Part of the Rover*, produced in 1681,[32] but the first extensive use of Harlequin and his fellows in the Restoration appeared somewhat later in Edward Ravenscroft's (c.1654–1707) *Scaramouch a Philosopher, Harlequin a School-boy, Bravo, Merchant and Magician* (1677), subtitled 'A Comedy After the *Italian* manner', followed by Behn's *The Emperor of the Moon*, and William Mountfort's (c.1664–1692) *Life and Death of Doctor Faustus* (1697).

English playwrights denounced low comedy, whether farce or the improvisation and exaggerated movements of *commedia*. Although low comedy certainly had its financial rewards in that it was extremely popular with audiences, many playwrights were hardly willing to claim its literary merits, even if they found themselves writing it.[33] In his treatise on drama in *An Evening's Love, or the Mock Astrologer* (1671), John Dryden remarked that

> Comedy presents us with the imperfections of humane nature: Farce entertains us with what is monstruous [sic] and chimerical. The one causes laughter in those who can judge of men and manners [...]; the other produces the same effect in those who can judge of neither [...] The first works on the judgment and fancy; the latter on the fancy only.[34]

Low comedy, Dryden added, would continue to hamper the English stage until their playwrights end up translating French plays, '*for their Poets wanting judgement to make, or to maintain true characters, strive to cover their defects with ridiculous Figures and Grimaces*' (p. 204). Thomas Shadwell (c.1642–1692) also found that

> The rabble of little People, are more pleas'd with *Jack-Puddings* being

---

Drama of Shakespeare and Jonson (Bristol: University of the West England, 2006); and Juliana Tanase, 'The Italian Commedia and the Fashioning of the Shakespearean Fool', in *Shakespeare and the Italian Renaissance: Appropriation, Transformation, Opposition*, ed. by Michele Marrapodi (Burlington, VT: Ashgate, 2014), pp. 215–31.

[31] Aston Cokain [also Cokayn], *Trappolin creduto Principe. Or Trappolin suppos'd a Prince* in *A Chain of Golden Poems* (London: W. G. to be sold by Isaac Pridmore, 1658); Nahum Tate, *A Duke and No Duke* (London: for Henry Bonwicke, 1685).

[32] Aphra Behn, *The Second Part of the Rover* (London: for Jacob Tonson, 1681).

[33] Peter Holland, 'Farce', in *The Cambridge Companion to English Restoration Literature*, ed. by Deborah Payne Fisk (Cambridge: Cambridge University Press, 2000), pp. 107–26 (p. 107).

[34] Dryden, 'Preface', in *An Evening's Love, Or The Mock-Astrologer*, in *Works*, x, ed. by Maximillian E. Novak (1970), p. 203.

soundly kick'd, or having a Custard handsomely thrown in his face, than with all the wit in Plays: and the higher sort of Rabble [...] are more pleased with the extravagant and unnatural actions the trifles, and fripperies of a Play, or the trappings and ornaments of Nonsense, than with all the wit in the world.[35]

Although English playwrights may have denigrated the entertainment provided by low comedy as chimerical, they nevertheless engaged in the form because English audiences desired it. This led a number of playwrights to claim that audience demand for such comedy had corrupted the English theatre. Not surprisingly, then, when Aphra Behn penned her *Emperor of the Moon* and subtitled it farce, she noted in her dedication to the Marquess of Worcester, that '*I am sensible, my Lord, how far the Word Farce might have offended some* [...] *and have damn'd it (because the Persons in it did not all talk like Hero's) as too debas'd and vulgar to entertain a Man of Quality*' (p. 47–48). Fortunately, she adds, the Marquess is not such a '*Man of Quality*' as to cry out about the vulgarity of her play or the lack of heroic language, and would instead consider the '*Intent, Character, or Nature*' of what was being presented (p. 47).

4. The Politics of *Commedia dell'Arte*

Meredith Chilton has observed that, 'to laugh in the theatre is to laugh at others, to deride them, ridicule them, raise public opinion against them, and ostracize them from the community'.[36] There were, however, some limits that local authorities were unwilling for players to cross. As Peter Jordan points out, *commedia* actors of the late sixteenth- and early seventeenth-century Italian stage 'were careful not to make any direct assaults on the spiritual authority of the [Roman Catholic] Church, [so] an obvious secular target would have been the university academic par excellence from Bologna, the scholar-windbag'.[37] Even so, in 1664 the French actor and playwright Molière attempted to fight the abuse of Church authority with his play *Le Tartuffe*, a comedy 'rooted in Commedia traditions'. The play, which portrays a conman who uses religious language and appeals to piety to manipulate a Christian family, was attacked by Church censors and banned by Louis XIV.[38] Molière subsequently argued in

---

[35]   Thomas Shadwell, 'Preface', in *The Humorists: A Comedy acted by his Royal Highnesses Servants* (1671), in *The Complete Works of Thomas Shadwell*, ed. by Montague Summers, 5 vols (London: The Fortune Press, 1927), I, pp. 172–255 (p. 185).
[36]   Meredith Chilton, *Harlequin Unmasked: The Commedia dell'Arte and Porcelain Sculpture* (New Haven: Yale University Press, 2002), p. 14.
[37]   Peter Jordan, 'Pantalone and il Dottore: The Old Men of Commedia', in *The Routledge Companion to Commedia dell'Arte*, ed. by Chaffee and Crick, pp. 62–69 (p. 68).
[38]   Elizabeth C. Goldsmith, 'Writing for the Elite: Molière, Marivaux, and Beaumarchais', in *The Routledge Companion to Commedia dell'Arte*, ed. by Chaffee and Crick, pp. 321–28 (pp. 322–23).

written pleas to the King that those who condemned his piece were engaging in the same nefarious behaviour as his eponymous villain. The playwright was seeking to expose such abuses. Molière maintained that his play had inspired backlash precisely because it denounced the techniques his hypocritical censors were wielding against him.[39] The King later allowed Molière's troupe to perform a modified version of the play, prompting the playwright to thank the monarch for redeeming him in the eyes of pious Christians who had wrongly disparaged his comedy.[40]

Through its humour, *commedia* has long addressed the political, not simply by the actions of the plot nor the grimaces and gestures of the actors, but via an understanding of the development and meaning of the characters themselves. For example, the Dottore character was typically portrayed as an educated older man and 'a philosopher, astronomer, man of letters, cabalist, barrister, grammarian, diplomat and physician'.[41] He wore a flesh-coloured mask with a red nose, or, if an actor chose not to wear the mask, he often coloured his cheeks red.[42] Bucknell adds that the Doctor was habitually dressed in a black tunic with a very large white ruffle at the neckline; he usually wore a wide black belt and often donned a black academic cape or robe; as part of his persona, he sometimes carried an enema syringe. He was exceptionally verbose, frequently speaking in meaningless words, and was highly opinionated and confrontational.[43] Although the Dottore character may well have appeared as a doddering old man, he also represented a figure of authority, one who demanded filial obedience.[44]

Harlequin, on the other hand, represented the underprivileged social classes, as Michele Bottini has argued. Bottini points out that in early sacred imagery in Italy, 'good' was represented as saints and angels with their faces clearly represented, while 'evil' was represented by devils who wore masks.[45] 'The problem for the Church then became that the [common] people ended up recognizing themselves in the diabolical personages' of early *commedia*, the dark-faced people labouring in the fields under the Sun, as opposed to the white-faced ruling class, so that the 'eternal battle between Good and Evil

[39] Molière, 'Second Placet, présenté au Roi dans son camp devant la ville de Lille en Flandre', in *Le Tartuffe*, ed. by Jean Serroy (Paris: Gallimard, 1997), p. 47.

[40] Molière, 'Troisième Placet, présenté au Roi', in *Le Tartuffe*, ed. by Serroy, p. 48.

[41] Pierre Louis Ducharte, *The Italian Comedy: The Improvisation Scenarios, Lives, Attributes, Portraits and Masks of the Illustrious Characters of the Commedia dell'arte*, trans. by Randolph T. Weaver (London: George G. Harrap, 1929), p. 196.

[42] Peter A. Bucknell, *Commedia Dell'Arte at the Court of Louis XIV: A Soft Sculpture Representation* (London: Stainer & Bell, 1980), p. 33; Ducharte, pp. 200–01.

[43] Bucknell, pp. 200–01.

[44] Jordan, 'Pantalone and il Dottore', pp. 65–66.

[45] Michele Bottini, 'You must have heard of Harlequin ...', in *The Routledge Companion to Commedia dell'Arte*, ed. by Chaffee and Crick, pp. 55–61 (p. 56).

ended up looking more like an eternal battle between servants and masters'.[46] Peter Jordan notes that the Church was concerned about the ideas being presented through the performances of the *commedia* actors, particularly through the wearing of masks, the 'untold evil of the masked actor', and the presence of women on stage, who presented 'sinful temptations'.[47] Harlequin typically wore a black mask, whether a full or half mask, and brightly coloured, irregularly patched clothing in a distinctive pattern.[48] While patched clothing itself implied the working classes, his brightly coloured patches drew particular attention to his attire and thus the social class he represented. Through his subversion of the establishment, Harlequin became on stage the 'champion of the popular masses, who [saw] him as a representation of themselves as well as a hope of change'; Harlequin and his mask functioned as 'the point of reference and the last hope for a social redemption' for those who lived everyday lives in a similar social condition.[49]

Commedia dell'arte, then, like drama in general, is by its very public and performative aspects a visible and direct medium for social causes and political ideology. Ellen McClure points out the strong affinity in France between the theatre and the state. 'Plays were performed not merely for the king's personal enjoyment but often to send messages, more or less bluntly, to ambassadors visiting the country', she argues.[50] Ambassadors to France were expected to attend these performances and their seating was carefully regulated. In one specific example McClure provides, Louis XIV commanded Molière to compose a play with Turkish elements to point out to the Turkish ambassador the 'affronts' he 'had committed during his official reception and stay in France'.[51] While the French King enjoyed theatre performances and on occasion used them to his advantage to correct the manners of ambassadors, he was also quick to reprimand the players when they crossed the line. 'Criticism of the régime, on French soil, was sternly repressed', and satirical works overtly targeting the King and his politics were generally printed outside the country.[52]

Two examples of the affinity between the stage and politics in England involve Robert Devereux, Second Earl of Essex (1565-1601) and James Scott, First Duke of Monmouth and First Duke of Buccleuch (1649-1685). In 1601, Essex managed

---

[46] Bottini, p. 56.

[47] Peter Jordan, *The Venetian Origins of the Commedia dell'Arte* (New York: Routledge, 2014), pp. 183–84.

[48] Bucknell, p. 15.

[49] Goldsmith, pp. 322–23.

[50] Ellen McClure, *Sunspots and the Sun King: Sovereignty and Mediation in Seventeenth-Century France* (Urbana: University of Illinois Press, 2006), p. 194.

[51] McClure, p. 195.

[52] Bruce Griffiths, 'Sunset: From Commedia dell'Arte to Comédie Italienne', in *Studies in the Commedia dell'Arte*, ed. by David George and Christopher J. Gossip (Cardiff: University of Wales Press, 1993), pp. 91–105 (p. 104).

to convince the Chamberlain's Men to stage a performance of Shakespeare's *Richard II*, with its deposition scene, just prior to their plans to seize the court and the Tower of London and force Queen Elizabeth I (1533–1603) to dismiss her advisor, Robert Cecil (1563–1612), in favour of Essex.[53] During the Rye House Plot of 1663, an anonymous tip was sent to Sir Leoline Jenkins (c.1625-1685), a Secretary of State for Charles II, observing that Monmouth, who was asserting his right to the throne in preference to James, Duke of York, was hiding in one of the two patent theatres.[54]

Further seventeenth-century English examples which demonstrate the intersection of politics and the stage are found in the plays themselves, such as John Dryden's *Amboyna, or the Cruelties of the Dutch to the English Merchants* (1672),[55] a play which supported England's entry into the Third Dutch War, as did Behn's comedy *The Dutch Lover* (1673). Thomas Shadwell's *The Libertine* (1675) attacked the libertinism associated with the court,[56] while his contemporaries recognised his *Lancashire Witches* (1682) as Whig propaganda.[57] A number of plays were produced during the Popish Plot and Exclusion Crisis (1678–1681) that reflected plots against the state, including, for example, Dryden and Nathaniel Lee's (c.1653–1692) *The Duke of Guise* (1682) and Lee's own *Constantine the Great* (1683), Thomas Southerne's (1660–1746) *The Loyal Brother* (1682), Thomas Otway's (1652–1685) *Venice Preserv'd; or a Plot Discovered* (1682), and John Crowne's (c.1641–1712) *City Politiques* (1683). Behn observed the political potential of theatre performance in the dedication to Laurence Hyde, First Earl of Rochester (1641–1711), of her comedy *The Luckey Chance, Or An Alderman's Bargain* (1687):

> [Plays] are Secret Instructions to the People, in things that 'tis impossible to insinuate into them any other Way. 'Tis Example that prevails above Reason or Divine Precepts [...] Plays have been ever held most important to the very Political Part of Government.[58]

If in the seventeenth-century, then, audiences and playwrights alike viewed the theatre unequivocally as a site of political expression, for authorities, the theatre presented a more amorphous setting, at times a collaborator while at others suspect, perhaps even dangerous.

---

[53]   Carole Levin, *The Heart and Stomach of a King: Elizabeth I and the Politics of Sex and Power* (Philadelphia: University of Pennsylvania Press, 1994), pp. 154–56; Robert Lacey, *Robert, Earl of Essex* (New York: Atheneum, 1971), p. 282.

[54]   *Calendar of State Papers Domestic*, vol. 25: 1 July–30 September 1683, p. 109. The note is recorded on 13 July.

[55]   Derek Hughes, *English Drama 1660–1700* (Oxford: Clarendon Press, 1996), p. 91.

[56]   Susan J. Owen, *Restoration Theatre and Crisis* (Oxford: Clarendon Press, 1996), pp. 107, 176–78.

[57]   Owen, p. 185.

[58]   Aphra Behn, *The Luckey Chance, Or An Alderman's Bargain* (London: R. H. for W. Canning, 1687), unpaginated ([pp. 1–2]).

As for Harlequin and Scaramouch, they took widely to the English stage in the late seventeenth and early eighteenth centuries, eventually in pantomime format, presenting identifiable political messages to their audiences.[59] Bakhtin argued that laughter liberates,[60] but playwrights and audiences alike also recognised its subversive qualities. Overtly, humour is a powerful release and a signal of pleasure, but covertly humour 'can be a powerful weapon, more devastating than the sharpest logic, because it is insidiously ingratiating; we laugh, we remember, and we ultimately believe'.[61] There is much more to slapstick and pigsbladder than the guffaws of diversion, for 'no laughter-inducing device may be regarded as innocent', nor should we overlook the significance of the social 'location' of the comic characters.[62] While the buffoon-like characters may seem innocent, their comic behaviour should be regarded circumspectly, since the humour also presents significant potential for political and/or social commentary.

5. The Comedy of Science

The English thought of 'science' as essentially a 'certain knowledge' that incorporated a wider body of learning — not only the scientific disciplines we think of today, such as chemistry, biology, and so forth, but also history and the arts. This meant that in his *Defence of Poesie* (1595), Philip Sidney (1554–1586) could write about poetry as a science, and his contemporary poets and scholars alike could refer to the seven liberal arts as 'the seven liberal sciences'.[63] Baking, brewing, and soapmaking, for example, were also viewed as science, so that 'the difference between *scientia* and *ars* is reduced to one of procedure, while the knowledge produced by both is shown to be qualitatively the same'.[64] With the establishment of the Royal Society, the seventeenth

---

[59] John O'Brien, *Harlequin Britain: Pantomime and Entertainment 1690–1760* (Baltimore: Johns Hopkins University Press, 2004); Judy A. Hayden, 'Of Windmills and Bubbles: Harlequin Faustus on the Eighteenth-Century Stage', *Huntington Library Quarterly*, 77.1 (2014), 1–16; and 'Harlequin, The Whigs, and William Mountfort's Doctor Faustus', *Studies in English Literature*, 49.3 (2009), 573–93.

[60] Mikhail Bakhtin, *Rabelais and His World*, trans. by Hélène Iswolsky (Bloomington: Indiana University Press, 1984), p. 94.

[61] Katherine Usher Henderson and Barbara F. McManus, *Half Humankind: Contexts and Texts of the Controversy about Women in England, 1540–1640* (Urbana-Champaign: University of Illinois Press, 1985), p. 34.

[62] Chilton, *Harlequin Unmasked*, p. 15.

[63] Judy A. Hayden, 'Intersections and Cross-Fertilization', in *Travel Narratives, the New Science, and Literary Discourse 1569–1750*, ed. by Judy A. Hayden (Burlington, VT: Ashgate 2012), pp. 1–21 (pp. 1–3).

[64] Carlo Mazzio, 'Shakespeare and Science, c.1600', *South Central Review*, 26.1/2 (2009), pp. 1–23 (p. 3); Henry S. Turner, *The English Renaissance Stage: Geometry, Poetics, and the Practical and Spatial Arts 1580–1630* (Oxford: Oxford University Press, 2006), pp. 61–62.

century began to witness a movement toward a new science that attracted the minds of many who discussed and debated new theories (such as Copernicus' theory of heliocentrism), who engaged in experiments to test old and new ideas, who developed new technology (such as the telescope and microscope), and who used these technologies to make new discoveries (such as geography of the lunar surface [selenography], made possible by the telescope), all of which culminated in new perceptions of science itself, of nature, and of the cosmos.

The purpose behind rethinking science in the seventeenth century is an important one as it pertains to our work here. In the early sixteenth century, the Dutch humanist Erasmus wittily pointed out that natural philosophers build 'countless universes and measur[e] the sun, moon, stars and planets by rule of thumb or bit of string', yet they only find that 'Nature has a fine laugh at them and their conjectures'.[65] Humanists viewed laughter as having 'a deep philosophical meaning', with just as essential a place in literature as the serious; later seventeenth-century 'scientists', however, held that

> the essential truth about the world and about man cannot be told in the language of laughter. Therefore, the place of laughter in literature belongs only to the low genres, showing the life of private individuals and the inferior social levels.[66]

Robert Hooke (1635–1703) observed in his *Micrographia* (1665) that science 'deserved the attention of "the most *serious* part of men"',[67] while Robert Boyle (1627–1691) concurred, describing things 'that tickle the Spleene of deluded mortals, and begets their mirth' as 'worthless trifles'.[68]

In maintaining this sense of the seriousness of science, the Royal Society worked to eradicate laughter from their observations. In his *History of the Royal Society For the Improving of Natural Knowledge* (1667), Thomas Sprat (1635–1713) decries laughter, particularly that directed at the Royal Society.[69] He observes that the 'present *Genius* of the *English Nation*' is so focused on humour in their writing that there are few who do not suffer from this 'infection'; however, he argues, if they would turn their interests to the study of nature, they could instead increase their knowledge (p. 413). The '*Wits* and *Railleurs* of this *Age*', he continues, should unite their interests with those of the Royal Society, for by denigrating the promotion of experiments and making them ridiculous because they are '*new*', they do injury to the Society (p. 417). Laughter, Sprat

---

[65] Desiderius Erasmus, *In Praise of Folly* (1511), trans. by Betty Radice, with an introduction and notes by A. H. T. Levi (London: Penguin, 1993), p. 151.

[66] Bakhtin, p. 67.

[67] Findlen, 'Between Carnival and Lent: The Scientific Revolution at the Margins of Culture', *Configurations*, 6.2 (1998), 243–67 (p. 254).

[68] Findlen, p. 263.

[69] Thomas Sprat, *History of the Royal Society of London, For the Improving of Natural Knowledge* (London: T. R. for J. Martyn and J. Allestry, Printers to the Royal Society, 1667).

points out, 'is the easiest and slendrest fruit of *Wit*' (p. 418). Sprat vents against such infectious laughter as he has seen from the 'wits' of the age and argues that not everything should be the grounds for laughter:

> In plain terms, a universal abuse of every thing, though it may tickle the fancy never so much, is *inhuman madness*; as one of the *Ancients* well expresses it, who calls such mirth *humanis Bacchari rebus*. If all things were made the subjects of such humour, all worthy designs would soon be laugh'd out of the World [...] All good Enterprises ought to find assistance when they are begun, applaus when they succeed, and even pity and prais if they fail. (pp. 418–19)

After all, Sprat points out, experiments, such as those conducted by the Society, are *'advantageous to the Interest of our Nation'* (p. 419). In his commendatory poem for Sprat's volume, Abraham Cowley expresses a similar opinion, pointing out that

> Mischief and tru Dishonour fall on those
> Who would to laughter or to scorn expose
> So Virtuous and so Noble a Design.[70]

By the second half of the seventeenth century, 'Laughter, with all its ambivalence and irony about the state of the world [...] was no longer the hallmark of the thinking individual who came to define the scientist'.[71]

This seriousness of the men of science, however, became part and parcel of the laughter on the printed page, as might be witnessed in a number of satires, such as Margaret Cavendish's (*c.*1624–1673) *The Description of a New World, Called the Blazing-World* (1666), Samuel Butler's (1612–1680) 'The Elephant in the Moon' (*c.*1671), or Daniel Defoe's (*c.*1660–1731) *The Consolidator: Or, Memoirs Of Sundry Transactions From The Moon* (1705). Importantly for this study, however, are the playwrights who also satirised those serious men of science and/or their ideas on the stage, from Edward Howard's (1624–1712) *The Six days Adventure, or the New Utopia* (1671) to Thomas Shadwell's well-known *The Virtuoso* (1676), and from Aphra Behn's *The Emperor of the Moon* to Thomas D'Urfey's (1653–1723) *Wonders in the Sun; or, The Kingdom of the Birds* (1706), to name but a few.

6. A Brief Historical Note on the Texts

For this edition, we chose to use the unsigned, undated version of *Arlequin, Empereur dans la lune* printed in Troyes by the Garnier publishing house, rather than Evaristo Gherardi's (1663–1700) version in *Le Théâtre Italien de*

---

[70] Abraham Cowley, 'To the Royal Society', in Sprat, *History of the Royal Society,* unpaginated [sig. B3], stanza viii.
[71] Findlen, pp. 250–51.

Gherardi (1700).[72] Although Gherardi's six-volume collection may contain one of the largest compilations of French scenes of the *comédiens italiens*, 'it is difficult to determine how much of this troupe's repertoire was performed in Italian, [and] how much in French'.[73] Furthermore, there are those who argue that Gherardi's text is the least authoritative.[74] Virginia Scott has observed, for example, that one of the plays in Gherardi's collection, *Colombine avocat pour et contre*, may have had far fewer scenes in its 1685 production than those published by Gherardi in his 1700 edition.[75] Scott argues that while Gherardi's 1700 edition is 'the principal source of materials for description and analysis of the Italian's repertory after 1680, it should be used with a certain discretion'.[76]

Evaristo Gherardi was the son of Italian actors, who, in 1689, after the death of Dominique Biancolelli, took the role of Arlequin for the Italian troupe in Paris, the *comédiens italiens*, a role in which he became immensely successful.[77] In 1691–92, reports of disruption and fights within the troupe began to circulate, in which Gherardi was involved, claiming among other things that some of the actors called him names and interrupted him during his performance.[78] Gherardi's determination in 1694 to publish a collection of the early French scenes of the *comédiens italiens* could not have helped their troupe's intense internecine struggles, particularly after some of the actors petitioned the King to forbid Gherardi from publishing his edition.[79] His fellow actors claimed that Gherardi exercised 'unheard-of infidelity' in obtaining 'all the plays and separate scenes performed over the last thirty years on the stage of the Italian actors'. Gherardi alleged that he paid the authors for their scenes over a number of years, but his troupe argued that they were not his to publish because they belonged to the troupe as a whole.[80] The French government's decision was that 'Gherardi had "adroitly swiped" the manuscripts from the individual charged

[72]   Anne Mauduit de Fatouville, *Arlequin, Empereur dans la lune*, in *Le Théâtre Italien de Gherardi, ou le Recueil Général de toutes les Comédies et Scènes Françoises jouées par les Comédiens Italiens du Roi, pendant tout le temps qu'ils ont été au Service*, ed. by Evaristo Gherardi, 6 vols (Paris: Jean-Bapt. Cusson et Pierre Witte, 1700), I, pp. 136–204.
[73]   *Musical Theatre at the Court of Louis XIV: Le Mariage de la Grosse Cathos*, trans. and ed. by Rebecca Harris-Warrick and Carol G. Marsh (Cambridge: Cambridge University Press, 2005), p. 12.
[74]   Scott, *The Commedia dell'Arte in Paris*, p. 279.
[75]   Scott, *The Commedia dell'Arte in Paris*, pp. 279–80.
[76]   Scott, *The Commedia dell'Arte in Paris*, p. 280.
[77]   Jeffrey S. Ravel, *The Contested Parterre: Public Theatre and French Political Culture 1680–1791* (New York: Cornell University, 1999), p. 115.
[78]   *French Theatre in the Neo-Classical Era, 1550–1789*, Document 337, p. 321.
[79]   Evaristo Gherardi, *Le Théâtre Italien, ou le Recueil de toutes les scènes françoises* (Paris: Guillaume de Luyne, 1694), pp. 1–26; Ravel, p. 116; *French Theatre in the Neo-Classical Era*, Document 338, pp. 321–22; Scott, *The Commedia dell'Arte in Paris*, pp. 276–78.
[80]   Ravel, p. 116.

with their safekeeping'.[81] Later, however, some of the Italian actors agreed that Gherardi could publish his 1694 volume of scenes as long as he shared the profits; others in the troupe, when they heard this decision, became angry.[82] After the King banned the *comédiens italiens* from Paris in 1697, Gherardi published his six volume compilation, *Le Théâtre Italien de Gherardi* (1700).

The edition of *Arlequin, Empereur dans la lune* from which we worked is similar in many respects to Gherardi's version in his six-volume collection published in 1700. Both texts feature eight scenes and both are largely in French with some small fragments of Italian discourse. A number of scholars have utilised Gherardi's text in working with Behn's play, with the understanding perhaps that this is the text to which Behn had access or because it appeared to them that this was the only published version of the play. We believe the Troyes edition, although undated, was published by Fatouville, probably the Monsieur D*** of the title page (see Appendix B), or conceivably one of his co-authors of the early scenes, close to the date of the first performance in 1684. While we transcribed and translated Gherardi's version as well as the Garnier edition as we explored the French scenes to determine which we would include here, we eventually decided to use the Garnier edition for a number of reasons.

First, Gherardi's single volume of scenes published in 1694 contains only four scenes of *Arlequin, Empereur dans la lune*, in about 26 pages; this suggests either that he did not have access to the full number of scenes, or that the other scenes had not yet been translated and recorded in French, although we believe they were, since this was the task for which Fatouville was hired, at least as early as 1683. Even so, in spite of the popularity of this particular play, Gherardi was unable to obtain access to and publish the eight scenes until after 1697.

Second, there would be good reason in 1683 or 1684 for Fatouville to take his material outside of Paris to Troyes. Troyes was one of several principal printing cities, and one reason to publish there would have been to prevent angering the Italian troupe, as Domenico Biancolelli did when he published the final act of *La matrone d'Éphèse, ou Arlequin Grapignan* in 1683, one of the first of the collections of French scenes by Monsieur D***,[83] and, of course, as Gherardi did in 1694. *Arlequin Grapignan* was published in Paris by Claude Blageart (*c.*1630–1685), although it was eventually suppressed.[84] The Italian troupe feared audiences would not attend their plays if the texts became 'public and common property'.[85] The French troupe, on the other hand, were distressed about the large crowds the Italians were drawing, which they determined was

---

[81] Ravel, p. 116.
[82] *French Theatre in the Neo-Classical Era*, Document 338i, p. 322.
[83] Scott, *The Commedia dell'Arte in Paris*, pp. 277, 281–82.
[84] Scott, *The Commedia dell'Arte in Paris*, pp. 277, 281–82.
[85] *French Theatre in the Neo-Classical Era*, Document 338, p. 322.

owing to the new French content, so they complained to the King.[86] Given the immense popularity of *Arlequin, Empereur dans la lune*, and the objection by the *comédiens italiens* to the publication of their material, Fatouville's scenes would have found a safer market with a printer outside Paris, like the Garnier family in Troyes.

In addition, Garnier was engaged in the highly competitive market of the *bibliothèque bleue*, the blue books or chapbooks designed for the mass population, which included saints' lives, romances, stories and tales, and plays, 'much of it distributed throughout the countryside by peddlers'.[87] Paris printers felt threatened by the provincial presses and tried to get the government to enforce a 1667 ban on licensing new printers in the provinces. If Rouen, from where Fatouville is believed to have come, was one of the major provincial printing cities in France at this time, the question becomes why Fatouville did not publish with a printer there. Perhaps his plan was to further disguise the identity of the author of the French scenes by removing the printing of them to Troyes, but more likely it was because Rouen printers ignored the ban and the royal licensing procedure and produced poor quality texts.[88] Furthermore, Rouen had an early reputation for printing conservative and reactionary (if not unorthodox) texts, including Jansenist tracts.[89] As counsellor at the *Cour des Aides* in the city of Rouen, it would not have been in his best interest to publish his manuscript there.

Finally, and perhaps most relevant to our choice, is that the close similarity between Behn's *Emperor of the Moon* and Fatouville's *Arlequin*, even to the same wording at times, suggests that Behn had access to most if not all of the printed scenes, whether from witnessing a performance herself or from a published copy of the scenes provided her by Thomas Betterton (*c*.1635–1710). In *Love-Letters Between a Nobleman and his Sister* (1684), attributed to Behn, the author states that she had been in Paris 'last spring'.[90] In August 1683, Charles II sent Betterton to Paris, taxing him to bring back French opera for the English stage, but Betterton did not go alone; rather, he took a number of people with him, purportedly actors. The Newdigate Letters report Betterton leaving England on 14 August 1683: 'Batterton wth other acto^rs are gone ov^er to fetch ye design' of French opera.[91] Behn may have been invited as well, since, as Mary Anne O'Donnell notes, the playwright seems to have disappeared from the publishing

---

[86]   *French Theatre in the Neo-Classical Era*, Document 340, p. 323.
[87]   Jane McLeod, *Licensing Loyalty: Printers, Patrons, and the State in Early Modern France* (University Park: The Pennsylvania State University Press, 2011), p. 18.
[88]   McLeod, p. 105.
[89]   McLeod, p. 42–43.
[90]   Aphra Behn, 'The Epistle', in *Love-Letters Between a Noble-Man And his Sister* (London: Printed and are to be sold by Randal Taylor, 1684), unpaginated [pp. 1–17], ([p. 1]).
[91]   John Harold Wilson, 'Theatre Notes from the Newdigate Newsletters', *Theatre Notebook*, 15.3 (1961), 79–84 (p. 82).

scene between August of 1682 and early 1684; certainly, O'Donnell observes, Behn 'was not publishing in 1683'.[92] Betterton and the actors were still in Paris at least in September 1683, where, if they visited the Italian troupe, they probably would have seen Fatouville's *Arlequin Protée* (1683).[93] When Betterton's group returned to England is unclear, but he may have been back in London at least by October or November for the new theatre season.[94]

That Behn claims in her dedication that she began her play for Charles II, who died 6 February 1685, suggests that she had access to the French *Arlequin* prior to that date. This access occurred, then, long before Gherardi printed either his one volume or multi-volume collection of scenes. As a follow-up note, Betterton was sent back to Paris in July 1685,[95] where he may have witnessed a performance of *Arlequin*; he would have had an opportunity to obtain a copy of the published scenes if the Garnier edition was indeed published in 1684, as we suggest. That Betterton owned a number of French and Italian plays can be demonstrated by the listings in the auction catalogue, *Pinacotheca Bettertonæana*, Betterton's library of about 550 books, which were auctioned off after his death in 1710. Unfortunately, many of the plays are listed in bundles and without playwrights' names or play titles, such as '[t]hirteen more [plays], in French and Italian', or a bundle of quartos marked 'twelve *French* and *English* Plays', so it is impossible to know if Fatouville's scenes are among those collections.[96]

Nevertheless, we believe the Garnier edition from Troyes was probably published close to the production date of *Arlequin*, while Gherardi's multi-volume collection was published sixteen years after the first performance of *Arlequin* and after the Italian troupe had been banned from Paris. Given that Betterton and probably Behn were in France at some point between 1683 and 1685 and had the opportunity not only to witness *Arlequin*, but even to obtain a copy of the scenes, we determined that the Garnier edition is the text we would use for this volume. Certainly Gherardi did not have the full scenes of *Arlequin* for his single-volume edition in 1694, but whether he obtained them from his troupe after 1697, or simply used the scenes from the Garnier edition for the publication in 1700, we have no way of knowing.

---

[92]   Mary Anne O'Donnell, 'Aphra Behn: The Documentary Record', in *The Cambridge Companion to Aphra Behn*, ed. by Derek Hughes and Janet Todd (Cambridge: Cambridge University Press, 2004), pp. 1–11 (p. 6).

[93]   David Roberts, *Thomas Betterton: The Greatest Actor of the Restoration Stage* (Cambridge: Cambridge University Press, 2010), p. 145.

[94]   *The London Stage, 1660–1800*, ed. by William Van Lennep, Emmett L. Avery, and others, 5 vols in 11 (Carbondale: Southern Illinois University Press, 1960–1968), I: *Part I: 1660–1700*, ed. by Van Lennep (1965), p. 333.

[95]   Frans Muller, 'Flying Dragons and Dancing Chairs at Dorset Garden: Staging *Dioclesian*', *Theatre Notebook*, 47.2 (1993), 80–95 (p. 83).

[96]   Jacob Hooke, *Pinacotheca Bettertonæana: Or, A Catalogue of the Books, Drawings, Prints, and Paintings of Mr. Thomas Betterton, that Celebrated Comedian, lately Deceased* (1710), ed. by David Roberts (London: Society for Theatre Research, 2013), p. 162.

The edition of Aphra Behn's *The Emperor of the Moon* transcribed here was published in 1687, the first edition of the play. Since the English language had yet to be standardised, and because we wanted to present Behn's text in the same language and format in which she would have seen it through the publication process, we determined neither to modernise the language nor standardise the play's format. We did, however, add scene numbers where she had simply written 'scene' or where the incorrect scene number had been inserted. This, we hope, will help students and scholars in reading and writing about the play. On rare occasions, we felt it necessary to intervene in Behn's spelling for clarity. We determined 'cloths' could well be understood for 'clothes', for example, or 'ridle' for 'riddle'; however, a word like 'hast' for 'haste' might in some instances cause difficulty, so that the meaning 'I must hast[e]' is understood rather than 'I must have'. Other than in such infrequent incidences, the spelling, punctuation, and capitalisation are Behn's. Where there may remain some difficulty in the reader's understanding, we have included a footnote.

We would like to thank the Huntington Library in San Marino, California, for providing us access to the 1687 edition. The *Emperor of the Moon* was republished in 1688; a number of editions of the play have been printed over the centuries, including editions in London, Dublin, Paris, New York and so forth. In her second edition of *Aphra Behn: An Annotated Bibliography of Primary and Secondary Sources* (2003), Mary Ann O'Donnell provides publishing documentation and a scholarly bibliography on Behn's works. In her edition of Behn's collected works, Janet Todd offers the variants between the 1687 and 1688 editions of *Emperor of the Moon*.[97]

We would also like to thank the Bibliothèque nationale de France for permission to publish this English translation of the French scenes of Anne Mauduit de Fatouville's *Arlequin, Empereur dans la lune*. Although these scenes were originally printed in a combination of seventeenth-century French and Italian languages, they are translated here into modern English; the format of the scenes, including at times the rather extensive stage directions, is that which is found in the original volume.

---

[97] Janet Todd, 'Variants', in *The Works of Aphra Behn* (Columbus: Ohio State University Press, 1992–1996), VII, *The Plays 1682–1696* (1996), pp. 466–74.

THE EMPEROR OF THE MOON:
A CRITICAL DISCUSSION

Aphra Behn's *Emperor of the Moon* has recently attracted the critical attention it has long deserved. This late seventeenth-century operatic spectacle was so popular with audiences that it was restaged repeatedly well into the eighteenth century. The play has been studied through a number of lenses, more recently as a satire on Dryden's *Albion and Albanius* (1685).[1] Other scholars have considered the play as Behn's response to a backlash against farce, as a satire on the Royal Society and/or fantastic lunar voyages, as a study of monstrous identity, or as a portrayal of social class and upward social mobility.[2]

The Emperor of the Moon, however, also sheds light on Behn's rejection of the notion of a plurality of worlds, an idea that even in the late seventeenth century was still contentious.[3] Behn rebuffs the idea of inhabited other worlds, especially an inhabited Moon, as she draws throughout her play on contemporary astronomical texts, whether 'scientific' discussions or fantastic fiction, authored by men like Francis Godwin (1562–1633), Nicolas-Pierre-Henri de Montfaucon, the Abbé de Villars (1635–1673), John Wilkins (1614–1672), and Bernard le Bovier de Fontenelle (1657–1757). She provides a window to her opinion from the outset of the play through Elaria, the daughter of the virtuoso Doctor Baliardo, who discusses her father with Scaramouch, her father's 'man'. The two agree that Baliardo is a 'Lunatick',[4] who has become infected with the idea of an inhabited Moon from

> reading foolish Books, *Lucian's Dialogue of the Lofty Traveller*, who flew up
> to the Moon, and thence to Heaven; an Heroick business called, *The Man*

---

[1]   Al Coppola, 'Retraining the Virtuoso's Gaze: Behn's *Emperor of the Moon*, The Royal Society, and the Spectacles of Science and Politics', *Eighteenth-Century Studies*, 41.4 (2008), 481–506 (p. 482).

[2]   Steven Henderson, '"*Deceptio Visus*": Aphra Behn's Negotiation with Farce in *The Emperor of the Moon*', in *Aphra Behn (1640–1689): Identity, Alterity, Ambiguity*, ed. by Mary Ann O'Donnell and others (Paris: L'Harmattan, 2000), pp. 59–64; Barbara Benedict, *Curiosity: A Cultural History of Early Modern Inquiry* (Chicago: University of Chicago Press, 2001), pp. 59–60; Cynthia Lowenthal, *Performing Identities on the Restoration Stage* (Carbondale: Southern Illinois University Press, 2003), p. 14; Susan Staves, 'Behn, Women, and Society', in *The Cambridge Companion to Aphra Behn*, ed. by Hughes and Todd, pp. 12–18.

[3]   Judy A. Hayden, 'Harlequin Science: Aphra Behn's *Emperor of the Moon* and the Plurality of Worlds', *English*, 64.246 (2015), 167–282 (pp. 167–68).

[4]   The term 'lunatic' in the seventeenth century not only referred to madness but more specifically to someone who was deeply affected by the Moon, typically thought to be owing to the various lunar phases.

in the Moon, if you'll believe a *Spaniard*, who was carried thether, upon an
Engine drawn by wild Geese; with another Philosophical Piece, *A Discourse
of the World in the Moon*; with a thousand other ridiculous Volumes too
hard to name. (1.1.88–93)[5]

The texts to which Elaria refers here are Francis Godwin's *The Man in the
Moone* (1638), which had been reprinted in London in 1686;[6] a partial translation
of Lucian of Samosata's (125 AD–*c*.180 AD) *Certain Select Dialogues* (1663);[7] and
John Wilkins' *The Discovery of a World in the Moone* (London, 1638), all of
which were popular in England during the seventeenth century.[8] Behn draws
on other 'ridiculous volumes' as well, including those Elaria does not mention,
such as Fontenelle's *Entretiens sur la pluralité des mondes* (1686), which Behn
was to translate as *A Discovery of New Worlds* (1688), the Abbé de Villars' *Count
of Gabalis* (1680),[9] and Cyrano de Bergerac's (1619–1655) *The Comical History
Of The States And Empires Of The Worlds Of The Moon and Sun* (Paris, 1657),
republished in London in 1687.[10]

While some of these texts are humorous tall tales of lunar voyages, some deal
more seriously with astronomy, such as Wilkins' *A Discovery of a New World*
(1684), probably the 'Philosophical Piece' Elaria mentions that her father has
read. While Behn may have found the fiction of Lucian, the Abbé de Villars, and
Godwin humorous — and she does make various references to their ideas in her
farce — she was more concerned about the serious discussions of a plurality of
worlds. Wilkins, for example, defended the possibility of other worlds, arguing

---

[5]   References are to act, (interpolated) scene, and line number of the present edition.
[6]   Grant McColley, 'The Third Edition of Francis Godwin's *The Man in the Moon*', *The
Library*, s4, 17.4 (1937), pp. 472–75.
[7]   Lucian of Samosata, *Certain Select Dialogues of Lucian: Together with his True History*,
trans. by Francis Hickes (London: for Richard Davis, 1663).
[8]   John Wilkins, *The Discovery of a World in the Moone. Or, A Discourse Tending To Prove
that 'tis probable there may be another habitable World in that Planet* (London: E. G. for
Michael Sparke and Edward Forrest, 1638); the volume was republished a number of times
and reissued in 1684 as *A Discovery Of A New World, Or, A Discourse Tending to prove, that
'tis Probable there may be another Habitable World in the Moon* (London: T. M. & J. A. for
John Gillibrand, 1684) which included a second volume, *A Discourse Concerning a New
Planet, Tending to prove That 'tis probable our Earth is one of the Planets*. The 1684 volume
is used here unless otherwise noted.
[9]   Aphra Behn, *A Discovery of New Worlds. From the* French. *Made English by Mrs.* A.
Behn (London: for William Canning, 1688). Behn's 'Translator's Preface' is unpaginated;
the quoted pages are noted here in brackets. *Le Comte de Gabalis, ou Entretiens sur les
Sciences secrètes* (Paris, 1670), translated into English by Philip Ayers and published as *The
Count of Gabalis: Or, The Extravagant Mysteries Of The Cabalists, Exposed in Five Pleasant
Discourses On The Secret Sciences* (London: for B. M., Printer to the Cabalistical Society of
the Sages, 1680).
[10] Savinien Cyrano de Bergerac, *Histoire comique des états et empires de la Lune et du Soleil*
(Paris, 1657), trans. by A. Lovell as *The Comical History Of The States And Empires Of The
Worlds Of The Moon and Sun* (London: for Henry Rhodes, 1687).

that scripture did not prove otherwise. '[I]f the Holy Ghost had intended to reveal unto us any Natural Secrets, certainly he would never have omitted the Mention of the Plannets' (p. 24), he writes, adding later that 'Absurdities have followed, when Men look for the Grounds of Philosophy in the Words of Scripture' (p. 28). Philosophers should not expect to find scriptural proof of other inhabited worlds since Moses and the prophets could not impart any more to the 'Ignorant and Ruder sort of People' than what was visible to them; therefore, Wilkins concludes, 'the silence of Scripture, concerning any other World, is not Sufficient Argument to prove that there is none' (pp. 25, 28).

The *Emperor of the Moon* was first performed in spring 1687,[11] prior to the publication of Behn's translation of Fontenelle's *Entretiens sur la pluralité des mondes* the following year. Whether she had begun her translation of the *Entretiens* when she sat down to complete her play is uncertain, but she protests the notion of a plurality of worlds in her 'Translator's Preface' to Fontenelle's text, where she points out that those who subscribe to the theory of inhabited worlds fail to recognise scripture and church authorities on the issue.

> We live in an Age, wherein many believe nothing contained in that holy Book, others turn it into Ridicule [...] I think it is the Duty of all good Christians to acquiesce in the Opinion and Decrees of the Church of Christ, in whom dwells the Spirit of God, which enlightens us to Matters of Religion and Faith; and as to other things contained in the Holy Scriptures relating to Astronomy, Geometry, Chronology, or other liberal Sciences, we leave those Points to the Opinions of the Learned [...] and this with all Submission to the Canons of General Councils, and Decrees of the Church. ([pp. 24–25])

Fontenelle, she complains, 'ascribes all to Nature, and says not a Word of God Almighty, from the Beginning to the End; so that one would almost take him to be a Pagan' ([p. 10]).

Behn does not directly address 'matters of religion' in *The Emperor of the Moon*; rather, she mocks those otherworldly texts with which many in her audience would have been familiar. At the same time, however, she responds somewhat anxiously to the opinions presented by men like Wilkins, and particularly Fontenelle, replying in various scenes and snippets to what she viewed as their fanciful assertions.

1. Staging the Spectacle: The Dorset Garden Theatre

The decreasing audience attendance in the latter decades of the seventeenth century became a serious problem for the two theatre companies, the King's Company, who were playing at the Theatre Royal, and the Duke's Company,

---

[11]   Van Lennep gives the first performance of *Emperor of the Moon* as possibly March 1687, although the play was licensed 6 April 1687; *London Stage, Part I*, pp. 356–57.

who were staging their plays at the Dorset Garden Theatre. A number of playwrights attributed poor audience attendance to the political chaos caused by the Popish Plot and Exclusion Crisis (1678–1681). John Crowne, for example, noted in the prologue to his play *The Ambitious Statesman* (1679) that '*now the Nation in a tempest rowles*', and as a result '*our poor play house, [is] fallen to the ground*'.[12] Anthony Carey, Viscount Falkland (1656–1694), who wrote the prologue for Thomas Otway's (1652–1685) *The Souldiers Fortune* (1681), observed the '*hard Fate of our abandon'd Stage*', where audiences are '*ravisht from our Arms*'.[13]

When the King's Company halted performances for part of 1679, the lack of competition between the theatres did not contribute to an increase in attendance at the Dorset Garden, as one might assume, for Behn noted the following in her epilogue to *The Feign'd Curtizans* (1679): '*So hard the Times are, and so thin the Town, | Though but one Playhouse, that must too lie down*'.[14] The King's Company, which was suffering from dissention within its own community as well as economic mismanagement, was hard hit.[15] The two theatre companies finally merged in 1682 to form the United Company. The players moved for the most part to the larger Theatre Royal for their performances, while the Dorset Garden Theatre, home of the former Duke's Company, was reserved largely for operas and spectacles.

Charles II regularly attended the theatre and was one of its most active patrons. In fact, he was not averse to offering advice or making requests, intervening in casting and even assisting a playwright in the composition of a play;[16] Behn refers to the King in her dedication to *The Emperor of the Moon* as '*that Great Patron of Noble Poetry, and the Stage*' (p. 47). The King let it be known that he was particularly fond of French theatre and sent Thomas Betterton to France in 1662 and again in 1671 to study French scenes and machines. The new staging equipment Betterton developed after his Paris visits was used for a number of operatic entertainments, such as Elkanah Settle's (1648–1724) *Empress of Morocco* (1673), Thomas Shadwell's *Psyche* (1674), and Charles Davenant's (1656–1714) *Circe* (1677), to name but a few.[17]

---

[12]   John Crowne, 'Prologue', to *The Ambitious Statesman, or The Loyal Favorite*, in *The Dramatic Works of John Crowne*, ed. by James Maidment and William Hugh Logan, 4 vols (Edinburgh: William Paterson 1873–1874), III (1874), pp. 131–241 (p. 148).

[13]   Anthony Carey, Viscount Falkland, 'Prologue', in Thomas Otway, *The Souldiers Fortune: A Comedy*, in *The Works of Thomas Otway*, ed. by Montague Summers, 3 vols (Bloomsbury: The Nonesuch Press, 1926), II, pp. 231–310 (p. 239, ll. 3–4).

[14]   Aphra Behn, 'Epilogue', in *The Feign'd Curtizans, or, A Night's Intrigue* (London: for Jacob Tonson, 1679), p. 72; *London Stage*, I, Part I, pp. 271 and 279.

[15]   *London Stage*, I, Part I, p. 271.

[16]   *London Stage*, 'Introduction', I, Part I, p. clii.

[17]   Robert Hume, 'The Dorset Garden Theatre: A Review of Facts and Problems', *Theatre Notebook*, 30.2 (1979), pp. 4–17, and 'Nature of the Dorset Garden Theatre', *Theatre Notebook*,

In 1685, John Dryden prepared to stage his long awaited operatic celebration of Charles II, *Albion and Albanius* (1685).[18] Dryden's spectacle, however, was marred with the death of the King in February 1685.[19] Although Dryden added lines 'to recognize the death of Charles and the accession of James', the play was simply not to have its full run, for after only two days on the boards, it was interrupted again, this time by the Monmouth rebellion in June 1685.[20] Even so, the machines and scenes that were constructed for Dryden's ill-fated *Albion and Albanius* were well-suited for the spectacle of Behn's third act. For example, in Act One of Dryden's opera, a number of machines descend: one with Mercury in a chariot drawn by ravens, a further chariot drawn by peacocks bringing Juno on stage, and a machine large enough for three people in which Iris appears. In Act Three, scene one, a large oval-shaped machine descends.

The machines that dazzled audiences in Dryden's opera became vehicles by which Behn's characters could descend onto the stage. Thus, 'Keplair *and* Gallileus *descend on each side* [*of the stage*], *opposite to each other, in Chariots*', while a large zodiac also arrives with its chorus of singers and dancers. A '*Globe of the Moon*' follows, in which the audience can see the Emperor and the Prince. Dryden's opera required a large company of singers and dancers, scenes depicting the heavens, and a scene with a walk of high trees. In the third act spectacle of Behn's *The Emperor of the Moon*, the scene draws off to a '*large Walk of Trees*', no doubt the same scene used in *Albion and Albanius*, and she employs a large cast of singers for her zodiac spectacle.

Although Behn's play was performed more than 130 times between 1687 and 1749,[21] much of the interest in the theatre itself remained subdued, so that few new plays were undertaken. As Derek Hughes points out, there was also a decline in tragedy in the period between 1682 and 1688, and most of the comedy produced during this period was 'farcical or lightweight'.[22] Behn acknowledges in the dedication to *The Emperor of the Moon* that she chose to write farce owing to poor audience attendance. While London in earlier days was able '*to keep so many play houses alive*', she points out, there is now hardly sufficient audience interest to '*supply one*' (p. 48). In the prologue to *Emperor of the Moon*, she declares that theatre audiences want neither tragedy nor comedy, so her only recourse was farce (p. 49); but even farce was struggling on the stage, so that 'There's nothing lasting but the Puppets Show' (p. 50). Shadwell observed

36.3 (1982), pp. 99–109; John R. Spring, 'Dorset Garden Theatre: Playhouse or Opera House', *Theatre Notebook*, 34.2 (1980), pp. 60–69.

[18]   John Dryden, *Albion and Albanius*, in *The Works of John Dryden*, XV, ed. by Earl Miner and George R. Guffey (1976), pp. 1–55.

[19]   Earl Miner and George R. Guffey, 'Commentary', *Albion and Albanius*, p. 323.

[20]   Miner and Guffey, 'Commentary', p. 323.

[21]   Frederick Link, *Aphra Behn* (New York: Twayne Publishers, 1968), p. 80.

[22]   Derek Hughes, *English Drama 1660–1700* (Oxford: Clarendon Press, 1996), p. 306.

in his *Squire of Alsatia* (1688) that comedies could no longer fill the theatre and farce was all the rage, adding in his prologue that audiences were tired of '*wholesome Food*' and desired trash.[23] In *Don Sebastian: King of Portugal* (1690), Dryden also noted the changes in the theatre, grumbling that it was difficult to please audiences as comedy was '*almost spent*', while '*Love and Honour (the mistaken Topicks of Tragedy)*' were so '*worn out, that the Theatres cou'd not support their charges*', and thus the '*Audience forsook them*'.[24]

2. Adapting the French Text

Although Behn claims in her dedication to *Emperor of the Moon* that she took only '*A very barren and thin hint of the Plot from the Italian*' and that '*all the Words are wholly new, without one from the Original*' (p. 47), this is absolutely not the case. The English translation of Fatouville's French scenes in the present edition demonstrate just how far Behn extended that 'hint'. Her claim may simply have been meant to acknowledge that she had used a source and thus to deflect criticism about the playwright's 'borrowing', a criticism levelled recurrently at playwrights in general, but particularly at Behn and Dryden. That most of her critics probably would not have had access to her French source may have encouraged her to bolster her claim.

Even so, Behn's revisions of Fatouville's French text of *Arlequin* significantly enhanced her play, particularly for the elaborate operatic spectacle of the third act on the Dorset Garden stage, employing to advantage the impressive new stage equipment. Her alterations include revising, cutting, or condensing a number of speeches, creating a carefully scripted plot, adding new scenes, and infusing the play with much more action than we see in the French scenes alone. Fatouville had relied on a minimal number of *commedia* characters, as Louis XIV had drawn up a series of rules in 1684 for his Italian actors 'to establish good order', and those rules included that the Italian troupe 'be composed always of a fixed number of twelve actors and actresses who are agreeable to him [the King] to serve in his royal houses when it pleases him'.[25]

Fatouville's listed characters, twelve in all, included Harlequin (*Arlequin*), the Doctor (*Docteur*), his daughter Isabelle and his niece Eularia, the ladies' servant Colombine, the Doctor's own servant Pierrot, Scaramouche, a clerk and policeman (*commissaire*), ending his play with three anonymous 'Knights of the

---

[23] Thomas Shadwell, 'The Epistle Dedicatory', in *The Squire of Alsatia. A Comedy* (1688), *Works*, ed. by Summers, IV, pp. 191–283 (p. 204).

[24] Dryden, 'The Preface', in *Don Sebastian, King of Portugal*, in *Works*, XV, pp. 57–219 (p. 65).

[25] *French Theatre in the Neo-Classical Era*, Document 295, pp. 292–93; Scott, *The Commedia dell'Arte in Paris*, p. 242.

Sun' (*Chevaliers du Soleil*).[26] Behn keeps many of these *commedia* characters, such as Doctor Baliardo and Harlequin, but scripts Scaramouch as the Doctor's 'man' rather than Pierrot, perhaps because the Scaramouch character had already established a presence for English audiences. In Fatouville's text, Scaramouche only appears in the final scene, suggesting that this character's key role was largely in the improvised Italian scenes, which were not printed. Pasquariel shows up periodically in the French scenes, a thirteenth character, although he is not noted in the list of characters, nor does he speak in these scenes; neither does Scaramouche, which raises the question of whether the playwright had forgotten that he had used Pasquariel earlier instead of Scaramouche, or, perhaps more likely, that these scenes were produced when the 'rules' for the *Comédie-Italienne* were implied or preferred, but before they were actually instituted.[27] However, since only the French scenes were printed, both Pasquariel and Scaramouche probably assumed a larger role in the improvised Italian scenes.

In Behn's farce, Scaramouch plays a major role as a facilitator for the young *innamorati*, while also vying with Harlequin for the two zanies' mutual love interest, Mopsophil. Behn transposes or even renames some of the characters, so that the Doctor's daughter here becomes Elaria, his niece Bellemante, and their governess Mopsophil. In the French text, Isabelle mentions Cinthio in scene four, but he does not appear on stage in Fatouville's printed text. Behn adds Cinthio as a main character, along with Don Charmante, as the lovers of Elaria and Bellemante, respectively; she also creates the character Florinda, a cousin to the young ladies. Behn retains the clerk and the officer, but adds Pedro, who is sometimes referred to as Peter, as Doctor Baliardo's 'boy'. Pedro is the Spanish version of the French 'Pierrot' (Peter), although Pierrot has a much larger role in the French text than in Behn's adaptation. Unconstrained by the French authority's rules for the regulation of the *Comédie-Italienne*, she adds a number of characters, such as those minor actors who populate the stunning operatic spectacle of the final scene, including 'Gallileus', 'Keplair', 'Stentraphon', and a host of pages, singers, dancers, musicians, and so forth.

Behn's four young lovers in this play are *commedia* characters known as *innamorati* or lovers. The *innamorati* were young and of the better classes,

---

[26] To differentiate in our discussion between the Harlequin character of the original French scenes and that of Behn's English adaptation, throughout this essay we have used 'Arlequin' in reference to the French scenes and 'Harlequin' in reference to the English farce. *Arlequin* italicised is a reference to the French text itself. Scaramouch is spelled with an 'e' in the French text, Scaramouche, and without in the English.

[27] 'The troupe will always be composed of twelve actors and actresses, that is to say two women to play the serious roles, two other women for the comic roles, two men to play the lovers' roles, two others to play the comic roles, two others to guide the plot and two others to play the fathers and old men.' *French Theatre in the Neo-Classical Era*, Document 295, p. 292.

typically appearing in groups of four, in which there were two couples. Eularia
and Cinzio were standard *innamorati* characters (as was the male Florindo,
rather than Behn's female Florinda). The names Charmante and Bellemante
are more rarely found in *commedia* scenes. This may well be because while
a certain number of the *commedia* players were stock characters, performers
also invented and developed their own names and personas, so that there were
multiple lesser-known *innamorati*. Given that the actors playing Charmante and
Bellemante were William Mountfort and his wife Susanna Percival Mountfort,
who had married 2 July 1686, these names may have had a more intimate
meaning — affectionate tags the couple developed themselves specifically for
this role.[28] Charmante is the feminised version of the masculine Charmant in
French, or 'lovely', a name that reminds one of the Prince Charming of fairy
tales. That Behn feminised Charmante's name may reflect a further intimate
tease or tag by the newly-married actors themselves.

Behn's play hinges on her lunatic doctor, but, however silly Doctor Baliardo
may appear at times, he is not a virtuoso in the manner of Sir Nicholas
Gimcrack in Thomas Shadwell's *The Virtuoso* (1676).[29] Sir Nicholas knows
nothing worthwhile; in fact, he claims, 'I never invented so much as an Engine
to pair Cream-cheese with. We Virtuoso's never find out anything of use, 'tis
not our way' (v.169). His experiments are pointless and his claims outrageously
false. For example, he alleges that he is so advanced in the art of flying that he
can outfly 'that pond'rous Animal call'd a *Bustard*; nor should any Grey-hound
in *England* catch me in the calmest day' (ii.126). In fact, he has so improved
the art of flying that it should shortly be as common 'to fly to the World in
the Moon, as to buy a pair of Wax Boots to ride into Sussex with' (ii.126). In
experimenting with the transfusion of blood, Sir Nicholas claims he exchanged
sheep's blood with a human male, resulting in the man bleating 'perpetually'
and having 'Wool growing on him in great quantities' (ii.129–30). Shadwell's
virtuoso was never inducted into the Royal Society, referred to in the play as
'The Colledge', for notwithstanding his being 'a rare Mechanick Philosopher', as
Lady Gimcrack notes, he was refused entry because 'they envy'd him' (ii.125).

Behn's learned doctor is not only a lunatic, but he is caught up in alchemy as
well, as his exchanges with Scaramouch in Act Three, scene two demonstrate,
but he does not profess outrageous claims, nor does he boast of the outcomes
of any experiments. Thus, while some have suggested that the Royal Society of
London is the focus of Behn's satire, her learned doctor's emphasis is less on

---

[28] 'William Mountfort', in *A Biographical Dictionary of Actors, Actresses, Musicians,
Dancers, Managers & Other Stage Personnel in London, 1660–1800*, ed. by Philip H. Highfill,
Jr, and others, 16 vols (Carbondale: Southern Illinois University Press, 1973–1993), x (1984),
pp. 354–59 (p. 356).
[29] Thomas Shadwell, *The Virtuoso*, in *Works*, ed. by Summers, iii, pp. 95–182. Subsequent
references to this play are by act and page numbers.

any society or experimentation than it is directed to his study of the Moon and his desire to join his daughter and niece in marriage to lunar royalty, that he might have 'super' grandsons. In addition, Behn's friendships with members of the Society, such as Thomas Sprat, who Janet Todd claims may have arranged for Behn's burial in the cloisters of Westminster Abbey, would not suggest a send-up of the organisation to which her friends and patrons belonged.[30] A number of the dedicatees to her works were Society members, such as Henry Howard, Seventh Duke of Norfolk (1655–1701), Robert Spencer, Second Earl of Sunderland (1641–1702), and, of course, Charles Somerset, Marquess of Worcester (1660–1698), to whom *Emperor of the Moon* was dedicated and who had been inducted into the Society at the age of thirteen.

In the French *Arlequin*, the Doctor's study and the marriages of his daughter and his niece seem less the core of the scenes than is the ridiculous competition between Arlequin and Pierrot for the love of Colombine. Nor does the elaborate peeping into the Emperor's closet of Behn's play occur in the French *Arlequin*, where the arrival of the purported ambassador in the French farce occurs later in the action. In the French scene, entitled 'With the Envoy and Arlequin's Travels in the Empire of the Moon', Arlequin dupes the Doctor into believing that he has come as representative of the Emperor of the Moon to seek his daughter Isabelle in marriage. Arlequin pretends to communicate with the Emperor through a 'trumpet', aided perhaps by Pasquariel rather than Pierrot, although the speaker of the lines is not identified; however, Pasquariel dresses Arlequin in the costume of the Emperor at the end of scene five, so he is the likely participant in the scheme. In the process of 'communicating' with the Emperor of the Moon, Arlequin cons the Doctor out of gold coins and a diamond ring. In return for his daughter Isabelle in marriage, the Emperor will reward the Doctor with Scorpio's place in the zodiac. Fatouville's brief proposal of an earthly/lunar union becomes in Behn's play the foundation of the ruse around which her two sets of young lovers cozen the tyrannical Doctor.

3. Critical Analysis

In the opening scene of the French *Arlequin*, the Doctor and Pierrot enter the garden to study the Moon, where the Doctor attempts to teach Pierrot such concepts as generation and corruption; for Pierrot, however, the 'science' behind the hypotheses that the Doctor presents is beyond his comprehension and causes him to conclude that the Moon is like an omelette. This scene ends with the Doctor announcing his plans to marry Colombine to one of three men: a farmer, a baker, or an apothecary — although he favours the farmer. Arlequin and Pierrot gambol throughout the following scenes, as they contest

---

[30] Janet Todd, *The Secret Life of Aphra Behn* (London: André Deutsch, 1996), p. 435.

each other's right to Colombine's affections. Over the course of *Arlequin, Empereur dans la lune*, Arlequin disguises himself in the professions of each of Colombine's three suitors as he vies for her hand.

Behn adapts the French text, so that Doctor Baliardo plays a larger role, not only as the lunatic virtuoso obsessed with the study of the Moon, but also as an authoritarian patriarch, who restricts the freedom of his daughter Elaria and his niece Bellemante, so they have little prospect for love. It is to the *zanni* Scaramouch then that Elaria and Bellemante must turn to further their secret correspondences and assignations with Don Cinthio and Don Charmante, respectively. The breaks in the main plot come with the outrageous schemes of Harlequin and Scaramouch to outclass each other in their contest for Mopsophil, the governess of the young ladies, who is looking for love herself. All this is capped with the elaborate scheme the young men concoct to wed the ladies and to enlighten and cure Baliardo of his lunar infection.

Through Scaramouch's clowning repartee, we learn that Elaria's father 'Religiously believes there is a World there [in the Moon], that he discourses as gravely of the People, their Government, Institutions, Laws, Manners, Religion and Constitution, as if he had been bred a *Machiavel* there' (I.I.84–86). Elaria's discourse here has something in common with that of the Marquise in Fontenelle's *Entretiens sur la pluralité des mondes*, where she tells the Philosopher that she would have the four moons of Jupiter 'to be Colonies of *Jupiter* and [the inhabitants] receive their Laws and Manners from thence, and pay Homage and Respect to *Jupiter*' (p. 117). From Lucian's *Dialogues* to Godwin's 'gansas', the Doctor studies stories of lunar voyages and lunar peoples. He is a great scholar, Scaramouch acknowledges, 'as grave and wise a Man, in all Argument and Discourse, as can be met with, yet name but the Moon, and he runs into Ridicule, and grows as mad as the Wind' (II.[3].167–69). Scaramouch prepares the audience for the fun that is to follow when he informs Elaria that Cinthio and Charmante are preparing a 'Farce, which shall be called [...] *the World in the Moon*' (I.I.99). The title suggests Wilkins' 1638 publication, *The Discovery of a World in the Moone*, and may well serve as a covert signal to that text. To forward the charade, Scaramouch adds, '*Charmante* is dressing himself like one of the Caballists of the *Rosacrusian* [sic] Order, and is coming to prepare my credulous Master for the greater imposition' (I.I.104–06).

The garden scene in Act One, scene two of Behn's play is surely one of the most comical in the farce. It is indebted to the opening scene of *Arlequin*, although Behn adds considerable detail as she prepares her audience for the spectacle in Act Three. Like the French scene, Baliardo and Scaramouch have set up a telescope to view the Moon; but while in the French scene the Doctor and Pierrot argue philosophical concepts like generation and corruption, Behn's farce moves directly into the action with the arrival of a lunar visitor — Charmante, disguised in peculiar attire, who enters the garden, declaring that he is the Ambassador of the Moon. He has come because Baliardo's reputation for great learning has brought him to the attention of the Caballa of Iredonozar's, Emperor of the lunar world, Eutopia (1.2.25–26). Behn appropriates the name from contemporary lunar fiction, for Irdonozur is the name of the first great lunar monarch in Francis Godwin's *Man in the Moone*.[31] Drawing on the Abbé de Villars' *Count de Gabalis*, who in turn borrowed from Paracelsus, Charmante insists on the truth of the Rosicrucian notion of divine beings, those salamanders, gnomes, sylphs, and nymphs, whose 'conjunction with mortals' begets noble and/or immortal men.[32] Charmante not only offers Baliardo the opportunity to enjoy one of these divine spirits himself, but also the prospect of uniting his daughter and niece with these beings, which leads the Doctor to disclose that he would like to have 'a Hero to my Grandson' (1.2.102–03). Behn pushes this amusing scene even further when Charmante directs the Doctor to peer through the telescope, while he secretly claps images to the lens — a nymph painted on one glass and the Emperor himself on another — claiming that these are inhabitants of Eutopia. When Baliardo observes that the Emperor appears 'sad and pensive', Charmante remarks that the Emperor's love fit is on, as he is infatuated with a mortal woman, leaving Baliardo to hope the mortal is his daughter Elaria (1.2.107–09).

The first grand spectacle in the play comes in Act Two, when Doctor Baliardo returns home unexpectedly, having been intentionally misled by Scaramouch that his brother was ill and near death; however, having met his brother's valet along the way, the Doctor has been speedily undeceived. On his return, Baliardo hears the musicians the young couples have invited for their evening's entertainment, which Scaramouch claims is 'the tuning of the Spheres, some serenade, Sir, from the Inhabitants of the Moon' (II.[3].81–82). In his *Discovery of a New World* (1684), Wilkins points out that 'there is no Musick of the Spheres', although he acknowledges that Plutarch believed a man might hear such harmony 'if he were an Inhabitant in the Moon'; however, Wilkins adds, 'because it is not now, I think, Affirm'd by any, I shall not therefore bestow either Pains or Time in Arguing against it' (pp. 42–43). In elaborate

---

[31] Francis Godwin, *The Man in the Moone* (1638), ed. by William Poole (Peterborough, Ontario: Broadview Press, 2009), p. 102.

[32] Abbé de Villars, *The Count of Gabalis*, pp. 14–18, 27–33. Villars draws here on Paracelsus' doctrine of spirits and the four humours. The Rosicrucians held Paracelsus in deep regard and some scholars have suggested they did likewise with the Abbé de Villars. See Paracelsus, 'A Book on Nymphs, Sylphs, Pygmies and Salamanders and on other Spirits', in *Four Treatises of Theophrastus von Hohenheim called Paracelsus*, ed. by Henry Sigerest (Baltimore: John Hopkins University Press, 1996), pp. 213–54; *Paracelsus: Essential Theoretical Writings*, ed. by Andrew Weeks, *Aries Book Series*, vol. 5 (Boston: Brill, 2008); Franz Hartmann, *The Life and Doctrines of Philippus Theophrastus, Bombast of Hohenhem* [*sic*] *known by the name of Paracelsus* (1891. New York: John W. Lovell, 1963).

scenic staging, Scaramouch shows the Doctor the ornate hangings in which he has placed the lovers and the dancers, alleging that these must have come from the cabalists. Scaramouch's success in hiding the lovers is undone, though, when Harlequin, one of the figures in the hanging, hits the Doctor on the head with his truncheon.

The Doctor's comical interview of Harlequin as a *Fille de Chambre*, a scene which comes largely from the French *Arlequin*, is interrupted by Charmante's second visit as the ambassador from the Moon. On this second and last visit, the 'ambassador' assures the Doctor that his daughter and niece are the chosen ones and that he should prepare for his celestial guests and the wedding to follow (II.[5].172–74). In the operatic masque which concludes the play, Behn engages in the concept of observing the heavens as an opera, an idea that also arises in the first night's discussion between the philosopher-speaker and the Marquise in Fontenelle's *Entretiens*, where the speaker remarks that

> Nature is a great Scene, or Representation, much like one of our *Opera's*; for, from the place where you sit to behold the *Opera*, you do not see the Stage, as really it is, Since every thing is disposed there for the representing agreeable Objects to your sight, from a large distance, while the wheels & weights, which move and counterpoise the Machines are all concealed from our view. (pp. 9–10)

Kepler and Galileo, interpreters to the great Iredonozar in Behn's play, carry perspectives as if viewing the mechanics of the zodiac. The zodiac, that great 'Circle of fixed Stars' of Fontenelle's text (p. 28), appears as a main feature in Behn's masque, as it descends and delivers the twelve signs — the singers of the masque — who declare in a song that the zodiac is commanded by the 'Force of Love'. The Moon appears to descend and the Emperor Iredonozar and the Prince of Thunderland disembark, where Baliardo, believing his daughter is about to marry the Emperor and his niece the Prince, gives his permission for the unions.

Behn's masque ends as two Knights of the Sun suddenly enter the scene to engage in battle. In the last scene of the French text, three unidentified Knights of the Sun engage Arlequin, Scaramouche, and the Doctor in battle. The *commedia* characters are easily defeated, and the Knights take Eularia and Isabelle with them, leaving Colombine for the 'Cowardly knight', Arlequin. In Behn's *Emperor of the Moon*, however, there are but two Knights of the Sun, Harlequin and Scaramouch, who compete against each other for Mopsophil. Their battle begins the 'great reveal' which concludes with Scaramouch divulging his identity by removing his helmet and thus inadvertently enlightening Doctor Baliardo of his folly. 'Oh, I am undone and cheated in every way', Baliardo cries out (III.[3].187).

The *commedia* doctor, Harold Knutson points out, 'is a permanent misfit, and his intrusion into polite society can only result in ridicule and humiliation'.[33] And so he is here as the blocking figure opposing the two young couples. There is no Emperor of the Moon just as there is no Moon world; such ideas are ridiculous inventions, simply stories 'To puzzle Fools withal—the Wise laugh at 'em', claims Cinthio (III.[3].210). In showing Baliardo the nature of his folly, they prevented 'a Scandal on your Learned Name' (III.[3].215), the same concern Behn expressed about Fontenelle, who, she asserts in her introduction to *A Discovery of New Worlds*, had compromised his reputation because he

> pushed his wild Notion of the Plurality of Worlds *to that heighth* [sic] *of Extravagancy, that he most certainly will confound those Readers, who have not Judgment and Wit to distinguish between what is truly solid (or, at least, probable) and what is trifling and airy.* ([p. 9])

Behn's Doctor Baliardo vows to give up his study once he is brought to realise the notion of a plurality of worlds is ridiculous. He resolves to burn all his books and his study, to 'be sure the Wind | Scatter the vile Contagious Monstrous Lies' (III.[3].218–19). While the 'lies' in the books that support a plurality of worlds may well be flame worthy and although he is heard muttering quietly to himself, 'I see there's nothing in Philosophy' (III.[3].225), Baliardo does not mention his telescope nor any of his other 'little divels', as Mopsophil refers to his various 'scopes' (I.1.116–17). Thus, Behn intimates here that she does not reject astronomy as unworthy of study, but rather that pluralist notions are merely 'Fantoms of mad Brains' (III.[3].209).

4. Gender, Knowledge, and Free Hearts

In *Emperor of the Moon*, as in many of her other works, Behn forwards her case for gender equality. The play opens with a song by Elaria, who laments that women were born as '*free as Man to Love and Range*', and it is only custom that constrains them. That custom is the great oppressor of women, Behn points out in a number of her works, such as the epilogue to her play *Sir Patient Fancy* (1678):

> We once were fam'd in Story, and cou'd write
> Equall to men; cou'd Govern, nay cou'd Fight.
> We still have passive Valour, and can show
> Wou'd Custom give us leave the Active too.[34]

Elaria's song ends with a compromise of sorts—she will pretend to be a constant lover, while secretly enjoying the liberty of a free heart.

---

[33] Harold C. Knutson, *The Triumph of Wit: Molière and Restoration Comedy* (Columbus: Ohio State University Press, 1988), pp. 124–25.

[34] Aphra Behn, 'Epilogue', in *Sir Patient Fancy: A Comedy* (London: for Richard Tonson and Jacob Tonson, 1678), p. 92.

An intellectual life for women through a masculine education is the subtext of a number of Behn's works. For example, she writes in the dedication to Sir Roger Puleston of her translation *Agnes de Castro: or, The Force of Generous Love* (1688) that '*I hope the Men will not say our Sex are wholly incapable of arriving to the Excellency of their Works; or that we cannot give just and true Ideas of the Noblest Passions*'.[35] Behn rejects the idea that intellectual capacity and the female gender are incompatible. She calls attention to her point directly in the epistle to her play *The Dutch Lover* (1673), inquiring why '*waving [sic] the examination, why women having equal education with men*', they are '*not as capable of knowledge*'.[36] Line Cottegnies has pointed out that Behn edited Fontenelle's text so that references to 'men' become 'men and women', thus making 'women feature in the philosophical discourse on an equal footing with men'.[37]

Even so, Behn adopts on occasion the traditional self-effacing rhetorical stance frequently found in women's writing as she argues for female equality; however, she often assumes this stance to undercut the pretence of this posture with a demonstration of women's true abilities and understanding. For example, in her poem 'To The Unknown DAPHNIS on his Excellent Translation of *Lucretius*' (c.1683), she writes that

> Till now, I curst my Birth, my Education,
> And more the scanted Customes of the Nation:
> Permitting not the Female Sex to tread,
> The Mighty Paths of Learned Heroes Dead.[38]

Behn praises the poet Thomas Creech (1659–1700) for having rendered Lucretius into English, advancing women's understanding by offering one more avenue through which women might read classical texts. The subtext of this poem concedes overtly that women are 'of feebler Seeds design'd', but intimates as well that this is merely a cultural construct, for women were not created this way. Given a masculine education, Behn implies, she could have read the original for herself. She adopts a similar rhetorical strategy in the dedication of her translation of Fontenelle's *Entretiens*, where she asks William Douglas, Earl of Drumlangrig, for his pardon 'in a *Woman*, who is not supposed to be well

---

[35]   Aphra Behn, 'To Sir Roger Puleston, Baronet', in *Agnes de Castro: or, The Force of Generous Love*, in *Works* (London: for William Canning, 1688), unpaginated [pp. 1–6], ([p. 6]).
[36]   Aphra Behn, 'An Epistle to the Reader', in *The Dutch Lover: A Comedy* (London: for Thomas Dring, 1673), unpaginated [pp. 1–9], ([p. 7]).
[37]   Line Cottegnies, 'Aphra Behn's French Translations', in *The Cambridge Companion to Aphra Behn*, ed. by Hughes and Todd, pp. 221–34 (p. 228).
[38]   Aphra Behn 'To Mr. Creech (*under the Name of* Daphnis) *on his Excellent Translation of Lucretius*', in *Poems Upon Several Occasions: With A Voyage To The Island of Love* (London: for R. Tonson and J. Tonson, 1684), pp. 50–57 (p. 51).

versed in the Terms of Philosophy, being but a new beginner in that Science' (sigs A3–A3^v). Having offered the requisite rhetorical curtsy, she forges ahead with a display of her mathematical skill.

In her *Emperor of the Moon*, Behn draws on a correlation between mathematics and reason. Astronomy was closely allied with mathematics, and as Nicholas Jardine notes, both astronomy and mathematics were part of the *quadrivium* in the early modern university curriculum.[39] The *commedia* doctor typically carries or wears something to identify his purported expertise,[40] so the wearing of mathematical instruments would have been one way to signify the Doctor's association with astronomy. Such props, however, also offered the playwright an opportunity to provide personal comment on the intersection of intellect, gender, and reason. After all, the astronomer/mathematician here is the 'lunatick', the one who reads 'foolish books' and is 'infected' with silly ideas. Those empowered with reason in this play are Elaria and Bellemante, the Doctor's daughter and niece, and, of course, their servant Mopsophil.

As the music of the spectacle begins in Act Three, Elaria asks whether this could be enchantment. Baliardo responds by saying 'Let not thy Female Ignorance prophane the highest Mysteries of Natural Philosophy: To Fools it seems Inchantment' (III.[3].10–11). As an aside, however, he adds '[I] must conceal my Wonder — that Joy of Fools — and appear wise in Gravity' (III.[3].13–14). Not only does the irony here bring the message home, but the paradox of his remark provides the context for the spectacle and the humour which follow. As Behn moves her characters through this last act, she does not moderate her derision of the scientific texts with which she peppers her play, nor has she yet finished with the spheres of Wilkins and Fontenelle. Thus, when Bellemante hears the music of the farce the young men have arranged, she asks, 'Whence comes this charming Sound, Sir?' Baliardo replies, 'From the Spheres — it is familiar to me' (III.[3].16). When the spectacle ends, however, the Doctor learns that this charming sound of the spheres was nothing more than the musicians hired by Don Cinthio and Don Charmante as part of the wedding opera.

Although there is no suggestion in the play that either Elaria or Bellemante had been provided with the masculine education for which Behn had long argued, she nevertheless demonstrates that these young women possess far more reason than the men. That Cinthio and Charmante lack reason at times or are driven by unrestrained emotion or enormous ego and, hence, make poor assumptions is discernible in Act One, scene three, for example, where Bellemante writes poetry on love. When Scaramouch secretly adds lines, she

---

[39] Nicholas Jardine, 'The Places of Astronomy in Early Modern Culture', *Journal for the History of Astronomy*, 29.1 (1998), 49–62 (p. 49); and Poole, 'Introduction', in *Man in the Moone*, p. 34.

[40] Lynne Lawner offers images of the doctor in *Harlequin on the Moon: Commedia dell'Arte and the Visual Arts* (New York: Harry N. Abrams, 1998), pp. 50–52.

determines that some invisible Cupid must be aiding her poetic efforts. Just as Bellemante decides the game is harmless, Charmante enters, grabs the tablet, and immediately demands the identity of her secret lover. His irrational fury leads Bellemante to question herself, asking 'How was I mistaken in this Man?' (1.[3].59). Fuming, Charmante refuses to hide in the closet when Baliardo approaches, endangering both Bellemante and himself, so that Bellemante must shove him in before her uncle appears. In the same scene, Elaria is surprised by Cinthio, and fearing discovery by her father, shoves him into the same closet. In a typical comedic scene of mistaken identity, both men believe the other is a secret lover and neither will listen to reason, so that Elaria finally concludes of Cinthio, 'Go peevish Fool [...] Let thy own Torments be my just Revenge' (1.[3].173–75).

Not only are the two young women endowed with judgment and reason, they are spirited and quick-witted as well — nor can the fast-thinking Mopsophil be excluded here. In Act Two, when the evening of dancing and courtship is interrupted by the unexpected return of Baliardo, Mopsophil comes to the young ladies' rescue. Having listened to Baliardo's plan to surprise the women in their rooms, she coaches them to pretend to sleep. Elaria and Bellemante concoct 'dreams' to tell the eavesdropping Doctor about a celestial visitation; Elaria claims to have been visited by a 'Demi-God' and Bellemante assures her uncle that she danced to 'the Musick of the Spheres' (II.[4].25–28). The obsessed Doctor, desiring such a liaison be true, determines nonsensically that Elaria's and Bellemante's dreams occurred because either the Emperor 'descended to Court my Daughter Personally', or else he sent the dreams by 'sublime Intelligence' (II.[4].38–41).

5. Telescopes and this 'Earthly Globe'

The twenty-foot telescope that Scaramouch drags into the garden in Act One was no doubt part of the frolic of Behn's farce, but perhaps the fun is less owing to the telescope itself than to the actors in the roles. The humour in the garden scene undoubtedly stemmed from the antics of the actor Anthony Leigh (d.1692), who played Scaramouch and who was one of the most popular comic actors of his day. Dragging the telescope on stage, no doubt with exaggerated effects, simply amplified the comedy.

By the mid-seventeenth century, the telescope had become popular, so that many in London had perhaps visited at least one of the various optical makers' shops. Before Behn's play was on stage, telescopes were well within the price range of the curious. In August 1666, for example, Samuel Pepys recorded climbing to the roof of his house with Richard Reeves, an optical instrument maker, and peering through Reeves' telescope. So pleased was Pepys by the experience, that he subsequently purchased a twelve-foot telescope.[41] Pepys had first visited Reeves' shop in February 1664, and after viewing microscopes, decided to purchase one along with a 'scotoscope', a type of camera obscura, for which he paid five pounds and 10 shillings, later recording having been 'mightily pleased'.[42]

As early as 1650, the optics-maker Johann Wiesel was selling telescopes as long as sixteen feet.[43] Albert Van Helden points out that in 1656, the Dutch mathematician and astronomer Christiaan Huygens (1629–1695) had a telescope made that was twenty-three feet in length; by 1660, Van Helden observes, the length of a good telescope had increased to twenty-five feet, and by 1670, the average length was forty to fifty feet.[44] In May of 1661, the diarist John Evelyn records having looked through Charles II's thirty-five foot telescope, while the astronomer Johannes Hevelius (1611–1687) built one that was as long as 140 feet.[45] Thus, the length of the telescope Scaramouch dragged onstage in *Emperor of the Moon* was not necessarily extraordinary or comic in itself; the manner in which it arrived, however, was.

While the telescope, then, opened the heavens to remarkable views and new discoveries, it also engendered heated debate, particularly about heliocentrism, for example, but also about the notion of a plurality of worlds. In 1641, during his travels abroad, for example, John Evelyn ascended the tower of the 'Vroû Kirk or Notre Dame' in Amsterdam to obtain a better view of the countryside, recording in his diary after the experience that he was 'much Confirmed in my Opinion of the Mones [*sic*] being of such a substance as this Earthly Globe'.[46] Evelyn's opinion, which was neither new nor unusual, reflected the view of many who had read Galileo's telescopic study of the Moon, *Sidereus Nuncius*.

> [W]e certainly see the surface of the Moon not to be smooth, even, and perfectly spherical, as the great crowd of philosophers have believed about this and other heavenly bodies, but, on the contrary, to be uneven, rough and crowded with depressions and bulges. And it is like the face of the Earth itself, which is marked here and there with chains of mountains and depths of valleys.[47]

---

[41] Samuel Pepys, *The Diary of Samuel Pepys*, ed. by William Matthews and Robert Latham, 11 vols (Berkeley: University of California Press, 1970–1983), VII: *1666* (1972), pp. 240–41.

[42] Pepys, *Diary*, V: *1664* (1971), pp. 223, 240, and n. 1.

[43] Inge Keil, 'Johann Wiesel's Telescopes and His Clientele', in *From Earth-Bound to Satellite: Telescopes, Skills, and Networks*, ed. by Alison D. Morrison-Low and others (Leiden and Boston: Brill, 2012), pp. 21–39 (pp. 26–27).

[44] Albert Van Helden, 'The Telescope in the Seventeenth Century', *Isis*, 65.1 (March 1974), 38–58 (pp. 46–47).

[45] Evelyn, *Diary of John Evelyn*, III: *Kalendarium 1650–1676*, pp. 285–86; Van Helden, 'The Telescope', pp. 46–47.

[46] Evelyn, *Diary*, I: *Introduction and De vita propria*, p. 50.

[47] Galileo Galilei, *Sidereus Nuncius, or, The Sidereal Messenger*, trans. with introduction, conclusion, and notes by Albert Van Helden (Chicago: University of Chicago Press, 1989), p. 40.

Galileo's statement, later corroborated by Johannes Kepler, confirmed for many the notion of the Moon as another Earth, so that as 'the affinity between the earth and other planets increased with every telescopic discovery' so men began 'to extrapolate earthly attributes to the planets'.[48]

The Moon's resemblance to Earth, then, led many to conclude that the Moon, too, must be inhabited, and thus literary references to the Moon as a new world proliferated.[49] Wilkins, for example, after reading some of the astronomers of the day, such as Galileo and Kepler, recorded that 'it was not only possible [...] but probable' that the moon was inhabited (p. 15); Wilkins follows up his declaration in 'Proposition XIII' with the fulfilment of a promise he made earlier in his text, to 'say somewhat of the Inhabitants'. He prefers to follow 'Campanella's Second Conjecture' as 'more probable, that the Inhabitants of that World are not Men as we are, but some other kind of Creatures which Bear some Proportion, and Likeness to our Natures' (p. 145); or 'It may be the Inhabitants of the Plannets are of a Middle Nature between' Men and Angels (p. 146). Fontenelle also advocated for an inhabited Moon in his *Entretiens*, through the Philosopher speaker of his text:

> Well, said I, since the Sun, which is now immoveable, and no longer a Planet; and that the Earth, that moves round the Sun, is now one, be not surpriz'd if I tell you, the Moon is another Earth, and is, by all appearance, inhabited. (p. 41)

While literary notions of a plurality of worlds may have proliferated, Behn patently objected to the notion, demonstrating her opposition, for example, in her review of Fontenelle's *Entretiens*, pronouncing that

> [I]f he [Fontenelle] had let alone his learned Men, Philosophical Transactions, and Telescopes in the Planet Jupiter, and his Inhabitants not only there, but in all the fixed Stars, and even in the Milky-Way, and only stuck to the greatness of the Universe, he had deserved much more Praise. ([pp. 10–11])

The telescope may well have been a 'discovery machine', as Toby E. Huff claims, but it also made the new astronomy more disquieting — even dangerous to some.[50] Aphra Behn no doubt sensed that disquiet, for she admonishes Fontenelle for turning his work of 'Natural Philosophy' into ridicule with his 'wild fancy' when he could have treated it in a manner 'to make everyone understand him' ([p. 9]). Such a treatment, she argues, makes him appear almost a 'Pagan'

---

[48]   Van Helden, 'The Telescope', p. 57.
[49]   Robert S. Westman, *The Copernican Question: Prognostication, Skepticism, and Celestial Order* (Berkeley: University of California Press, 2011), p. 502.
[50]   Toby E. Huff, *Intellectual Curiosity and the Scientific Revolution: A Global Perspective* (Cambridge University Press, 2011), p. 18; Thomas S. Kuhn, *The Copernican Revolution: Planetary Astronomy in the Development of Western Thought* (Cambridge, MA: Harvard University Press, 1957), p. 226.

([p.9]). While in her play she does not seem to reject the telescope or the new astronomy, Behn does express concern about the new shape of the universe that men like Godwin and Wilkins proposed, or Fontenelle's universe filled with inhabited planets — from Mercury to Jupiter and Saturn — a plurality of worlds pushed to the limits of extravagance. No doubt, then, the French scenes of *Arlequin, Empereur dans la lune* appealed to her for they furnished the thread with which she could weave a farce that hinged upon a lunatic, a man driven to madness by his belief in an inhabited Moon.

6. Politics and the Art of *Commedia*

As noted above, Behn, like her peers, understood the political context that drama could provide. In her dedication of *The Luckey Chance* (1687) to Laurence Hyde, First Earl of Rochester, she argues for the political benefit, if not political necessity, of plays and similar public performances:

> It being undeniable then, that Plays and publick Diversions were thought by the Greatest and Wisest of States, one of the most essential Parts of good Government, and in which so many great Persons were interested.[51]

While acknowledging Rochester as faithful to the Stuarts, she signifies that her own Stuart loyalty had not flagged, notwithstanding the growing opposition to James.

Behn had long been an ardent adherent of James, Duke of York, and her loyalism can be observed in *The Second Part of the Rover* (1681), for example, which she dedicated to the Catholic James, who was sent into exile in Scotland owing to the Exclusion Crisis and the concerns about a Catholic plot. She claims that the Duke's exile is needless since the fears that led to his circumstances were simply an occasion to '*Play the old Game o're again*', a reference to the English Civil War.[52] Behn praises James for having disregarded his personal safety, a reference to the Duke's tenure as Lord High Admiral of the Navy, ending her dedication with a pronouncement that she '*will eternally pray for the Life, Health and Safety of Your Royal Highness*' ([p. 3]).

Charles Somerset, Marquess of Worcester, to whom *The Emperor of the Moon* is dedicated, was a Member of Parliament and a colonel of a regiment of foot, although at twenty-seven years old, the Marquess had yet to make his mark. Even so, both Worcester and his father, the Duke of Beaufort, receive abundant praise in Behn's dedication. The Duke opposed the Exclusion Bill of 1679 introduced in the Commons by Anthony Ashley Cooper, First Earl of

---

[51] Behn, 'The Epistle Dedicatory', in *The Luckey Chance, Or An Alderman's Bargain*, [p. 2].
[52] Behn, 'The Epistle Dedicatory', in *The Second Part of The Rover*, [p. 1]; Tim Harris, *Restoration: Charles II and his Kingdoms, 1660–1685* (London: Allen Lane, 2005), pp. 251–52.

Shaftesbury (1621–1683), who became a leader of the opposition and a noted Whig. Shaftesbury's goal was to prevent the Catholic James from inheriting the throne.[53] In June 1685, Beaufort defended Bristol during the Duke of Monmouth's rebellion, earning him the praise and gratitude of James. Praising Worcester's birth and his *'Illustrious Father'*, Behn assures the Lord Marquess that she is certain his acts *'will Equal those of his Glorious Father'*, whose *'unshaken Loyalty* [...] *have rendred him to us, something more than Man'* (p. 46). This pronouncement of Stuart loyalty is followed by a complaint that *'the only Diversion of the Town now, is high Dispute, and publick Controversies in Taverns, Coffee-houses, &c.'* (p. 47), a reference to the growing controversy over religion and the monarchy.

The prologue and the dedication to *Emperor of the Moon* should be read in tandem and not as separate pieces, since they work together to point out the current state of affairs as Behn perceives them. If the prologue offers a brief summary of the declining state of the English stage from heroic tragedy to farce, it reflects as well the shape of the political — and social — state, where the general population, much like audiences, have 'malicious grown, | Friends Vices to expose' while hiding their own (ll. 15–16). The 'feign'd Niceness' of those who spread secrets about town in 'gross Lampoon' is 'but cautious Fear, | Their own Intrigues shou'd be unravel'd here' on the stage (ll. 25–26). This is the mirror she holds up to the audience, whose misapprehensions, as well as mis-representations, have brought about the demise of the stage, a stage that in earlier times, she claims in her dedication, was also the sign *'of a flourishing State'* (p. 47). Having made her accusations in the first part of her prologue about the ungrateful times, Behn announces that since nothing else has sped with the public, she offers now the 'speaking Head', and thus rises Stentor, the puppet head with the 'Northern Strain' (a reminder of the recent exile of James), who sings 'Sawny' and cries 'God Bless the King' (p. 50).

Stentor re-appears in the operatic final act as a character speaking through a stentraphon,[54] and is given the character name 'Stentraphon'. His appearance in the final scenes of the spectacle, where he requests permission from Baliardo for the marriages to occur, circles back to the prologue and the thrust of the message — a dying stage, a threatened state, and a discontented 'rabble'. In relinquishing his daughters, Baliardo ends his tyranny and sets his world upright. Such is often the role of the Dottore in *commedia dell'arte*, who can be (and is here) a figure of authority who demands obedience.[55]

Since drama is frequently imbued with a political context, and given Behn's

---

[53]   Lionel K. J. Glassey, 'Shaftesbury and the Exclusion Crisis', in *Anthony Ashley Cooper, First Earl of Shaftesbury 1621–1683*, ed. by John Spurr (New York: Routledge, 2016), pp. 207–31.

[54]   A kind of megaphone or trumpet used to amplify the voice.

[55]   Jordan, 'Pantalone & il Dottore', pp. 65–66.

devout allegiance to the Stuarts, it would not be surprising if woven into the humour and the spectacle one might find her political voice, and indeed one does. When James, Duke of York, succeeded to the throne as James II in 1685, his succession was not only peaceful, but his Parliament was relatively compliant.[56] In fact, Tim Harris notes, 'Few English monarchs have come to the throne in as strong a position as did James II'.[57] But the situation for the King turned quickly. His commission of Catholic officers in the army, his resolve to maintain a standing army, and his ambition for religious toleration, for example, were met with opposition from his Tory allies.[58] Within a few months of his reign, he had begun to lose his support. During 1686, the Tories and the Anglican ministers became stronger in their opposition to James' push toward religious toleration; he responded with harsh criticism of the Anglican Church ministry and granted dispensation to Dissenters.[59] William Gibson claims that 'In France, James found a model of kingship which he hoped to emulate', pointing out Louis XIV's revocation of the Edict of Nantes, which removed 'religious tolerance from his Protestant subjects'.[60] Relying on his prerogative powers, James replaced Anglican judges and justices of the peace with Catholics, which could only further antagonise those who would have supported him.

Enter Doctor Baliardo. But not as James II. This is absolutely *not* a case of the King as a *commedia* character. Rather, what is here — both in Baliardo and James — is an example of misdirected focus and an abuse of authority. Baliardo's all-consuming interest in lunar inhabitants and marriages between his daughter and niece to lunar royalty, just like James' unrelenting focus on Catholicism, had to be interrupted. Baliardo, then, is prevented from further error through the intercession of those who are loyal to and loved him. As Ferdinand explains, it is not

> [...]   in the Power of Herbs or Minerals,
> Of Reason, common Sense, and right Religion,
> To draw you from an Error that unman'd you. (III.[3].192–94)

Dramatic performances can and frequently do comment on politics and the

---

56   Geoffrey Holmes, *The Making of a Great Power: Late Stuart and Early Georgian Britain 1660–1722* (London: Longman, 1993), p. 163; Mark Kishlansky, *A Monarchy Transformed: Britain 1603–1714* (London: Allen Lane, 1996), p. 267.
57   Tim Harris, *Politics Under the Later Stuarts: Party Conflict in a Divided Society 1660– 1715* (London: Longman, 1993), p. 119.
58   Harris, *Politics Under the Later Stuarts*, pp. 124–26. See also John Miller, *James II* (New Haven: Yale University Press, 2000), p. 148.
59   John Miller, *Popery and Politics in England 1660–1688* (Cambridge: Cambridge University Press, 1973), pp. 208–11. See also Harris, *Politics under the Later Stuarts*, pp. 124–26.
60   William Gibson, *James II and the Trial of the Seven Bishops* (Basingstoke Hampshire: Palgrave Macmillan, 2009), p. 52.

state, and this is particularly so in *commedia dell'arte*. For example, Louis XIV of France danced and was costumed as the Sun King (*Le Roy Soleil*) in *La Nuit*, a court ballet in 1653, when he was fifteen years old. He later danced in court performances as the sun god Apollo as a continuation of his royal symbolism, and he was also frequently painted as a Roman emperor, a warrior hero.[61] Bent Holm suggests, however, that the symbolism in Arlequin's costume as Emperor of the Moon in Fatouville's *Arlequin* might be a parody of the royal symbolism in the ballet *La Nuit*.[62] The basic structure of Arlequin's costume, as illustrated in Gherardi's volume, and which provides the image on the cover of this volume, is a helmet decorated with exaggerated plumage, while the body of the costume is a Roman-style tunic and skirt. Does the costume depict both sunbeams and moonbeams, or is the emblem on the tunic simply the Man in the Moon, accompanied by various moonbeams? 'The *Empereur de la lune* can be seen as the reverse of *Le Roy Soleil*', Holm argues, asserting that these are both sunbeams and the Moon, 'an inverse replica of the Majesty in its symbolic appearance or identity'.[63] Whatever the case, the *Chevaliers du Soleil*, or Knights of the Sun, arrive at the end of this last French scene, defeat the 'Cowardly knight' Lunar Emperor, and take from him Isabelle and Eularia.

A number of satiric prints of the French King depict him among other images as Phaeton, whose attempts to control the chariot of the sun failed miserably and led to disaster.[64] And in Fatouville's earlier comedic scenes in *Arlequin Protée*, which premiered in 1683, Arlequin appears as a Roman emperor, who eventually reveals that his grand attire of Roman skirt and plumes were 'hired from a second-hand dealer'.[65] While Arlequin in these *commedia dell'arte* performances is absolutely not Louis XIV, any more than Baliardo is James II, the playwrights can and do draw on symbolism in their plots and scenes to depict the politics and political issues they see as troubling for the state.

Playwrights also employ the trope of the private family as an analogy for the public political body, and they used their productions this way as a mirror to the court.[66] As Richard Braverman points out, 'Political and literary discourse share common ground by virtue of an analogy that cuts across both to give

---

[61]   Bent Holm, 'Picture and Counter-Picture: An Attempt to Involve Context in the Interpretation of Théâtre Italien Iconography', *Theatre Research International*, 22.3 (1997), 220–33 (pp. 220–21).

[62]   Holm, p. 223.

[63]   Holm, p. 223.

[64]   Holm, p. 223.

[65]   Holm, p. 221.

[66]   Gordon J. Schochet, 'Patriarchalism, Politics and Mass Attitudes in Stuart England', *Historical Journal*, 12.3 (1969) 413–41 (pp. 424 and 428–30); Susan Dwyer Asmussen, *An Ordered Society: Gender and Class in Early Modern England* (Oxford: Blackwell, 1988), pp. 55–56 and 63–64; Michael McKeon, 'Historicizing Patriarch: The Emergence of Gender Difference in England, 1660–1760', *Eighteenth-Century Studies*, 28.3 (1995), 295–322.

human form to abstract relationships: the analogy of the polity as a family'.[67]
Thus, in *The Emperor of the Moon*, Baliardo's autocracy as the patriarch of the
family might be viewed as a trope for the tyranny of political authority. Baliardo's
attempts to frame the young women's future to gratify his own desires not only
impacts his family's best interests and crushes the affections of his daughter and
niece, but it forces them to rebel. Thus, the message here can be extended to the
public political body — that they, too, will rebel when pressured by the tyranny
of a patriarch who has miscalculated his people's wishes and is racing headlong
toward self-destruction. But reformation is possible, according to Behn, and the
'family' may still be saved through the intervention of those who are closest to
and most loyal to Baliardo in the private sphere of the theatre, like those closest
to the King in the public, political sphere of the state, who might do much to
change the tide of opposition.

As John Miller has noted, James believed that 'converts would flock to the
[Catholic] church once they could see Catholicism as it really was and not as
its enemies said it was'.[68] However, Protestants did not believe their religion
was inaccurate or wrong, and this was something that 'James II could not
or would not understand'.[69] Behn's dedication in this play demonstrates her
understanding of the potential political backlash, as she points out Worcester's
'refin'd Sence, and Delicacy of Judgement', arguing that he is one who will
be able to see *'beyond the Show and Buffoonry'* (p. 47). That Behn appeals to
Worcester to look beyond the laughter and buffoonery is significant, for James
had written to Worcester's father, Henry Somerset, Duke of Beaufort, as head of
a noted Protestant family, to ask him to 'speak to M.P.s about repealing two test
acts and the penal laws so that the king's "Catholic subjects may be in the same
condition the rest of my subjects are"'.[70] Behn would certainly not have known
about this letter, but she did indeed know about Beaufort's loyalty to the Stuarts
and that Stuart kings had relied on this family, as they had on other loyal
aristocratic families, in times of crises. It is perhaps with a specific purpose,
then, that she chose to dedicate this play to Worcester, through whom she could
direct her own appeal, supporting her plea by providing extensive praise of the
Duke his father for his long-standing political support of the Stuart monarchy.
There is indeed more behind the gestures and the grimaces, the exaggerated
movements and the plot action, than simply comedic gambolling.

[67] Richard Braverman, *Plots & Counterplots: Sexual Politics and the Body Politic in English Literature, 1660–1730* (Cambridge: Cambridge University Press, 1993), p. 11.
[68] Miller, *Popery and Politics*, p. 244; see also Harris, *Politics Under the Later Stuarts*, pp. 124–26.
[69] Miller, *Popery and Politics*, p. 249.
[70] Miller, *Popery and Politics*, p. 213.

Often the solution or resolution to the problem in a dramatic performance is brought about through uniting the right couples, followed by singing and/or dancing. While the enjoyment of this play may well hinge upon the machinations of the young couple, the plot is not simply about uniting the young lovers. Rather, the pomp and circumstance of the final operatic scene, like much of the horseplay through which the comic fools cavort, leads to the unmasking of Baliardo's tyranny. Baliardo is not 'unmanned', as he initially believes; rather, he is brought to recognise that his beliefs have oppressed those who are truly loyal. Supported by his faithful friends and family, who are there to see that he 'shall no longer be impos'd upon', Baliardo vows to 'Scatter the vile Contagious Monstrous Lies' (III.[3].219). Those who have become his allies and have assisted him in this 'Glorious Miracle' are invited to revel with him and see his 'happy Recantation', a significant choice of expression since the term not only expresses the disavowing of one's opinions or ideas, but was often used as well in the context of renouncing or abjuring one's religion.

Harlequin, long associated with the popular masses, and Scaramouch are instrumental in facilitating an end to the tyranny suffered by the young ladies, largely through their enabling of the lovers' intrigues. Holm has pointed out that the Harlequin figure serves in some *commedia* plays as an 'anti-king' or lord of misrule.[71] Behn provides a similar 'anti-king', a counter-picture of the figure of authority in her farce, a zanni ambassador from the Emperor of the Moon. He must be defeated, as he is by his Knight of the Sun opponent Scaramouch, the same false figure who had pronounced him ambassador in Act Three (III.[2].244). Harlequin's is a false apotheosis, as false as — and a reflection of — the counterfeit, 'upside-down realm' created by Cinthio and Charmante. Neither world is genuine. Harlequin and Scaramouch enter the final scene claiming to be Knights of the Sun and hence princely neighbours to the Emperor of the Moon and the Prince of Thunderland. But both these false worlds are exposed when the fictitious Ambassador-cum-Knight (and Prince of the Sun) Harlequin is defeated by Scaramouch. This reveal is critical in that it immediately brings about the revelation of the other false authority, Cinthio as ruler of the lunar world.

Kings had long been associated with the Sun in literary allegories, and so it was not unusual that Louis XIV had himself acknowledged as the Sun King. But in *Emperor of the Moon*, the royalty of the Sun is false — just as counterfeit as the royalty of the Moon — and so both are exposed in the final scene, where legitimacy is laid bare. Baliardo's true identity had been overpowered by false belief, having allowed the rightful world in which he lived to become subsumed by a world he anticipated, but that would never, could never, be. Thus, the figure of authority in this play, the person on whom this stage-play world depends,

---

[71]   Holm, p. 222.

suffers from the tyranny that is often borne of false belief. Behn seems to have understood well the importance of this idea, for in her function as poet, she observes in her epilogue that she, like poets of an earlier age, can by a 'gentler force the Soul [subdue]' (l. 32).

Behn's political voice resounds loudly in the plot of *The Emperor of the Moon*, then, just as it does in her epilogue, where she argues that her status is not simply as playwright, but, like the playwrights of Rome, she is much like a minister of state. In '*flourishing* Rome', she argues, playwrights were prized and counted as important as armies, for it was their task to subdue men's souls. Poets, then, seek '*fruitful drops*' from the court's purse, since '*honest Pens do his* [the king's] *just cause afford* | *Equal Advantage with the useful Sword*' (ll. 39–41). But as much as she makes a claim that her work is for the political state as well as the public stage, she also understands that a stronger voice is required in this particular, and contentious, political moment. Hence, beneath the gentle praise of Worcester in her dedication, one can hear an urgent tone, a plea perhaps that hers is a play of '*Critical Nature*', and that to effect change will require not only '*the Patronage of a great Title, but of a great Man, too*' (p. 46).

THE
EMPEROR
OF THE
MOON:
A
FARCE.

As it is Acted by Their

𝕸𝖆𝖏𝖊𝖘𝖙𝖎𝖊𝖘 𝕾𝖊𝖗𝖛𝖆𝖓𝖙𝖘,

AT THE
QUEENS THEATRE.

Written by Mrs. *A. Behn.*

L O N D O N:

Printed by *R. Holt*, for *Joseph Knight*, and *Francis Saunders*, at the *Blew-Anchor* in the lower Walk of the *New Exchange*, 1687.

Title page to Aphra Behn's *Emperor of the Moon* (1687). RB 112066. The Huntington Library, San Marino, California.

To The Lord Marquess of Worcester, &c.[1]

My Lord,

It is a common Notion, that gathers as it goes, and is almost become a vulgar Error, That Dedications in our Age, are only the effects of Flattery, a form of Complement, and no more; so that the Great, to whom they are only due, decline those Noble Patronages that were so generally allow'd the Ancient Poets; since the Awful Custom has been so scandaliz'd by mistaken Addresses, and many a worthy Piece is lost for want of some Honourable Protection, and sometimes many indifferent ones traverse the World with that advantagious Passport only.

This humble Offering, which I presume to lay at your Lordship's Feet, is of that Critical Nature, that it does not only require the Patronage of a great Title, but of a great Man too, and there is often times a vast difference between those two great Things; and amongst all the most Elevated, there are but very few in whom an illustrious Birth and equal Parts compleat the Hero; but among those, your Lordship bears the first Rank, from a just Claim, both of the Glories of your Race and Vertues. Nor need we look back into long past Ages, to bring down to ours the Magnanimous deeds of your Ancestors: We need no more than to behold (what we have so often done with wonder) those of the Great Duke of Beauford, your Illustrious Father,[2] whose every single Action is a glorious and lasting President to all the future Great; whose unshaken Loyalty, and all other eminent Vertues, have rendred him to us, something more than Man, and which alone, deserving a whole Volume, wou'd be here but to lessen his Fame, to mix his Grandeurs with those of any other; and while I am addressing to the Son, who is only worthy of that Noble Blood he boasts, and who gives the World a Prospect of those coming Gallantries that will Equal those of his Glorious Father; already, My Lord, all you say and do is admir'd, and every touch of your Pen reverenc'd; the Excellency and Quickness of your Wit, is the Subject that fits the World most agreeably. For my own part, I never presume to contemplate your Lordship, but my Soul bows with a perfect Veneration to your mighty Mind; and while I have ador'd the delicate Effects of your uncommon Wit, I have wish'd for nothing more than an Opportunity of expressing my infinite Sense of it; and this Ambition, my Lord, was one Motive of my present Presumption in the Dedicating this Farce to your Lordship.

I am sensible, my Lord, how far the Word Farce[3] might have offended some, whose Titles of Honour, a Knack in dressing, or his Art in writing a Billet Deux,[4]

---

[1] Charles Somerset, Marquess of Worcester (1661–1698). At the age of 13, he was elected a Fellow of the Royal Society of London. He died in a coaching accident in 1698.

[2] Henry Somerset, First Duke of Beaufort (1629–1700). Charles, Marquess of Worcester, was his second son.

[3] Farce is comedy that largely uses extravagant and/or absurd ideas or behaviour, often bordering on buffoonery and, on occasion, crudity.

[4] Behn probably means billet-doux here, i.e. love letters.

had been his chiefest *Talent*, and who, without considering the *Intent*, *Character*, or *Nature* of the thing, wou'd have cry'd out upon the *Language*, and have damn'd it (because the *Persons* in it did not all talk like *Hero's*) as too debas'd and vulgar to entertain a *Man* of *Quality*; but I am secure from this *Censure*, when your *Lordship* shall be its *Judge*, whose refin'd *Sence*, and *Delicacy* of *Judgment*, will, thro' all the humble *Actions* and trivialness of *Business*, find *Nature* there, and that *Diversion* which was not meant for the *Numbers*, who comprehend nothing beyond the *Show* and *Buffoonry*.

A very barren and thin hint of the *Plot* I had from the *Italian*,[5] and which, even as it was, was acted in France *eighty odd times without intermission*.[6] 'Tis now much alter'd, and adapted to our *English Theatre* and *Genius*, who cannot find an *Entertainment* at so cheap a *Rate* as the *French* will, who are content with almost any *Incoherences*, howsoever shuffled together under the *Name* of a *Farce*; which I have endeavour'd as much as the thing wou'd bear, to bring within the compass of *Possibility* and *Nature*, that I might as little impose upon the *Audience* as I cou'd; all the *Words* are wholly new, without one from the *Original*. 'Twas calculated for *His late Majesty* of *Sacred Memory*,[7] that Great *Patron* of Noble *Poetry*, and the *Stage*, for whom the *Muses* must for ever mourn, and whose *Loss*, only the *Blessing* of so *Illustrious* a *Successor* can ever repair; and 'tis a great *Pity* to see that best and most useful *Diversion* of Mankind, whose *Magnificence* of old, was the most certain sign of a *flourishing State*, now quite undone by the *Misapprehension* of the *Ignorant*, and *Mis-representings* of the *Envious*, which evidently shows the *World* is improv'd in nothing but *Pride Ill Nature*, and affected *Nicety*; and the only *Diversion* of the *Town* now, is high *Dispute*, and *publick Controversies* in *Taverns*, *Coffee-houses*,[8] &c. and those things which ought to be the greatest *Mysteries* in *Religion*, and so rarely the *Business* of *Discourse*, are turn'd into *Ridicule*, and look but like so many *fanatical Stratagems* to ruine the *Pulpit* as well as the *Stage*. The *Defence* of the first is left to the *Reverend Gown*, but the departing *Stage* can be no otherwise restor'd, but by some leading *Spirits*, so *Generous*, so *Publick*, and so *Indefatigable* as that of your *Lordship*, whose *Patronages* are sufficient to support it, whose *Wit* and *Judgment* to defend it, and whose *Goodness* and *Quality* to justifie it; such *Encouragement* wou'd inspire the *Poets* with new *Arts* to please, and the *Actors* with *Industry*. 'Twas this that occasion'd so many *Admirable Plays* heretofore, as *Shakespear's*, *Fletcher's*, and

---

5   Behn suggests *commedia dell'arte*; see the Introduction above for more on the Italian players.

6   Fatouville's *Arlequin, Empereur dans la lune*.

7   Charles II (1630–1685) died on 6 February, 1685.

8   Coffee houses were popular gathering places for poets, playwrights, and the 'scientists' of the day. London had many of these, such as Garraway's, Jonathan's, White's, Button's, and so forth. A number of playwrights frequented Will's Coffee House, while men like Robert Hooke and Hans Sloane of the Royal Society patronised the Grecian Coffee House.

Johnson's,[9] *and 'twas this alone that made the Town able to keep so many Play-houses alive, who now cannot supply one.*[10] *However, my Lord, I, for my part, will no longer complain, if this Piece find but favour in your Lordship's Eyes, and that it can be so happy to give your Lordship one hours Diversion, which is the only Honour and Fame is wish'd to crown all the Endeavours of,*

> My Lord,
>> Your Lordship's
>>> Most Humble, and
>>>> Most Obedient
>>>>> Servant,
>>>>>> A. *Behn.*

---

[9]   William Shakespeare (1564–1616), John Fletcher (1579–1625), and Ben Jonson (1572–1637) were major playwrights in the early modern English theatre.
[10]   In 1682, the two public acting companies, the King's Company and the Duke's Company, joined to form the United Company.

PROLOGUE

Spoken by Mr. *Jevern*.

Long, and at vast Expence the industrious Stage
Has strove to please a dull ungrateful Age:
With Hero's and with Gods we first began,
And thunder'd to you in Heroick Strain.
Some dying Love-sick Queen each Night you injoy'd,   5
And with Magnificence, at last were cloy'd:
Our Drums and Trumpets frighted all the Women;
Our fighting scar'd the *Beaux* and *Billet Deux* Men.[11]
So Spark in an Intrigue of Quality,
Grows weary of this splendid Drudgery;   10
Hates the Fatigue, and cries a Pox upon her,
What a damn'd bustle's here with Love and Honour.
    In humbler Comedy, we next appear,
No Fop or Cuckold,[12] but slap-dash we had him here;
We show'd you all, but you malicious grown,   15
Friends Vices to expose, and hide your own;
Cry, Dam it——This is such, or such a one.
Yet netled,[13] Plague, What do's the Scribler mean?
With his damn'd Characters, and Plot obscene.
No Woman without Vizard in the Nation,[14]   20
Can see it twice, and keep her Reputation——that's certain
Forgetting——
That he himself, in every gross Lampoon,
Her lewder Secrets spread about the Town;
Whil'st their feign'd Niceness is but cautious Fear,[15]   25
Their own Intrigues shou'd be unravel'd here.
    Our next Recourse was dwindling down to Farce,

---

[11]   This should be 'billets-doux' in keeping with the plural 'beaux'; the meaning here is men (lovers) who woo or court through love notes and letters. Beaux also has a pejorative meaning: a fop-like person who pays disproportionate attention to his appearance and social connections and manners.

[12]   A cuckold is a derisive term for the husband of an adulterous wife.

[13]   Nettled is provoked, irritated, or annoyed.

[14]   The vizard was a mask, typically black and often of velvet, worn by ladies and prostitutes alike. That it was difficult to tell of which social class the vizard wearer was is the subject of a number of observations in the literature of this period. Behn often intentionally obscures the line between lady and prostitute.

[15]   Nice meaning coyness or reserved behaviour, but the term is also pejorative, meaning a pretence to virtue.

Then——Zounds,[16] what Stuff's here? 'tis all o're my——
Well, Gentlemen, since none of these has sped,
30   'Gad, we have bought a share i'th'speaking Head.
So there you'l save a Sice,[17]
You love Good Husbandry in all but Vice;
Whoring and Drinking, only bears a Price.

The Head rises upon a twisted Post, on a Bench from under
the Stage. After Jevern *speaks to its Mouth.*

	Oh! ——Oh! ——Oh!
35 *Stentor:*[18]	Oh! ——Oh! ——Oh!

After this it sings Sawny,[19] *Laughs, crys God bless the King in order.*

Stentor Answers. Speak lowder *Jevern*, if you'd have me repeat;
Plague of this Rogue, he will betray the Cheat.

He speaks lowder, it answers indirectly.

——Hum——There 'tis again,
Pox of your Echo with a Northern Strain.
40   Well,——This will be but a nine days wonder too;
There's nothing lasting but the Puppets Show.
What Ladies heart so hard, but it wou'd move,
To hear *Philander* and *Irene*'s Love.[20]
Those Sisters too, the scandalous Wits do say,
45   Two nameless, keeping[21] *Beaux*, have made so gay;
But those Amours are perfect Sympathy,
Their Gallants being as meer Machines as they.
Oh! how the City Wife, with her nown Ninny,[22]

---

[16]   Meaning 'God's wounds', considered a mild curse or oath.
[17]   The number six in dicing games.
[18]   Meaning loud; Stentor was a Greek herald in the Trojan War whose voice was as loud as fifty men collectively. Behn may refer here to the talking head mentioned in the Newdigate Letters of 26 March 1687, in which a man contrived a 'head' that one could speak into and the same words would echo back. See *The London Stage*, ed. Van Lennep, I, Part 1, pp. 156–57. A talking head was also part of a droll performed in Bartholomew Fair, where there was a 'Brazen Speaking Head in the Gallery'. See *The London Stage*, I, Part 1, pp. 400–01.
[19]   A sawny refers to a number of Scottish songs; it is also a derisive name for a Scottish person and a term for a fool. There are numerous 'Sawny' poems and ballads, such as 'Sawny will ne'r be my love again', 'Jennies answer to Sawny', and 'When Sawny first did woe me'.
[20]   Puppet shows were becoming popular entertainment, so much so that playwrights began to denounce them for appropriating their audiences.
[21]   Keeping is the private support of a woman for a man's personal (sexual) use. A 'keeper' is a man who engages in this practice.
[22]   'Nown' is probably a misprint for 'own'. A ninny is a fool or an idiot; hence, Behn points out that the city wives have fools for husbands.

Is charm'd with, Come into my Coach——————Mis *Jinny*, Mis *Jinny*.[23]
But overturning——————*Frible* crys[24]——————Adznigs,[25]
The jogling Rogue has murther'd all his Kids.
The Men of War cry Pox on't, this is dull,
We are for rough Sports, ——Dog Hector, and the Bull.[26]
Thus each in his degree, Diversion finds,
Your Sports are suited to your mighty Minds;
Whilst so much Judgment in your Choice you show,
The Puppets have more Sence than some of you.

---

[23] Mis, i.e. Miss, is a term for a young girl or lady, but it can also denote a whore of some quality.
[24] A frible or fribble is something or someone frivolous or ridiculous, but also a conceited cuckold. 'Overturning' here refers to an overturned coach. Behn was involved in such an accident in London's terrible frost of 1683–1684. See her poem 'Letter to Mr. Creech at Oxford, Written in the Last Great Frost', where she notes that she was slightly hurt. See *Miscellany, Being a Collection of Poems By Several Hands* (London: for J. Hindmarsh, 1685), pp. 73–77 (pp. 74–75).
[25] A mild oath or curse like 'zounds'. Also spelled 'gads nigs' or 'Godz neaks', etc.
[26] Bull-baiting was a popular form of entertainment, which took place in theatres during the off season. Dogs were set on bulls (or bears) tethered to a pole in the middle of the theatre.

PERSONS NAMES.[27]

Doctor Baliardo.	Mr. *Underhill.*
Scaramouch, *his Man.*	Mr. *Lee.*
Pedro, *his Boy.*	
Don Cinthio, Don Charmante,	Young Mr. *Powel.*
both Nephews to the Vice-Roy,	Mr. *Mumford.*
and Lovers of Elaria and Bellemante.	
Harlequin, *Cinthio's Man.*	Mr. *Jevern.*
Officer and Clark.	
Elaria, *Daughter to the* Doctor.	Mrs. *Cooke.*
Bellemante, *Niece to the* Doctor.	Mrs. *Mumford.*
Mopsophil, *Governante to the young Ladies.*	Mrs. *Cory.*

The Persons in the Moon, are Don Cinthio, *Emperor;* Don Charmante, *Prince of* Thunderland.

Their Attendants, Persons that represent the Court Cards.

Keeplair *and* Gallileus, *two Philosophers.*

Twelve Persons representing the Figures of the twelve Signs of the Zodiack.

Negroes, and Persons that Dance.

Musick, Kettle-Drums, and Trumpets.

The SCENE, NAPLES.

---

27   The actors here noted are Cave Underhill (1634–c.1710), Anthony Leigh (d.1692), George Powell (c.1668–1714), William Mountfort (c.1664–1692), Thomas Jevon (c.1652–1688), Sarah Cooke (d.1688), Susannah Percival Mountfort (1667–1703), wife of William Mountfort, and Katherine Mitchell Corey (fl.1660–1692). None of the minor actors, such as Kepler (Keplair) and Galileo (Gallileus), are named in Behn's list of performers.

FARCE.

ACT I. SCENE I.

A Chamber.

Enter Elaria *and* Mopsophil.

I.

A Curse upon that faithless Maid,
Who first her Sexes Liberty betrayed;
Born free as Man to Love and Range,
Till Nobler Nature did to Custom change.
Custom, that dull excuse for Fools,
Who think all Vertue to consist in Rules.

II.

From Love our Fetters never sprung,
That smiling God, all wanton Gay and Young,
Shows by his Wings he cannot be
Confined to a restless Slavery;
But here and there at random roves,
Not fixt to glittering Courts or shady Groves.

III.

Than she that Constancy[28] Profest,
Was but a well dissembler at the best;
And that the imaginary sway
She feigned to give, in seeming to obey,
Was but the height of Prudent Art,
To deal with greater Liberty her Heart.

[*After the Song* Elaria *gives her Lute to* Mopsophil.[29]

Ela. This does not divert me:
  Nor nothing will, till *Scaramouch* return,
  And bring me News of *Cinthio.*
Mop. Truly I was so sleepy last Night, I know nothing of the adventure, for
  which you are kept so close a Prisoner to Day, and more strictly guarded
  than usual.
Ela. Cinthio came with Musick last Night under my Window, which my Father

---

28 Faithfulness to one's lover.
29 Since Elaria had the lute, which served as an accompaniment to the song, she was most likely the one singing.

hearing sallyed out with his *Mermidons* upon him; and clashing of Swords I heard, but what hurt was done, or whether *Cinthio* were discovered to him, I know not; but the Billet I sent him now by *Scaramouch*, will occasion me soon intelligence.

30 *Mop.* And see Madam where you[r] trusty *Roger* comes.

Enter Scaramouch peeping on all sides before he enters.

———You may advance, and fear none but your Friends.

Scar. Away and keep the door.   ([*Ex.* Mopsophil.)[30]

Ela. Oh dear *Scaramouch*! hast thou been at the Vice-Roys!

Scar. Yes, yes.———   [*In heat.*

35 *Ela.* And hast thou delivered my Letter, to his Nephew, Don *Cinthio*?

Scar. Yes, yes, what should I deliver else?

Ela. Well———and how does he?

Scar. Lord, how shou'd he do? Why, what a Laborious thing it is to be a Pimp?
                                [*Fanning himself with his Cap.*

Ela. Why, well he shou'd do.

40 *Scar.* So he is, as well as a Night adventuring Lover can be,———he has got but one wound, Madam.

Ela. How! wounded say you? Oh Heavens! 'Tis not Mortal?

Scar. Why, I have no great skill,———but they say it may be Dangerous.

Ela. I Dye with fear, where is he wounded?

45 *Scar.* Why, Madam, he is run———quit[e] thorough the———heart,———but the Man may Live, if I please.

Ela. Thou please! Torment me not with Ridles.

Scar. Why, Madam, there is a certain cordial Balsam,[31] called a fair Lady; which outwardly applyed to his Bosom, will prove a better cure than all your
50 Weapon or Sympathetick Powder,[32] meaning your Ladyship.

Ela. Is *Cinthio* then not wounded?

Scar. No otherwise than by your fair Eyes, Madam; he got away unseen and unknown.

Ela. Dost know how precious time is, and dost thou Fool it away thus? what said
55 he to my Letter?

Scar. What should he say?

Ela. Why a hundred dear soft things of Love, kiss it as often, and bless me for my goodness.

---

[30] This stage direction is missing in the original text. Numerous entrances, exits, and asides which were left out of the original have been added in brackets for clarity.

[31] A healing salve. Cordial is also a reference to the Latin *cordus*, the heart; Scaramouch suggests that the substance that best heals Cinthio is Elaria herself.

[32] Sympathetic powder is a reference to a type of magic, where a 'healing powder' is applied to the weapon which has caused an injury and thereafter heals the person injured.

Scar. Why so he did.

o   *Ela.* Ask thee a thousand question[s] of my health after my last nights fright.

Scar. So he did.

Ela. Expressing all the kind concern Love cou'd inspire, for the punishment
my Father has inflicted on me, for entertaining him at my Window last
Night.

5   *Scar.* All this he did.

Ela. And for my being confin'd a Prisoner to my Apartment, without the hope
or almost possibility of seeing him any more.

Scar. There I think you are a little mistaken, for besides the Plot that I have
laid to bring you together all this Night,——there are such Strategems

o   abrewing, not only to bring you together, but with your Fathers consent
too; Such a Plot, Madam.

Ela. Ay that wou'd be worthy of thy Brain; prethee what——

Scar. Such a device.

Ela. I'm impatient.

5   *Scar.* Such a Canundrum,——well if there be wise Men and Conjurers in the
World, they are intriguing Lovers.

Ela. Out with it.

Scar. You must know, Madam, your Father, (my Master, the Doctor,) is a little
Whimsical, Romantick, or Don Quick-sottish,[33] or so.——

o   *Ela.* Or rather Mad.

Scar. That were uncivil to be supposed by me; but Lunatick we may call him
without breaking the Decorum of good Manners;[34] for he is always
travelling to the Moon.

Ela. And so Religiously believes there is a World there, that he discourses as

5   gravely of the People, their Government, Institutions, Laws, Manners,
Religion and Constitution, as if he had been bred a *Machiavel* there.[35]

Scar. How came he thus infected first?

Ela. With reading foolish Books, *Lucian's Dialogue of the Lofty Traveller,* who
flew up to the Moon, and thence to Heaven;[36] an Heroick business called,

o   *The Man in the Moon,* if you'll believe a *Spaniard,* who was carried thether,

---

[33] Miguel de Cervantes Saavedra's (c.1547–1616) character, Alonso Quixano, having read
too many romances, suffers from madness and, changing his name to Don Quixote de la
Mancha, sets out on a knightly quest with a farmer, Sancho Panza, as his squire.

[34] A 'lunatick' was someone who had been physically affected by the Moon. The term
could also be used for men who pretended to knowledge of the Moon, such as Dr Baliardo.
Scaramouch is correct in referring to his employer as a 'lunatick'.

[35] Niccolò di Bernardo dei Machiavelli (1469–1527) outlined in *The Prince* harsh but
effective methods for obtaining and retaining political power.

[36] Lucian of Samosata's (125 AD–c.180 AD) wildly imaginary *Icaromenippus* is the tale of a
journey beyond the Earth.

upon an Engine drawn by wild Geese;[37] with another Philosophical Piece, *A Discourse of the World in the Moon;*[38] with a thousand other ridiculous Volumes too hard to name.

Scar. Ay, this reading of Books is a pernicious thing. I was like to have run Mad
95   once, reading Sir *John Mandivel;*[39]——but to the business,——I went, as you know, to Don *Cinthio's* Lodgings, where I found him with his dear Friend *Charmante,* laying their heads together for a Farce.

Ela. A Farce.——

Scar. Ay a Farce, which shall be called,——*the World in the Moon.* Wherein your
100 Father shall be so impos'd on, as shall bring matters most magnificently about.—

Ela. I cannot conceive thee, but the design must be good since *Cinthio* and *Charmante* own it.

Scar. In order to this, *Charmante* is dressing himself like one of the Caballists
105 of the *Rosacrusian* Order,[40] and is coming to prepare my credulous Master for the greater imposition. I have his trinckets here to play upon him, which shall be ready.

Ela. But the Farce, where is It to be Acted?

Scar. Here, here, in this very House; I am to order the Decoration, adorn a Stage,
110 and place Scenes proper.

Ela. How can this be done without my Father's knowledge?

Scar. You know the old Apartment next the great Orchard, and the Worm-eaten Gallery, that opens to the River; which place for several years no Body has frequented, there all things shall be Acted proper for our purpose.

Enter Mopsa *running.*

115 *Mop.* Run, Run *Scaramouch,* my Masters Conjuring for you like Mad below, he calls up all his little Divels with horrid Names, his *Microscope,* his *Horoscope,* his *Telescope,* and all his *Scopes.*

Scar. Here, here,——I had almost forgot the Letters; here's one for you, and one for Mrs. *Bellemante.*   [*runs out.*

---

[37]   Geese are the method of transportation to the Moon in Francis Godwin's *The Man in the Moone: or, A Discourse of a Voyage Thither* (1638).
[38]   Probably a reference to John Wilkins' first edition of *The Discovery of a World in the Moone* (1638).
[39]   Sir John Mandeville (*fl.* fourteenth century), who wrote *The Travels of Sir John Mandeville,* a fantastic travel narrative.
[40]   A cabal is a group of people who organise for some task or policy; here this may allude to the disliked CABAL of Charles II, which served between 1667 and 1673. The term is also a reference to members of the secret society of the Rosicrucian order. The Abbé Nicolas-Pierre-Henri de Montfaucon de Villars's (1635–1673) *Le Comte de Gabalis, ou, Entretiens sur les sciences secrètes* refers to the Rosicrucians as a 'certain Fraternity, or Cabal', of German extraction, who obliged themselves to fidelity and secrecy, and who wrote enigmatically in characters (sig. A2^{V}).

Enter Bellemante *with a Book.*

20   *Bell.* Here, take my Prayer Book, Oh *Matres chear.*[41]   [*Embraces her.*

    Ela. Thy Eyes are always laughing, *Bellemante.*

    Bell. And so would yours had they been so well employed as mine, this Morning.
        I have been at the Chapel; and seen so many Beaus, such a Number of
        Plumeys,[42] I cou'd not tell which I shou'd look on most, sometimes my
25   heart was charm'd with the gay Blonding,[43] then with the Melancholy
        Noire,[44] annon the amiable brunet, sometimes the bashful, then again the
        bold; the little now, anon the lovely tall! In fine, my Dear, I was embarass'd
        on all sides, I did nothing but deal my heart *tout au toore.*[45]

    Ela. Oh there was then no danger, Cousin.

30   *Bell.* No but abundance of Pleasure.

    Ela. Why, this is better than sighing for *Charmante.*

    Bell. That's when he's present only, and makes his Court to me; I can sigh to
        a Lover, but will never sigh after him,——but Oh the Beaus, the Beaus,
        Cousin, that I saw at Church.

35   *Ela.* Oh you had great Devotion to Heaven then!

    Bell. And so I had; for I did nothing but admire its handy work, but I cou'd
        not have pray'd heartily if I had been dying; but a deuce on't, who shou'd
        come in and spoyl all but my Lover *Charmante,* so drest, so Gallant, that
        he drew together all the scatter'd fragments of my heart, confin'd my
40   wandering thoughts, and fixt 'em all on him; Oh how he look't, how he
        was dress'd!

Sings

Chivalier, a Chevave Blond,
Plus de Mouche, Plus de Powdre
Pleus de Ribons et Cannous.[46]

45   ——Oh what a dear ravishing thing is the beginning of an Amour?

---

41   Probably *ma très chère*, i.e. 'my dear' or 'my dearest'.
42   The young men of the day often wore feathers in their hats, so hence the term plumey.
43   Blonde-haired.
44   Black- or dark-haired.
45   Probably *tout autour*, i.e. 'all around'. There were so many handsome men at church
that Bellemante's heart was divided between all of them. The expression 'deal my heart *tout
au toore*' is also a reference to card playing and dealing one's hearts (i.e. the suit of hearts)
around the table.
46   Cannous is cannons, wide breeches decorated with ribbons and lace, popular in France.
The French language here is incorrect, perhaps owing to the printer, for 'a' here is probably
'à' in the sense of 'with', while 'Mouche' (fly in French) is perhaps the black dots that men
and women wore on their whitened faces. Charmante is smartly dressed in the French style,
with 'powdre' (perhaps 'poudre' as in a powdered wig), the fashionable dots, ribbons and
cannons.

Ela. Thou'rt still in Tune, when wilt thou be tame, *Bellemante*?

Bell. When I am weary of loving, *Elaria*.

Ela. To keep up your Humor, here's a Letter from your *Charmante*.

Bel. reads. Malicious Creature, when wilt thou cease to torment me, and either
150   *appear less charming or more kind. I languish when from you, and am*
       wounded when I see you, and yet I am eternally Courting my Pain. Cinthio
       and I are contriving how we shall see you to Night. Let us not toyl in vain; we
       ask but your consent; the pleasure will be all ours; 'tis therefore fit we suffer
       all the fatigue. Grant this, and Love me, if you will save the Life of
155   *Your Charmante.*

       ——Live then *Charmante*! Live, as long as Love can last!

Ela. Well, Cousin, *Scaramouch* tells me of a rare design's a hatching, to relieve
       us from this Captivity; here are we mew'd up to be espous'd to two Moon-
       calfs for ought I know;[47] for the Devil of any Human thing is suffer'd to
160   come near us, without our Governante and Keeper, Mr. *Scaramouch*.

Bell. Who, if he had no more Honesty, and Conscience, than my Uncle, wou'd
       let us pine for want of Lovers; but thanks be prais'd the Generosity of our
       Cavaliers has open'd their obdurate Hearts with a Golden key,[48] that let's
       'em in at all opportunities. Come, come, let's in, and answer their Billet
165   Deux.   [*Exeunt.*

SCENE II. *A Garden.*

Enter Doctor, *with all manner of Mathematical Instruments, hanging at his*
    Girdle; Scaramouch *bearing a Telescope twenty (or more) Foot long.*[49]

Doct. Set down the Telescope.——Let me see, what Hour is it?

Scar. About six a Clock, Sir.

Doct. Then 'tis about the Hour, that the great Monarch of the upper World
       enters into his Closet;[50] Mount, mount the Telescope.

5   *Scar.* What to do, Sir?

Doct. I understand, at certain moments Critical, one may be snatch'd of such a
       mighty consequence to let the sight into the secret Closet.

Scar. How, Sir, Peep into the Kings Closet; under favour, Sir, that will be
       something uncivil.

10   *Doct.* Uncivil, it were flat Treason if it shou'd be known, but thus unseen, and
       as wise Politicians shou'd, I take Survey of all: This is the States-man's
       peeping-hole, thorow[51] which he Steals the secrets of his King, and seem

---

47   A moon-calf is a derogatory term for someone foolish, unstable, or fickle.
48   Money. Cinthio and Charmante have bribed the young ladies' governess and guardian.
49   Behn draws in this scene on scene one of the French *Arlequin*.
50   A closet is a small private room used as a place for study or private devotion.
51   Thorow meaning 'through'.

to wink at distance.

Scar. The very key-hole, Sir, thorow which with half an Eye, he sees him even at
    his Devotion, Sir.   [*A knocking at the Garden Gate.*

Doct. Take care none enter——   [Scar. *goes to the Door.*

Scar. Oh, Sir, Sir, here's some strange great Man come to wait on you.

Doct. Great Man! from whence?

Scar. Nay, from the Moon World, for ought I know, for he looks not like the
    People of the lower Orb.

Doct. Ha! And that may be: wait on him in.   [*Ex.* Scar.

> Enter Scaramouch *bare, bowing before* Charmante, *drest in a strange*
> *Fantastical Habit, with* Harl[e]quin *Salutes the* Doctor.

Char. Doctor *Baliardo,* most learned Sir, all Hail; Hail from the great
    Caballa——of *Eutopia.*

Doct. Most Reverend *Bard,* thrice welcome.   [*Salutes him low.*

Char. The Fame of your great Learning, Sir, and Vertue, is known with Joy to
    the renown'd Society.[52]

Doct. Fame, Sir, has done me too much Honour, to bear my Name to the
    renown'd *Caballa.*

Char. You must not attribute it all to Fame, Sir, they are too learned and wise
    to take up things from Fame, Sir; our intelligence is by ways more secret
    and sublime, the Stars, and little Dæmons of the Air inform us all things,
    past, present, and to come.

Doct. I must confess the Count of *Gabalist,* renders it plain, from Writ Divine
    and Humane, there are such friendly and intelligent Dæmons.[53]

Char. I hope you do not doubt that Doctrine, Sir, which holds that the
    Four Elements are Peopl'd with persons of a Form and Species more
    Divine than Vulgar Mortals——those of the fiery Regions we call the
    Salamanders, they beget Kings and *Heroes,* with Spirits like their Deietical
    Sires the lovely Inhabitants of the Water, we call Nymphs. Those of the
    Earth are Gnomes or Fayries. Those of the Air are Silfs. These, Sir, when
    in Conjunction with Mortals, beget Immortal Races.[54] Such as the first
    born man, which had continu'd so, had the first Man ne'er doated on a
    Woman.[55]

---

[52] 'Society' may be a tongue-in-cheek reference to the scientific Royal Society of London,
chartered in 1662 by Charles II, but more likely it is a suggestion of the society of the
Rosicrucian order, the 'great Caballa'.

[53] In the Abbé de Villars' *Count of Gabalis* a gentleman from the 'Cabal' (the Count of the
Cabal) visits the narrative's speaker to instruct him in the secrets of the society, so that he
might become one of its sages.

[54] The four inhabitants of the elements (sylphs, gnomes, nymphs, and salamanders) are
important features of the Abbé de Villars' narrative (pp. 13–17, 27–33).

[55] Adam's crime, according to the Count of Gabalis, was not in eating the apple but in his
relations with Eve, since God designed Adam to take his pleasure with the 'Nymphs and

Doct. I am of that opinion, Sir, Man was not made for Woman.

45 *Char.* Most certain, Sir, Man was to have been Immortalliz'd by the Love and Conversation of these Charming Silfs and Nymphs, and Woman by the Gnomes and Salamanders, and to have stock'd the World with Demy Gods, such as at this Day inhabit the Empire of the *Moon*.[56]

Doct. Most admirable Philosophy and Reason.——But do these Silfs and
50   Nymphs appear in shapes?

Char. Of the most Beautiful of all the Sons and Daughter of the *Universe*: Fancy, Imagination is not half so Charming: And then so soft, so kind! but none but the *Caballa* and their Families are blest with their Divine Addresses. Were you but once admitted to that Society.——

55 *Doct.* Ay, Sir, what Vertues or what Merits can accomplish me for that great Honour?

Char. An absolute abstinence from carnal thought, devout and pure of Spirit; free from Sin.[57]

Doct. I dare not boast my Vertues, Sir; Is there no way to try my Purity?

60 *Char.* Are you very secret.

Doct. 'Tis my first Principle, Sir——

Char. And one, the most material in our *Rosocrusian* order. Please you to make a Tryal.

Doct. As how, Sir, I beseech you?——

65 *Char.* If you be throwly[58] purg'd from Vice, the opticles of your sight will be so illuminated, that glancing through this *Telescope*, you may behold one of these lovely Creatures, that people the vast Region of the Air.[59]

Doct. Sir, you oblige profoundly.

Char. Kneel then, and try your strength of Vertue, Sir.— Keep your Eye fix't
70   and open.

[*He looks in the* Telescope. *While he is looking,* Charmante *goes to the Door to* Scaramouch, *who waited on purpose without, and takes a Glass with a picture of a Nymph on it, and a light behind it; that as he brings it, it shows to the Audience. Goes to the end of the* Telescope.

——Can you discern, Sir?

Doct. Methinks I see a kind of Glorious Cloud drawn up——and now——'tis gone again.

Sylphids' (pp. 110–11).

[56] Gabalis points out that had Adam mated with the elemental creatures, rather than a mortal woman, the universe would be populated with heroes or giants (p. 112).

[57] Gabalis also insists that his pupil '*must Renounce all Carnal Commerce with Women*' (p. 25).

[58] 'Thoroughly'.

[59] Gabalis assures his pupil that were he to become one of the philosophers, a sacred medicine would be applied to his eyes, after which he would be able to see these perfect creatures (p. 26).

Char. Saw you no fuger?[60]

'5   *Doct.* None.

Char. Then make a short Prayer to *Alikin*,[61] the Spirit of the East; shake off all
Earthly thoughts, and look again.[62]

> [He *prays*. Charmante *puts the Glass into the Mouth
> of the* Telescope.

Doct. ——Astonisht, Ravisht with delight, I see a Beauty young and Angel like,
leaning upon a Cloud——

3o   *Char.* Seems she on a Bed, then she's reposing, and you must not gaze——

Doct. Now a Cloud Veils her from me.[63]

Char. She saw you peeping then, and drew the Curtain of the Air between.

Doct. I am all Rapture, Sir, at this rare Vision——is't possible, Sir, that I may
ever hope the Conversation of so Divine a Beauty?

35   *Char.* Most possible, Sir; they will Court you, their whole delight is to
Immortallize— *Alexander* was begot by a *Salamander*, that visited his
Mother in the form of a Serpent, because he wou'd not make King *Philip*
Jealous,[64] and that famous Philosopher *Merlin*, was begotten on a Vestal
Nun, a certain Kings Daughter, by a most beautiful young *Salamander*; as

9o   indeed all the *Heroes*, and men of mighty minds are.[65]

Doct. Most excellent!

Char. The Nymph *Egeria* inamour'd on *Numa Pompilius*, came to him invisible
to all Eyes else, and gave him all his Wisdom and Philosophy.[66] *Zoriastes*,
Trismegistus, *Apuleius*, *Aquinius*, *Albertus Magnus*, *Socrates* and *Virgil*

95   had their *Zilphid*,[67] which foolish people call'd their Dæmon or Devil. But

---

[60]   Probably 'figure'.

[61]   In early regional dialect, the term 'alkin' meant the collective, as 'of every kind' or 'of
every sort'. Most likely here this is a spirit Behn created for this play.

[62]   Gabalis informs his pupil that for ascendancy over the salamanders, he needs to
'concentrate the Fire of the World (by Means of concave Mirrours) in a Globe of Glass' and
for the sylphs, gnomes, and nymphs he should 'shut up a Glass fill'd with conglobated Air,
Water, or Earth' (p. 47).

[63]   In Lucian's *Icaromenippus*, the Moon draws a veil of cloud when she sees a human on
Earth committing some atrocity, such as adultery or theft, so that other humans have no
light to see such men (p. 23).

[64]   Alexander the Great (356 BC–323 BC), King of Macedonia.

[65]   Merlin, from Arthurian lore, is described as both a prophet and a wizard or sorcerer.

[66]   Pompilius (753 BC–673 BC), a legendary King of Rome.

[67]   Zoroaster, founder of Zoroastrianism; Trismegistus, purported author of a series of
sacred texts on hermeticism; Apuleius (*c.*124 AD–170 AD), famous Latin novelist; St Thomas
Aquinas (1225–1274), influential Roman Catholic philosopher and theologian; Albertus
Magnus (1200–1280), German Catholic Bishop, an influential theologian and scholar in
fields as diverse as botany, astronomy, geography, and so forth; Socrates (*c.*470 BC–399 BC),
Greek philosopher, often recognised as one of the founders of Western philosophy; Virgil
(70 BC–19 BC), a Latin poet, famed for his *Georgics* and his *Aeneid*. Most of these figures on
whom Charmante draws are also found in the Abbé de Villars' *Le Comte de Gabalis*.

you are wise, Sir.———

Doct. But do you imagine Sir, they will fall in Love with an old Mortal?

Char. They love not like the Vulgar, 'tis the Immortal Part they doat upon.

Doct. But Sir, I have a Neece and Daughter which I love equally, were it not
100   possible they might be Immortalliz'd?[68]

Char. No doubt on't Sir, if they be Pure and Chast.

Doct. I think they are, and I'll take care to keep 'em so; for I confess Sir, I wou'd
      fain have a Hero to my Grandson.

Char. You never saw the Emperor of the Moon, Sir, the mighty *Iredonozar*?[69]

105 *Doct.* Never Sir; his Court I have, but 'twas confusedly too.

Char. Refine your Thoughts Sir, by a moments Pray, and try again.

> [*He Prays.* Char. *claps the Glass with the Emperour*
> *on it, he looks in and sees it.*

Doct. It is too much, too much for mortal Eyes! I see a Monarch seated on a
      Throne—But seems most sad and pensive.

Char. Forbear then Sir, for now his Love-Fit's on, and then he wou'd be
110   private.

Doct. His Love-Fit, Sir!

Char. Ay Sir, the Emperor's in Love with some fair Mortal.

Doct. And can he not command her?

Char. Yes, but her Quality being too mean, he struggles, tho' a King 'twixt Love
115   and Honour.[70]

Doct. It were too much to know the Mortal, Sir?

Char. 'Tis yet unknown, Sir, to the Caballists, who now are using all their Arts
      to find her, and serve his Majesty; but now my great Affair deprives me of
      you: To morrow Sir, I'll wait on you again; and now I've try'd your Vertue,
120   tell you Wonders.

Doct. I humbly kiss your Hands, most Learned Sir.

> [Charmante *goes out.* Doctor *waits on him to the Door, and returns, to*
> *him* Scaramouch. *All this while* Harlequin *was hid in the Hedges, peeping*
> *now and then, and when his Master went out he was left behind.*

Scar. So, so, *Don Charmante* has plaid his Part most exquisitely; I'll in and see
      how it works in his Pericranium.   ([*Aside.*)

---

[68]   Gabalis claims that the sylphs, gnomes, nymphs, and salamanders united with
mankind as a means of becoming immortal (pp. 32–33).

[69]   Irdonozur is the name of the lunar monarch in Godwin's *The Man in the Moone.* Behn
spells it Iredonozar here but Iredonozor later.

[70]   Marriage between royalty and a commoner was the subject of much debate in the
Restoration, largely owing to the barrenness of Charles II's queen, Catherine of Braganza
(1638–1705). There were those who urged him to divorce Catherine and marry one of his
more fertile mistresses, regardless of her social rank.

———Did you call Sir?

25 *Doct.* *Scaramouch*, I have, for thy singular Wit and Honesty, always had a Tenderness for thee above that of a Master to a Servant.

Scar. I must confess it, Sir.

Doct. Thou hast Vertue and Merit that deserves much.

Scar. Oh Lord, Sir!

30 *Doct.* And I may make thee great,———all I require, is, that thou wilt double thy diligent Care of my Daughter and my Neece, for there are mighty things design'd for them, if we can keep 'em from the sight of Man.

Scar. The sight of Man, Sir!

Doct. Ay, and the very Thoughts of Man.

35 *Scar.* What Antidote is there to be given to a young Wench, against the Disease of Love and Longing?

Doct. Do you your Part, and because I know thee Discreet and very Secret, I will hereafter discover Wonders to thee.———On pain of Life, look to the Girls; that's your Charge.

40 *Scar.* Doubt me not, Sir, and I hope your Reverence will reward my faithful Service with *Mopsophil*, your Daughters Governante, who is Rich, and has long had my Affection, Sir.

Har. Peeping, cries— Oh Traitor![71]

Doct. Set not thy Heart on Transitories mortal, there's better things in store

45 ———besides, I have promis'd her to a Farmer for his Son.———Come in with me, and bring the Telescope. [*Ex. Doctor and* Scaramouch.

[Harlequin *comes out on the Stage.*

Har. My Mistriss *Mopsophil* to marry a Farmers Son! What, am I then forsaken, abandon'd by the false fair One?———If I have Honour, I must die with Rage; Reproaching gently, and complaining madly.———It is resolv'd, I'll

150 hang my self———No,———When did I ever hear of a Hero that hang'd himself? no — 'tis the Death of Rogues. What If I drown my self?———No, ———Useless Dogs and Puppies are drown'd; a Pistol or a Caper on my own Sword wou'd look more nobly, but that I have a natural Aversion to Pain. Besides, it is as Vulgar as Rats-bane, or the sliceing of the Weasand.

155 No, I'll Die a Death uncommon, and leave behind me an eternal Fame. I have somewhere read an Author, either Antient or Modern, of a Man that laugh'd to death.[72]———I am very Ticklish, and am resolv'd———to dye that

---

[71] In the original text, Behn places this as an 'aside' rather than in the script itself.

[72] Death by laughing may refer to Pietro Aretino (1492–1556), an Italian poet and satirist, who purportedly suffocated from laughter. Montague Summers points to Bernardo Accolti (1465–1536), who flung himself backward in a chair laughing and broke his neck, and to the Scottish writer Thomas Urquhart (1611–1660) who died of laughter when he heard that Charles II was restored to the throne (Behn, *Works*, ed. by Summers, III, p. 497 n. 408).

Death.——Oh *Mopsophil*, my cruel *Mopsophil!*[73]

> [*Pulls off his Hat, Sword and Shooes.*

——And now, farewel the World, fond Love, and mortal Cares.

> [*He falls to tickle himself, his Head, his Ears, his Arm-pits, Hands, Sides, and Soles of his Feet; making ridiculous Cries and Noises of Laughing several ways, with Antick Leaps and Skips, at last falls down as dead.*[74]

Enter Scaramouch.

160 *Scar.* *Harlequin* was left in the Garden, I'll tell him the News of *Mopsophil.*

> [*Going forward, tumbles over him.*

Ha, whats here? *Harlequin* Dead!   [*Heaving him up, he flies into a Rage.*

Har. Who is't that thus wou'd rob me of my Honour?

Scar. Honour, why I thought thou'dst been dead.

Har. Why so I was, and the most agreeably dead.——

165 *Scar.* I came to bemoan with thee, the mutual loss of our Mistriss.

Har. I know it Sir, I know it, and that thou'rt as false as she: Was't not a Covenant between us, that neither shou'd take advantage of the other, but both shou'd have fair Play, and yet you basely went to undermine me, and ask her of the Doctor; but since she's gone, I scorn to quarrel for her

170   ——But let's like loving Brothers, hand in hand, leap from some Precipice into the Sea.

Scar. What, and spoil all my Cloths? I thank you for that; no, I have a newer way: you know I lodge four pair of Stairs high, let's ascend thither, and after saying our Prayers.——

175 *Har.* ——Prayers! I never heard of a dying Hero that ever pray'd.

Scar. Well, I'll not stand with you for a Trifle——Being come up, I'll open the Casement, take you by the Heels, and fling you out into the Street, ——after which, you have no more to do, but to come up and throw me down in my turn.

180 *Har.* The Atchievment's great and new; but now I think on't, I'm resolv'd to hear my Sentence from the Mouth of the perfidious Trollop, for yet I cannot credit it.

> I'll to the Gypsie, tho' I venture banging,
> To be undeceiv'd, 'tis hardly worth the hanging.   [*Exeunt.*

---

[73]   The idea of Harlequin tickling himself to death is from the French *Arlequin*, scene two.

[74]   In Fatouville's scene, Arlequin tries to smother himself but passes gas instead. Behn leaves out the fart joke.

SCENE II[I].[75] *The Chamber of* Bellemante.

Enter Scaramouch *groping.*

Scar. So, I have got rid of my Rival, and shall here get an Opportunity to speak with *Mopsophil*, for hither she must come anon, to lay the young Ladies Night-things in order; I'll hide my self in some Corner till she come.

[*Goes on to the further side of the Stage.*

Enter Harlequin groping.

Har. So, I made my Rival believe I was gone, and hid my self, till I got this Opportunity to steal to *Mopsophil*'s Apartment, which must be hereabouts, for from these Windows she us'd to entertain my Love.   [*Advances.*

Scar. Ha, I hear a soft Tread,——if it were *Mopsophil*'s, she would not come by Dark.   [*Har. advancing runs against a Table, and almost strikes himself backwards.*

Har. What was that?— a Table,— There I may obscure myself.——

[*Groping for the Table.*

——What a Devil, is it vanish'd?

Scar. Devil,——Vanish'd,——What can this mean? 'Tis a Mans Voice.——If it shou'd be my Master the Doctor, now I were a dead Man;——he can't see me, —and I'll put my self into such a Posture, that if he feel me, he shall as soon take me for a Church Spout as a Man.

[*He puts himself into a Posture ridiculous, his Arms a-kimbo, his Knees wide open, his Back-side almost touching the Ground, his Mouth stretched wide, and his Eyes stairing. Harl. groping, thrusts his Hand into his Mouth, he bites him, the other dares not cry out.*

Har. Ha, what's this? all Mouth, with twenty Rows of Teeth.——Now dare not I cry out, least the Doctor shou'd come, find me here, and kill me.——I'll try if it be mortal.

[*Making damnable Faces and Signs of Pain, he draws a Dagger. Scar. feels the Point of it, and shrinks back, letting go his Hand.*

Scar. Who the Devil can this be? I felt a Poniard,[76] and am glad I sav'd my Skin from pinking.[77]   [*Steals out.*

[*Harlequin groping about, finds the Table, on which there is a Carpet, and creeps under it, list[e]ning.*

Enter Bellemante, *with a Candle in one Hand, and a Book in the other.*[78]

---

[75]   Most of the scenes in this play are either unmarked or incorrectly marked.
[76]   A poniard is a short dagger or stiletto.
[77]   Pinking is a reference to piercing or stabbing.
[78]   The comical section which follows is missing stage directions noting the writing and speaking of these lines. These have been added parenthetically for clarity. Bellemante's

20   *Bell.* I am in a *Belle* Humor for Poetry to Night,——I'll make some Boremes[79]
     on Love.   [*She Writes and Studies.*
     Out of a great Curiosity,— A Shepherd did demand of me.——No, no,——*A*
     Shepherd this implor'd of me.—   [*Scratches out, and Writes anew.*
     Ay, ay so it shall go.——*Tell me, said he,*——*Can you Resign?*——Resign,
25   ay,——what shall Rhime to *Resign?*— *Tell me, said he,*—
                             [*She lays down the Tablets, and walks about.*
                  [Harlequin *peeps from under the Table, takes the Book,*
                        writes in it, and lays it up before she can turn.
        [*Reads.*] Ay, Ay,————So it shall be,————*Tell me, said he, my*
        Bellemante;——*Will you be kind to your* Charmante?
                             [(Bell.) *Reads those two Lines and is amaz'd.*
        ——Ha,— Heav'ns! What's this? I am amaz'd!
        ——And yet I'll venture once more—   [(*She*) *Writes and Studies.*
30   ——*I blush'd, and veil'd my wishing Eyes.*
                             [*Lays down the Book, and walks as before.*
        ——*Wishing Eyes*——
                       [*Har. Writes as before (and speaks the following line.)*
     [Har.] ——*And answer'd only with my Sighs.*
                             [*She turns and takes the Tablet.*
     [Bell.] ——Ha,——What is this? Witchcraft or some Divinity of Love? some
        Cupid sure invisible.——Once more I'll try the Charm.——
                                   [Bell. *Writes (and speaks)*]
35   *Cou'd I a better way my Love impart?*   [*Studies and walks.*
        ——*Impart*——
                             [He *writes (and speaks) as before.*
     [Har. *wri.*] —*And without speaking, tell him all my Heart.*
     [Bell.] —'Tis here again, but where's the Hand that writ it?   [*Looks about.*
        ——The little Deity that will be seen
40   But only in his Miracles. It cannot be a Devil,
     For here's no Sin nor Mischief in all this.

                  Enter Charmante. *She hides the Tablet, he steps to her,*
                        and snatches it from her and Reads.

     Char. Reads.   Out of a great Curiosity,
                         A Shepherd this implor'd of me.
                         Tell me, said he, my Bellemante.
45   Will you be kind to your Charmante?

---

pleasure in writing poetry and a demon writing on her tablets has some similarity to scene
four of Fatouville's *Arlequin.*
[79] 'Bouts rimés', a list of rhyming words given to a poet, whose job it was to create a poem
using these rhymes (Behn, *Works*, ed. by Summers III, p. 497 n. 410; Behn, *Works*, ed. by
Todd VII, p. 435 n. 23).

I blush'd, and veil'd my wishing Eyes,
And answser'd only with my Sighs.
Cou'd I a better way my Love impart?
And without speaking, tell him all my Heart.

Char. Whose is this different Character?[80]   [*Looks angry.*

Bell. 'Tis yours for ought I know.

Char. Away, my Name was put here for a blind.[81] What Rhiming Fop have you
    been clubbing Wit withal?[82]

Bell. Ah, *mon Dieu!*[83]——*Charmante* Jealous!

Char. Have I not cause? ——Who writ these Boremes?

Bell. Some kind assisting Deity, for ought I know.

Char. Some kind assisting Coxcomb,[84] that I know,
    The Ink's yet wet, the Spark is near I find.——

Bell. Ah, *Maluruse!*[85] How was I mistaken in this Man?

Char. Mistaken! What did you take me for, an easie Fool to be impos'd
    upon?— One that wou'd be cuckolded by every feather'd Fool; that you
    shou'd call a——*Beau un Gallant Huome.*[86] 'sdeath![87] Who wou'd doat
    upon a fond She-Fop?——A vain conceited Amorous Cocquett.[88]

                                 [*Goes out, she pulls him back.*

                Enter Scaramouch, running.

Scar. Oh Madam! Hide your Lover, or we are all undone.

Char. I will not hide, till I know the thing that made the Verses.

                [*The* Doctor *calling as on the Stairs.*

Doct. Bellemante, Neece,——Bellemante.

Scar. She's [He's] coming Sir.——Where, where shall I hide him?——Oh, the
    Closet's open!   [*Thrusts him into the Closet by force.*

           ([The Doctor enters.])

Doct. Oh Neece! Ill Luck, Ill Luck, I must leave you to night; my Brother the
    Advocate[89] is sick, and has sent for me; 'tis three long Leagues,[90] and dark

---

[80] Character refers to handwriting or penmanship.
[81] As a cover for another person.
[82] 'With whom have you been exchanging witticisms (i.e. here, poetic lines)?'
[83] I.e. my God!
[84] A coxcomb is a silly fool.
[85] The term is probably *malheureuse*, meaning unlucky or unhappy woman, something
like 'woe is me'.
[86] A handsome seducer. Charmante claims that Bellemante is taken in by good looks and
thus she is a poor judge of character.
[87] 'Sdeath is a mild oath meaning 'God's death'.
[88] A coquette is a flirtatious young woman.
[89] An advocate is a person who intercedes for someone else; here, probably an attorney
or solicitor.
[90] A league is a measure of distance, about three miles.

as 'tis, I must go.— They say he's dying.

[Pulls out his Keys; one falls down.[91]

Here, take my Keys, and go into my Study, and look over all my Papers, and bring me all those Mark'd with a Cross and Figure of Three,[92] they concern my Brother and I.

[She looks on Scaramouch, *and makes pitiful Signs, and goes out.*

75 ——Come *Scaramouch,* and get me ready for my Journey, and on your Life, let not a Door be open'd till my Return.   *[Ex.*

Enter Mopsophil. Har. *peeps from under the Table.*

Har. Ha! *Mopsophil,* and alone!

Mop. Well, 'tis a delicious thing to be Rich; what a World of Lovers it invites: I have one for every Hand, and the Favorite for my Lips.

80 *Har.* Ay, him wou'd I be glad to know.   *[And peeping.*

Mop. But of all my Lovers, I am for the Farmers Son, because he keeps a Calash— and I'll swear a Coach is the most agreeable thing about a man.

Har. Ho, ho!

Mop. Ah me,——What's that?   *[He answers in a shrill Voice.*

85 *Har.* The Ghost of a poor Lover, dwindle'd into a Hey-ho.

[He rises from under the Table and falls at her Feet. Scaramouch *enters. She runs off squeaking.*

Scar. Ha, my Rival and my Mistriss!— Is this done like a Man of Honour, Monsieur *Harlequin,* To take Advantages to injure me?   *[Draws.*

Har. All Advantages are lawful in Love and War.

Scar. 'Twas contrary to our League and Covenant;[93] therefore I defy thee as a

90 Traytor.

Har. I scorn to fight with thee, because I once call'd thee Brother.

Scar. Then thou'rt a Paltroon, that's to say, a Coward.

Har. Coward, nay, then I am provok'd, come on——

Scar. Pardon me, Sir, I gave the Coward, and you ought to strike.

[They go to fight ridiculously, and ever as Scaramouch *passes,* Harlequin *leaps aside, and skips so nimbly about, he cannot touch him for his Life; which after a while endeavouring in vain, he lays down his Sword.*

---

[91] That the Doctor drops one of his keys is noted within the lines of conversation in the 1687 play. As the action is essential to the plot, this has been set off as a stage direction for clarity.

[92] Crosses and figures of three are frequently used as symbols in alchemy.

[93] Scaramouch means their 'oath' or 'agreement', but the term also suggests the Solemn League and Covenant of 1643, a treaty established during the English Civil War by which the English and the Scottish parliaments agreed to various terms, including an alliance of their armies to defeat the Royalists.

95 ——If you be for dancing, Sir, I have my Weapons for all occasions.

> [Scar. *pulls out a Fleut Deux,*[94] *and falls to Playing. Har. throws down his [sword], and falls a Dancing; after the Dance, they shake Hands.*

Har. He my Bone Ame[95]— Is not this better than Duelling?

Scar. But not altogether so Heroick, Sir. Well, for the future, let us have fair Play; no Tricks to undermine each other, but which of us is chosen to be the happy Man, the other shall be content.   [Elaria *within.*

100 *Ela.* Cousin *Bellemante,* Cousin.

Scar. 'Slife,[96] let's be gone, lest we be seen in the Ladies Apartment.

> [Scar. *slips Harlequin behind the Door.*

Enter Elaria.

Ela. How now, how came you here?—   [(Scar.) *Signs to Har. to go out.*

Scar. I came to tell you, Madam, my Master's just taking Mule to go his Journey to Night, and that *Don Cinthio* is in the Street, [waiting] for a lucky
105 moment to enter in.

Ela. But what if any one by my Fathers Order, or he himself, shou'd by some chance surprise us?

Scar. If we be, I have taken order against a Discovery. I'll go see if the old Gentleman be gone, and return with your Lover.   [*Goes out.*

110 *Ela.* I tremble, but know not whether 'tis with Fear or Joy.

Enter Cinthio.

Cin. My dear *Elaria*——   [*Runs to imbrace her, she starts from him.*
——Ha,——shun my Arms, *Elaria*!

Ela. Heavens! Why did you come so soon?

Cin. Is it too soon, when ere 'tis safe, *Elaria*?

115 *Ela.* I die with fear——Met you not *Scaramouch*? He went to bid you wait a while; What shall I do?

Cin. Why this Concern? none of the House has seen me. I saw your Father taking Horse.

Ela. Sure you mistake, methinks I hear his Voice.

120 *Doct. below.*]—My Key—The Key of my Laboratory.— Why, Knave *Scaramouch,* where are you?——

Ela. Do you hear that, Sir?——Oh, I'm undone!— Where shall I hide you?— He approaches —   [*She searches where to hide him.*
——Ha,— my Cousins Closet's open,— step in a little.—

---

94   *Fleut Deux* should be *flûte-douce* and is a high-pitched flute (Behn, *Works,* ed. by Summers, III, p. 497 n. 413).
95   Meaning something like 'Hey, my friend'.
96   'Slife is a mild oath which means 'God's life'.

[He goes in, she puts out the Candle. Enter the Doctor. *She gets round the Chamber to the Door, and as he advances in, she steals out.*

125 *Doct.* Here I must have dropt it; a Light, a Light——there——

Enter Cinthio *from the Closet, pulls* Charmante *out, they not knowing each other.*

Cin. Oh this perfidious Woman! no marvel she was so surpris'd and angry at my Approach to Night.——

Char. Who can this be?——but I'll be prepar'd—— *[Lays his hand on his Sword.*

Doct. Why *Scaramouch*, Knave, a Light!   *[Turns to the Door to call.*

Enter Scaramouch *with a Light, and seeing the two Lovers there, runs against his Master, puts out the Candle, and flings him down, and falls over him. At the entrance of the Candle,* Charmante *slipt from* Cinthio *into the Closet.* Cinthio *gropes to find him; when* Mopsophil *and* Elaria, *hearing a great Noise, enter with a Light.* Cinthio *finding he was discover'd, falls to acting a Mad Man.* Scaramouch *helps up the* Doctor, *and bows.*

130   ——Ha,——a Man,——and in my House,——Oh dire Misfortune! ——Who are you, Sir?

Cin. Men call me *Gog Magog*,[97] the Spirit of Power;
        My Right-hand Riches holds, my Left-hand Honour.
        Is there a City Wife[98] wou'd be a Lady?——Bring her to me,
135   Her easie Cuckold shall be dub'd a Knight.

Ela. Oh Heavens! a mad Man, Sir.

Cin. Is there a Tawdry Fop wou'd have a Title?
        A rich Mechanick[99] that wou'd be an Alderman?[100] Bring 'em to me,
        And I'll convert that Coxcomb, and that Block-head, into, Your Honour,
140   and Right Worshipful.

Doct. Mad, stark mad! Why Sirrah, Rogue——*Scaramouch*——How got this mad Man in?

[While the Doctor turns to Scaramouch, Cinthio *speaks softly to* Elaria.

---

97   Gogmagog or Gog Magog means a man of immense strength and stature, according to the *OED*. Gog and Magog are also referenced in the Hebrew Bible (Ezekiel) and in the Book of the Apocalypse as enemies of God and Israel.
98   City wives were frequently mocked as lustful, greedy, and/or social climbers, whose lack of chastity frequently made their husbands cuckolds.
99   A mechanick is a tradesman. In Shakespeare's *A Midsummer Night's Dream*, for example, the 'mechanicals' are a weaver, a carpenter, a tinker, and so forth.
100   An alderman is an officer in a city or borough whose rank generally places him next to the mayor in authority.

Cin. Oh, thou perfidious Maid! Who hast thou hid in yonder conscious Closet?

[Aside to her.

Scar. Why Sir, he was brought in a Chair for your Advice, but how he rambl'd
45   from the Parlour to this Chamber, I know not.

Cin. Upon a winged Horse, Icliped *Pegasus*,[101]

           Swift as the fiery Racers of the Sun,

           ——I fly——I fly——

           See how I mount, and cut the liquid Sky.   [*Runs out.*

50 *Doct.* Alas poor Gentleman, he's past all Cure——But Sirrah, for the future, take
      you care that no young mad Patients be brought into my House.

Scar. I shall Sir,——and see——here's your Key you look'd for.——

Doct. That's well; I must be gone——Bar up the Doors, and upon Life or Death
      let no man enter.   [*Exit* Doctor, *and all with him, with the Light.*

[*Charmante peeps out*——*and by degrees comes all out, listing every step.*[102]

55 *Char.* Who the Devil cou'd that be that pull'd me from the Closet? but at last
      I'm free, and the Doctors gone; I'll to *Cinthio*, and bring him to pass this
      Night with our Mistrisses.   [*Exit.*

As he is gone off, enter Cinthio groping.

Cin. Now for this lucky Rival, if his Stars will make this last part of his
      Adventure such. I hid my self in the next Chamber, till I heard the Doctor
60   go, only to return to be reveng'd.

[He gropes his way into the Closet, with his
Sword drawn.

Enter Elaria with a Light.

Ela. Scaramouch tells me *Charmante* is conceal'd in the Closet, whom
      Cinthio surely has mistaken for some Lover of mine, and is jealous;
      but I'll send *Charmante* after him, to make my peace and undeceive
      him.   [*Goes to the Door.*

65   ——Sir, Sir, Where are you? they are all gone, you may adventure out.

[Cinthio comes out.

      ——Ha,——*Cinthio* here!——

Cin. Yes, Madam, to your shame——Now your Perfidiousness is plain——False
      Woman, 'Tis well your Lover had the Dexterity of escaping, I'd spoil'd his
      making Love else.   [*Gets from her, she holds him.*

70 *Ela.* Prethee hear me.

Cin. ——But since my Ignorance of his Person saves his Life, live and possess
      him, till I can discover him.   [*Goes out.*

---

[101]   'Icliped' means to be named. Pegasus is the winged horse of classical legend.
[102]   Charmante exits the closet slowly, listening carefully as he takes each step.

Ela. Go peevish Fool——
        Whose Jealousie believes me given to Change,
175   Let thy own Torments be my just Revenge.   [*Ex.*

The End of the first Act.

ACT II. SCENE I.

An Antick Dance.[103]
After the Musick has plaid. Enter Elaria *to her* Bellemante.

Ela. Heavens *Bellemante!* Where have you been?

Bell. Fatigu'd with the most disagreeable Affair, for a Person of my Humour, in the World. Oh, how I hate Business, which I do no more mind, than a Spark does the Sermon, who is ogling his Mistriss at Church all the while: I have been ruffling over twenty Reams of Paper for my Uncles Writings.

———

Enter Scaramouch.

Scar. So, so, the Old Gentleman is departed this wicked World, and the House is our own for this Night.——Where are the Sparks? Where are the Sparks?

Ela. Nay, Heaven knows.

Bell. How! I hope not so; I left *Charmante* confin'd to my Closet, when my Uncle had like to have surpriz'd us together: Is he not here?———

Ela. No, he's escaped, but he has made sweet doings.

Bell. Heavens Cousin! What?

Ela. My Father was coming into the Chamber, and had like to have taken *Cinthio* with me, when, to conceal him, I put him into your Closet, not knowing of *Charmante*'s being there, and which, in the Dark, he took for a Gallant[104] of mine; had not my Fathers Presence hinder'd, I believe there had been Murder committed; how ever, they both escap'd unknown.

Scar. Pshaw, is this all? Lovers Quarrels are soon adjusted; I'll to 'em, unfold the Riddle, and bring 'em back— take no care, but go in and dress you for the Ball; *Mopsophil* has Habits which your Lovers sent to put on: the Fidles Treat,[105] and all are prepar'd.——   [*Ex.* Scar.

Enter Mopsophil.

Mop. Madam, your Cousin *Florinda*, with a Lady, are come to visit you.

Bell. I'm glad on't, 'tis a good Wench, and we'll trust her with our Mirth and Secret.   [*They go out.*

---

[103] The precise meaning of 'Antick' is unclear. While the meaning could be 'old-fashioned', in his *A New Dictionary* (1699), B. E. notes 'antick postures or dresses' as 'odd, ridiculous or singular, the habits and motions of Fools, Zanies, or Merry-andrews' (p. 10). As this is a comedy, the dance was likely something unusual or ridiculous.

[104] 'Gallant' suggests lover or intimate male friend.

[105] Janet Todd points out that Behn probably means 'fiddlers' treat', or provisions for the fiddlers (see Behn, *Works*, ed. by Todd, VII, p. 436, note to line 24).

SCENE [II] *Changes. To the Street.*

Enter Page with a Flambeaux,[106] *follow'd by* Cinthio; *passes over the Stage.*
Scaramouch follows Cinthio *in a Campaign Coat.*[107]

Scar. 'Tis *Cinthio— Don Cinthio —*   [*Calls, he turns.*
——Well, whats the Quarrel?——How fell ye out?

Cin. You may inform your self I believe, for these close Intrigues cannot be carried on without your Knowledge.

5   *Scar.* What Intrigues Sir? be quick, for I'm in hast[e].

Cin. Who was the Lover I surpris'd i'th' Closet?

Scar. Deceptio visus,[108] Sir; the Error of the Eyes.

Cin. Thou Dog,——I felt him too; but since the Rascal scaped me——I'll be Reveng'd on thee——

> [*Goes to beat him, he running away, runs against* Harlequin,
> *who is entering with* Charmante, *and like to have thrown 'em
> both down.*

10   *Char.* Ha,——What's the matter here?——

Scar. Seignior Don *Charmante*——   [*Then he struts courageously in with 'em.*

Char. What, *Cinthio* in a Rage! Who's the unlucky Object?

Cin. All Man and Woman Kind: *Elaria's* false.

Char. Elaria false! take heed, sure her nice Vertue is Proof against the Vices of

15   her Sex.

      ——Say rather *Bellemante.*

    She who by Nature's light and wavering.

    The Town contains not such a false Impertinent.

    This Evening I surpris'd her in her Chamber

20   Writing of Verses, and between her Lines,

    Some Spark had newly pen'd his proper Stuff.

    Curse of the Jilt, I'll be her Fool no more.[109]

Har. I doubt you are mistaken in that, Sir, for 'twas I was the Spark that writ the proper Stuff. To do you Service——

25   *Char.* Thou!

Scar. Ay, we that spend our Lives and Fortunes here to serve you,——to be us'd

---

[106]   This should be the singular 'flambeau' or torch.

[107]   A campaign coat is a military coat, which, according to the *OED*, became a mode in city attire.

[108]   Latin phrase meaning faulty vision or an error of sight.

[109]   While the majority of this play is in prose, on occasion Behn uses verse, as she appears to do here. Mistaken identity and lovers' quarrels are the stuff of great tragedy. Hence, these six lines coming here in a farce suggest a playful sendup of tragedy, which had lost much of its popularity with audiences.

like Pimps and Scowndrels.——Come, Sir,——satisfie him who 'twas was
hid i'th Closet, when he came in and found you.

Cin. Ha,——is't possible? Was it *Charmante?*

30 *Char.* Was it you, *Cinthio?* Pox on't, what Fools are we, we cou'd not know one
another by Instinct?

Scar. Well, well, dispute no more this clear Case, but lets hasten to your
Mistrisses.

Cin. I'm asham'd to appear before *Elaria.*

35 *Char.* And I to *Bellemante.*

Scar. Come, come, take Heart of Grace; pull your Hats down over your Eyes;
put your Arms across; sigh and look scurvily; your simple Looks are ever
a Token of Repentance; come——come along.   [*Exeunt Omnes.*

SCENE [III] changes to the Inside of the House.

*The Front of the Scene is only a Curtain or Hangings to be
drawn up at Pleasure.*

Enter Elaria, Bellemante, Mopsophil, *and Ladies, dress'd in Masking Habits.*

Ela. I am extreamly pleas'd with these Habits,[110] Cousin.

Bell. They are *A la Gothic* and *Uncomune.*[111]

Lady. Your Lovers have a very good Fancy, Cousin, I long to see 'em.[112]

Ela. And so do I. I wonder *Scaramouch* stays so, and what Success he has.

5 *Bell.* [Y]ou have no cause to doubt, you can so easily acquit your self; but I, what
shall I do? who can no more imagine who shou'd write those Boremes,
than who I shall love next, if I break off with *Charmante.*

Lady. If he be a Man of Honour, Cousin, when a Maid protests her Innocence——

Bell. Ay, but he's a Man of Wit too, Cousin, and knows when Women protest

10 most, they likely lye most.

Ela. Most commonly, for Truth needs no asseveration.

Bell. That's according to the Disposition of your Lover, for some believe you

---

[110] Outfits or costumes.

[111] According to the *OED*, 'gothic' suggests old fashioned, i.e. from the Middle Ages,
or 'romantic' rather than classical. The term can also mean rude or savage, which is
probably not the case here. Neither Phillips' nor Coles' nor any other sixteenth- or
seventeenth-century dictionary we could find offers the term 'gothic' or 'gothick' to assist in
understanding Behn's meaning here. The term gothique does appear, however, in Furetière's
French dictionary from 1690, with the meaning 'in the style of the Goths' or barbarous. We
suggest, then, that the ladies are presumably dressed in old-fashioned clothing, perhaps
theatre company costuming from an earlier period. Bellemante's *uncomune* is incorrect
French; the term could be *peu communs*, meaning unusual.

[112] The lady is probably Florinda. 'Cousin' could mean a close friend or companion as well
as a relative.

most, when you most abuse and cheat 'em; some are so obstinate, they wou'd damn a Woman with protesting, before she can convince 'em.

15 *Ela.* Such a one is not worth convincing, I wou'd not make the World wise at the expence of a Vertue.

Bell. Nay, he shall e'en remain as Heaven made him for me, since there are Men enough for all uses.

Enter Charmante *and* Cinthio, *dress'd in their Gothic Habits.* Scaramouch, Harlequin *and Musick.* Charmante *and* Cinthio *kneel.*

Cin. Can you forgive us?   [Elaria *takes him up.*

20 *Bell.* That, *Cinthio,* you're convinc'd, I do not wonder; but how *Charmante's* Goodness is inspir'd, I know not.   [*Takes him up.*

Char. Let it suffice, I'me satisfy'd, my *Bellemante.*

Ela. 'Pray' know my Cousin *Florinda.*[113]   [*They salute the Lady.*[114]

Bell. Come, let us not lose time, since we are all Friends.

25 *Char.* The best use we can make of it, is to talk of Love.

Bell. Oh! We shall have time enough for that hereafter; besides, you may make Love in Dancing as well as in Sitting; you may Gaze, Sigh,——— and press the Hand, and now and then receive a Kiss, what wou'd you more?

Char. Yes, wish a little more.

30 *Bell.* We were unreasonable to forbid you that cold Joy, nor shall you wish long in vain, if you bring Matters so about, to get us with my Uncle's Consent.

Ela. Our Fortunes depending solely on his Pleasure, which is too considerable to lose.

Cin. All things are order'd as I have written you at large; our Scenes and all
35   our Properties are ready; we have no more to do but to banter the old Gentleman into a little more Faith, which the next Visit of our new Caballist *Charmante* will compleat.

[*The Musick plays. Enter some Anticks and dance.*[115]
They all sit the while.

Ela. Your Dancers have perform'd well, but 'twere fit we knew who we have trusted with this Evenings Intrigue.

40 *Cin.* Those, Madam, who are to assist us in carrying on a greater Intrigue, the gaining of you. They are our Kinsmen.

Ela. Then they are doubly welcome.

---

[113] The inverted commas here are also in the later 1688 edition, which suggests that perhaps this is not a printing error. Rather this term may be a shortened form of 'I pray you'.

[114] There were, in fact, two ladies, Florinda and her companion.

[115] 'Anticks' are probably the dancers in strange, old-fashioned or rustic costumes.

*[Here is a Song in Dialogue, with Fleut Deux and Harpsicals.[116]
Shepherd and Shepherdess; which ended, they all dance a
Figure Dance.[117]*

Cin. Hark, what Noise is that? sure 'tis in the next Room.

Doct. within.] Scaramouch, Scaramouch!   *[Scar. runs to the Door and
holds it fast.*

5 *Scar.* Ha,——the Devil in the likeness of my old Masters Voice, for 'tis
impossible it shou'd be he himself.

Char. If it be he, how got he in? did you not secure the Doors?

Ela. He always has a Key to open 'em. Oh! what shall we do? there's no escaping
him; he's in the next Room, through which you are to pass.

10 *Doct.* Scaramouch, Knave, where are you?

Scar. 'Tis he, 'tis he, follow me all——

*[He goes with all the Company behind the Front
Curtain.*

Without Doctor.] I tell you Sirrah, I heard the Noise of Fiddles.

Without Peter.] No surely Sir, 'twas a Mistake.   *[Knocking at the Door.*

*[Scaramouch having plac'd them all in the Hanging, in which they make the
Figures, where they stand without Motion in Postures.[118] He comes out. He
opens the Dore with a Candle in his Hand.*

Enter the Doctor *and* Peter *with a Light.*

Scar. Bless me, Sir! Is it you,——or your Ghost.

25 *Doct.* 'Twere good for you, Sir, if I were a thing of Air; but as I am a substantial
Mortal, I will lay it on as substantially——   *[Canes him. He cries.*

Scar. What d'ye mean, Sir? what d'ye mean?

Doct. Sirrah, must I stand waiting your Leisure, while you are Rogueing here? I
will reward ye.   *[Beats him.*

30 *Scar.* Ay, and I shall deserve it richly, Sir, when you know all.

Doct. I guess all, Sirrah, and I heard all, and you shall be rewarded for all.
Where have you hid the Fiddles, you Rogue?

Scar. Fiddles, Sir!——

Doct. Ay, Fiddles, Knave.

---

116 A harpsical or harpsichord is a keyboard instrument which produces sound through
the plucking of strings when the keys are pressed. Smaller versions include the virginal and
the spinet, one of which is probably the instrument here, as it would have to be moved on
and off stage.

117 A figure dance is a formalised patterned dance, often using the hands and arms to form
patterns and designs. Phillips defines dance as 'To move the Body in Measure and Figure
according to the Tune or Air that is plaid at the same time, for the Delight of the Spectators';
see Phillips, *The New World of Words: or, A Universal English Dictionary* (London, 1696).

118 He places them on pedestals or steps in the hanging as if they are figures woven into
the tapestry. They all freeze in some stance or posture.

65   *Scar.* Fiddles, Sir!——Where?

Doct. Here,—— here I heard 'em, thou false Steward of thy Masters Treasure.

Scar. Fiddles, Sir! Sure 'twas Wind got into your Head, and whistled in your
Ears, riding so late, Sir.

Doct. Ay, thou false Varlot, there's another Debt I owe thee, for bringing me so

70   damnable a Lye: My Brother's well——I met his Valet but a League from
Town, and found thy Rogury out.   [*Beats him. He cries.*

Scar. Is this the Reward I have for being so diligent since you went?

Doct. In what, thou Villain? In what?

                    [*The Curtain is drawn up, and discovers the Hangings*
                    where all of them stand.

Scar. Why look you, Sir, I have, to surprise you with Pleasure, against you came

75   home, been putting up this Piece of Tapestry, the best in *Italy*, for the
Rareness of the Figures, Sir.

Doct. Ha——Hum——It is indeed a stately Piece of Work; how came I by 'em?

Scar. 'Twas sent your Reverence from the *Vertuoso*,[119] or some of the Caballists.

Doct. I must confess, the Workmanship is excellent,— but still I do insist I heard

80   the Musick.

Scar. 'Twas then the tuning of the Spheres,[120] some serinade, Sir, from the
Inhabitants of the Moon.

Doct. Hum,—— from the Moon,—— and that may be——

Scar. Lord, d'ye think I wou'd deceive your Reverence?

85   *Doct.* From the Moon, a Serinade,—— I see no signs on't here, indeed it must
be so——I'll think on't more at leisure.——   [*Aside.*
—— Prithee what Story's this?   [*Looks on the Hangings.*

Scar. Why, Sir,——'Tis. ——

Doct. Hold up the Candles higher, and nearer.

                    [Peter *and* Scaramouch *hold Candles near. He takes a Perspective*
                    and looks through it; and coming nearer, Harlequin, *who is plac'd on*
                    a Tree in the Hangings, hits him on the Head with his Trunchion.[121]
                    He starts, and looks about. He sits still.

90   *Scar.* Sir.——

Doct. What was that struck me?

Scar. Struck you, Sir! Imagination.

Doct. Can my Imagination feel, Sirrah?

Scar. Oh, the most tenderly of any part about one, Sir!

---

[119]   A vertuoso, i.e. virtuoso, is a scholar or person of 'science', although the term came to
be used derisively to refer to those who pretended to knowledge.

[120]   It was long held that the turning of the heavenly spheres, overseen by a *primum mobile*,
created music. Copernican hypotheses disproved the notion of spherical layers, but the
concept remained in literary discourse.

[121]   A truncheon is a thick staff baton, or a club or cudgel.

5   *Doct.* Hum——That may be——

Scar. Are you a great Philosopher, and know not that, Sir?

Doct. This Fellow has a glimpse of Profundity——   [*Aside. Looks again.*

——I like the Figures well.

Scar. You will, when you See 'em by Day-light, Sir.   [*Har. hits him again. The*
                                                              Doctor *sees him.*

20   *Doct.* Ha,——Is that Imagination too———Betray'd, betray'd, undone; run for
my Pistols, call up my Servants *Peter,* a Plot upon my Daughter and my
Neece.   [*Runs out with* Peter.

[Scaramouch *puts out the Candle, they come out of the Hanging,*
which is drawn away. He places 'em in a Row just at the
Entrance.

Scar. Here, here, fear nothing, hold by each other, that when I go out, all may go;
that is, slip out, when you hear the Doctor is come in again, which he will
05   certainly do, and all depart to your respective Lodgings.

Cin. And leave thee to bear the Brunt?

Scar. Take you no care for that, I'll put it into my Bill of Charges, and be paid
all together.

Enter the Doctor *with Pistols, and* Peter.

Doct. What, by dark? that shall not save you, Villains, Traytors to my Glory and
10   Repose.——*Peter,* hold fast the Door, let none escape.   [*They all slip out.*

Pet. I'll warrant you, Sir.

                              [*Doctor gropes about, then stamps and calls.*

Doct. Lights there——Lights——I'm sure they cou'd not scape.

Pet. Impossible, Sir.

Enter Scaramouch *undress'd in his Shirt, with a Light. Starts.*

Scar. Bless me!——what's here?

15   *Doct.* Ha,—— Who art thou?   [*Amaz'd to see him enter so.*

Scar. I, who the Devil are you, and you go to that. [*Rubs his Eyes, and brings the*
                                        Candle nearer. Looks on him.*

——Mercy upon us!——Why what is't you, Sir, retun'd so soon?

Doct. Return'd!   [*Looking sometimes on him, sometimes about.*

Scar. Ay Sir, Did you not go out of Town last night, to your Brother the
20   Advocate?

Doct. Thou Villain, thou question'st me, as if thou knew'st not that I was
return'd.

Scar. I know, Sir! How shou'd I know? I'm sure I am but just wak'd from the
sweetest Dream———

25   *Doct.* You dream still, Sirrah, but I shall wake your Rogueship.——Were you

not here but now, shewing me a piece of Tapestry, you Villain?——
Scar. Tapestry!——

[*Mopsophil* listning all the while.

Doct. Yes Rogue, yes, for which I'll have thy Life——   [*Offering a Pistol.*
Scar. Are you stark mad, Sir? or do I dream still?
130 *Doct.* Tell me, and tell me quickly, Rogue, who were those Traytors that were hid
but now in the Disguise of a piece of Hangings.   [*Holds the Pistol*
to his Breast.

Scar. Bless me! you amaze me, Sir. What conformity has every Word you say, to
my rare Dream: Pray let me feel you, Sir,——Are you Humane?
Doct. You shall feel I am, Sirrah, if thou confess not.
135 *Scar.* Confess, Sir! What shou'd I confess?——I understand not your Caballistical
Language; but in mine, I confess that you have wak'd me from the rarest
Dream——Where methought the Emperor of the Moon World was in
our House, Dancing and Revelling; and methought his Grace was fallen
desperately in Love with Mistriss *Elaria*, and that his brother, the Prince,
140 Sir, of *Thunderland*, was also in Love with Mistriss *Bellemante*; and
methoughts they descended to court 'em in your Absence.——And that
at last you surpris'd 'em, and that they transform'd themselves into a Suit
of Hangings to deceive you. But at last, methought you grew angry at
something, and they all fled to Heaven again; and after a deal of Thunder
145 and Lightning, I wak'd, Sir, and hearing Humane Voices here, came to see
what the Matter was.

[*This while the Doctor lessens his signs of Rage by degrees, and
at last stands in deep Contemplation.*

Doct. May I credit this?
Scar. Credit it! By all the Honour of your House, by my unseparable Veneration
for the Mathematicks, 'tis true, Sir.
150 *Doct.* ——That famous *Rosacrusian*, who yesterday visited me, told me——the
Emperor of the Moon was in Love with a fair Mortal——This Dream is
Inspiration in this Fellow——He must have wonderous Vertue in him, to
be worthy of these Divine Intelligences.   [*Aside.*
——But if that Mortal shou'd be *Elaria*! but no more, I dare not yet
155 suppose it——perhaps the thing was real and no Dream, for oftentimes
the grosser part is hurried away in Sleep, by the force of Imagination, and
is wonderfully agitated——This Fellow might be present in his Sleep,
——of this we've frequent Instances——I'll to my Daughter and my
Neece, and hear what knowledge they may have of this.
160 *Mop.* Will you so? I'll secure you, the Frolick shall go round.[122]   [(*Exit.*)

---

[122]   Mopsophil will protect the two young ladies by assuring that the ruse continues.

Doct. Scaramouch, If you have not deceiv'd me in this Matter, time will convince
     me farther; if it rest here, I shall believe you false——

Scar. Good Sir, suspend your Judgment and your Anger then.

Doct. I'll do't, go back to Bed——   [*Ex.* Doctor *and* Peter.

65 *Scar.* No, Sir, 'tis Morning now — and I'm up for all day.——This Madness is a
     pretty sort of a pleasant Disease, when it tickles but in one Vein— Why
     here's my Master now, as great a Scholar, as grave and wise a Man, in all
     Argument and Discourse, as can be met with, yet name but the Moon, and
     he runs into Ridicule, and grows as mad as the Wind.

70   Well *Doctor,* if thou can'st be madder yet,
            We'll find a Medicine that shall cure your Fit.
            —Better than all *Gallanicus.*[123]   [*Goes out.*

SCENE [IV] Draws Off.[124]

Discovers Elaria, Bellemante, *and* Mopsophil *in Night-Gowns.*

Mop. You have your Lessons, stand to it bravely, and the Town's our own,
     Madam.   [*They put themselves in Postures of Sleeping, leaning on the*
                                            Table, Mopsophil *lying at their Feet.*

Enter Doctor, *softly.*

Doct. Ha, not in Bed! this gives me mortal Fears.

Bell. Ah, Prince——   [*She speaks as in her Sleep.*

5 *Doct.* Ha, Prince!   [*Goes nearer and listens.*

Bell. How little Faith I give to all your Courtship, who leaves our Orb so soon.
                                                     [*In a feign'd Voice.*

Doct. Ha, said she Orb?

Bell. But since you are of a Cœlestial Race,
            And easily can penetrate
10   Into the utmost limits of the Thought,
            Why shou'd I fear to tell you of your Conquest?
            ——And thus implore your Aid.   [*Rises and runs to the* Doctor. *Kneels,*
                                                and holds him fast. He shews signs of Joy.

---

[123] Scaramouch refers to Galen (129 AD–c.210 AD), a Greek philosopher and physician, who
had a major influence on Western medicine.
[124] Typically Behn writes 'scene change' or simply 'scene' and location. Here she refers to
the previous scene being 'drawn off', or the shutters being removed, to reveal a new scene on
the inner stage. Franz Muller argues that the Dorset Garden Theatre probably had two inner
stages (three shutter positions) which would allow for multiple changes of scene on stage. See
Muller, 'Flying Dragons and Dancing Chairs at Dorset Garden: Staging Dioclesian', *Theatre
Notebook*, 47 (1993), 80–95 (p. 88). Hence, here the shutters of the previous scene have been
drawn back to reveal the young ladies in one of their bedrooms in their nightwear.

Doct. I am Ravish'd!

Bell. Ah, Prince Divine, take Pity on a Mortal————

15 *Doct.* I am rapt!

Bell. And take me with you to the World above.

Doct. The Moon, the Moon she means, I am Transported, Over-joy'd, and Ecstacy'd.   [*Leaping and jumping from her Hands, she seems to wake.*

Bell. Ha, my Uncle come again to interrupt us!

20 *Doct.* Hide nothing from me, my dear *Bellemante*, since all already is discover'd to me————and more.————

Ela. Oh, why have you wak'd me from the softest Dream that ever Maid was blest with?

Doct. What————what my best *Elaria*?   [*With over-joy.*

25 *Ela.* Methought I entertain'd a Demi-God, one of the gay Inhabitants of the Moon.

Bell. I'm sure mine was no Dream————I wak'd, I heard, I saw, I spoke————and danc'd to the Musick of the Spheres, and methought my glorious Lover ty'd a Diamond Chain about my Arm————and see 'tis all substantial.
          [*Shows her Arm.*

30 *Ela.* And mine a Ring, of more than mortal Lustre.

Doct. Heaven keep me moderate! least excess of Joy shou'd make my Vertue less.
          [*Stifling his Joy.*

————There is a wonderous Mystery in this.
A mighty Blessing does attend your Fates.
Go in, and pray to the chast Powers above
35 To give you Vertue fit for such Rewards.   [*They go in.*

————How this agrees with what the learned Caballist inform'd me of last Night! He said, that great *Iredonozor*, the Emperor of the Moon, was inamour'd on a fair Mortal. It must be so— and either he descended to Court my Daughter Personally, which, for the Rareness of the Novelty, she
40 takes to be a Dream; or else, what they and I beheld, was Visionary, by way of a sublime Intelligence.————And possibly————'tis only thus————the People of that World converse with Mortals.————I must be satisfy'd in this main Point of deep Philosophy.

I'll to my Study,————for I cannot rest,
45 Till I this weighty Mystery have discuss'd.   [*Ex. very gravely.*

SCENE [V]. *The Garden.*

Enter Scaramouch *with a Ladder.*

Scar. Tho' I am come off *en Cavalier*[125] with my Master, I am not with my

---

[125] Without repercussions or consequences.

Mistriss, whom I promised to console this Night, and is but just I shou'd
make good this Morning; 'twill be rude to surprize her Sleeping, and more
Gallant to wake her with a Serinade at her Window.

> [*Sets the Ladder to her Window, fetches his Lute,*
> *and goes up the Ladder. He Plays and Sings this Song.*

When Maidens are young and in their Spring
Of Pleasure, of Pleasure, let 'em take their full Swing,
   full Swing,——full Swing,——
  And Love, and Dance, and Play, and Sing.
  For Silvia, believe it, when Youth is done,
There's nought but hum drum, hum drum, hum drum;
There's nought but hum drum, hum drum, hum drum.

Then Silvia *be wise——be wise——be wise,*
Tho' Painting and Dressing, for a while, are Supplies,
   And may——surprise——
  But when the Fire's going out in your Eyes,
  It twinkles, it twinkles, it twinkles, and dies.
And then to hear Love, to hear Love from you,
I'd as live[126] *hear an Owl cry——Wit to woo,*
  Wit to woo, Wit to woo.

Enter Mopsophil *above.*

Mop. What woful Ditty-making Mortal's this?
  That ere the Lark her early Note has sung,
  Does doleful Love beneath my Casement Thrum.——[127]
  ——Ah, Seignior *Scaramouch*, is it you?
Scar. Who shou'd it be, that takes such pains to sue?
Mop. Ah, Lover most true Blew.

Enter Harlequin *in Womens Cloths.*

Har. If I can now but get admittance, I shall not only deliver the young Ladies
  their Letters from their Lovers, but get some opportunity, in this Disguise,
  to slip this *Billet Deux* into *Mopsophil's* Hand, and bob[128] my Comrade
  Scaramouch.——Ha,——What do I see?—My Mistriss at the Window,
  courting my Rival! Ah Gypsie!——

---

[126] The word is probably lief, rather than live, and means 'I would prefer to' or 'I would
rather'.
[127] Mopsophil's speech comically suggests the balcony scene in Shakespeare's *Romeo and
Juliet* (2.2).
[128] To 'bob' someone is to cheat or out-do them.

Scar. —But we lose precious time, since you design me a kind Hour in your Chamber.

Har. Oh Traytor!——

Mop. You'll be sure to keep it from *Harlequin.*

35   *Har.* Ah yes, he, hang him Fool, he takes you for a Saint.

Scar. Harlequin!——Hang him, shotten Herring.[129]

Har. Ay, a Cully, a Noddy.[130]

Mop. A meer Zany.[131]

Har. Ah, hard hearted Turk.[132]

40   *Mop.* Fit for nothing but a Cuckold.

Har. Monster of Ingratitude! How shall I be reveng'd?

[*Scar. going over the Balcony.*

——Hold, hold, thou perjur'd Traytor.   [*Cryes out in a Womans Voice.*

Mop. Ha,——Discover'd!——A Woman in the Garden!

Har. Come down, come down, thou false perfidious Wretch.

45   *Scar.* Who, in the Devils Name, art thou? And to whom dost thou speak?

Har. To thee, thou false Deceiver, that has broke thy Vows, thy Lawful Vows of Wedlock——   [*Bawling out.*

Oh, oh, that I shou'd live to see the Day!——   [*Crying.*

Scar. Who mean you, Woman?

50   *Har.* Whom shou'd I mean, but thou—— my lawful Spouse?

Mop. Oh Villain!——Lawful Spouse!— Let me come to her.   [*Scar. comes down, as* Mopsophil *flings out of the Balcony.*

Scar. The Woman's mad——hark ye Jade——how long have you been thus distracted?

Har. E're since I lov'd and trusted thee, false Varlot.

55   ——See here,— the Witness of my Love and Shame.   [*Bawls and points to her Belly.*

Just then Mopsophil *enters.*

Mop. How! With Child!——Out Villain, was I made a Property?[133]

Scar. Hear me.

Har. Oh, thou Heathen Christian!——Was not one Woman enough?

---

[129]   An old or spoiled (rotten) herring.

[130]   Cully and noddy are terms for fool or idiot.

[131]   The meaning of 'zany' is fool, trickster, or imitator; Mopsophil's use of the term is ironic here since both Harlequin and Scaramouch are zani or zanni, those silly but often cunning servants/tricksters of *commedia dell'arte*. Zanni was also a term for *commedia dell'arte* itself.

[132]   To call someone 'Turk' was to denigrate them as cruel or cruel-hearted.

[133]   To make someone a property is to incorporate them unwillingly and/or unknowingly in a deceit. Scaramouch has made Mopsophil complicit in the abandonment of this 'pregnant lover'.

Mop. Ay, Sirrah, answer to that.

Scar. I shall be sacrific'd.——

Mop. I am resolv'd to marry to morrow——either to the Apothecary or the Farmer, men I never saw, to be reveng'd on thee, thou tarmagant Infidel.

Enter the Doctor.[134]

Doct. What noise, what Out-cry, what Tumult's this?

Har. Ha,—the Doctor!—What shall I do?—   [*Gets to the Door,*
                                                *Scar. pulls her (*Har.*) in.*
                                                           ([*Aside.*)

Doct. A Woman——some Bawd I am sure——
     Woman, what's your Business here?——ha—

Har. I came, an't like your Seigniorship, to Madam the Governante here, to serve her in the Quality of a *Fille de Chambre*, to the young Ladies.[135]

Doct. A *Fille de Chambre*! 'tis so, a she Pimp,——

Har. Ah, Seignior——   [*Makes his little dapper Leg instead of a*
                                                           Curtsie.[136]

Doct. How now, what do you mock me?

Har. Oh Seignior!——   [*Gets nearer the Door.*

Mop. Stay, stay, Mistriss, and what Service are you able to do the Seigniors Daughters?

Har. Is this Seignior Doctor *Baliardo*, Madam?

Mop. Yes.

Har. Oh! He's a very handsome Gentleman——indeed——

Doct. Ay, ay, what Service can you do, Mistriss?

Har. Why Seignior, I can tye a Cravat the best of any Person in *Naples*, and I can comb a Periwig——and I can——[137]

Doct. Very proper Service for young Ladies; you, I believe, have been *Fille de Chambre* to some young Cavaliers.[138]

Har. Most true, Seignior, why shou'd not the Cavaliers keep *Filles de Chambre*, as well as great Ladies *Vallets de Chambre*?[139]

Doct. Indeed 'tis equally reasonable.——'Tis a Bawd.——   [*Aside.*
——But have you never serv'd Ladies?

Har. Oh yes! I serv'd a Parsons Wife.

---

[134]   This portion of Behn's scene owes much to scene three in Fatouville's *Arlequin*.
[135]   A 'fille de chambre' is a lady's maid.
[136]   He bows, a male gesture, instead of a female curtsy, as a lady would have offered.
[137]   A cravat is a tie and a periwig is a wig worn as a headdress. While both women and men wore wigs as elaborate headdresses, Harlequin means a man's wig here.
[138]   The Doctor suggests that if Harlequin were a 'lady's maid' to young gentlemen, 'her' service would be sexual in nature.
[139]   A valet is an attendant largely responsible for the clothing, dressing, and appearance of his employer.

Doct. Is that a great Lady?

Har. I surely, Sir, what is she else? for she wore her Mantoes of *Brokad de or,*
90   Petticoats lac'd up to the Gathers, her Points, her Patches, Paints and
Perfumes, and sate in the uppermost Place in the Church to.[140]

Mop. But have you never serv'd Countesses and Dutchesses?

Har. Oh, yes, Madam! the last I serv'd, was an Aldermans Wife in the City.

Mop. Was that a Countess or a Dutchess?

95   *Har.* Ay, certainly— for they have all the Money; and then for Cloths, Jewels,
and rich Furniture, and eating, they outdo the very *Vice Reigne* her self.[141]

Doct. This is a very ignorant running Bawd,——therefore first search her for
Bellets Deux, and then have her Pump'd.[142]

Har. Ah, Seignior,——Seignior.——

[Scar. *searches him, finds Leters.*

100   *Scar.* ——Ha,—— to *Elaria*——and *Bellemante?*——

[*Reads the Outside, pops 'em into his Bosom.*

——These are from their Lovers——

——Ha, ——a Note to *Mopsophil,* — Oh, Rogue! have I found you?——

Har. If you have, 'tis but Trick for your Trick, Seignior *Scaramouch,* and you
may spare the Pumping.

105   *Scar.* For once, Sirrah,[143] I'll bring you off,[144] and deliver your Letters. ([To Har.)
—Sir, do you not know who this is?——Why 'tis a Rival of mine, who put
on this Disguise to cheat me of Mistriss *Mopsophil.*
—— See here's a Billet to her.——

Doct. What is he?

110   *Scar.* A Mungrel Dancing-Master; therefore, Sir, since all the Injury's mine, I'll
pardon him for a Dance, and let the Agility of his Heels save his Bones,
with your Permission, Sir.

Doct. With all my Heart, and am glad he comes off so comically.

[Harlequin *Dances.*

[*A knocking at the Gate.* Scar. *goes and returns.*

Scar. Sir, Sir, here's the rare Philosopher who was here yesterday.

115   *Doct.* Give him Entrance, and all depart.   ([*All exit except the* Doct.)

Enter Charmante.

---

[140]   A *manto* is a headdress and *Brokad de or* [brocade d'or] is gold cloth; points are laces
and ribbons; black patches on the face were fashionable; to paint is to wear cosmetics,
particularly a white wash or cream applied to the face. This alludes to the extravagance and
haughtiness of some parsons' wives.

[141]   A *vice-reine* is the wife of a viceroy.

[142]   To be 'pumped' is to be held under a stream of water from a pump as punishment.

[143]   An address to someone of lower status.

[144]   I.e. 'I will save you from this situation'.

Char. Blest be those Stars! that first conducted me to so much Worth and
    Vertue, you are their Darling, Sir, for whom they wear their brightest
    Lustre. Your Fortune is establish'd, you are made, Sir.

Doct. Let me contain my Joy——   [*Keeping in an impatient Joy.*
20   ——May I be worthy, Sir, to apprehend you?

Char. After long Searching, Watching, Fasting, Praying, and using all the
    virtuous means in Nature, whereby we solely do attain the highest
    Knowledge in Philosophy; it was resolv'd, by strong Intelligence——you
    were the happy Sire of that Bright Nymph, that had infascinated, charm'd
25   and conquer'd the mighty Emperor *Iredonozor*——the Monarch of the
    Moon.

Doct. I am——undone with Joy! ruin'd with Transport——   [*Aside.*
    ——Can it——can it, Sir,——be possible——   [*Stifling his Joy, which*
                                                    breaks out.

Char. Receive the Blessing, Sir, with moderation.
30 *Doct.* I do, Sir, I do.

Char. This very Night, by their great Art, they find He will descend, and
    show himself in Glory. An Honour, Sir, no Mortal has receiv'd this sixty
    hundred years.

Doct. Hum———Say you so, Sir? no Emperor ever descend[ed] this Sixty
35   hundred years?   [*Looks sad*
    ——Was I deceiv'd last night?   [*Aside.*

Char. Oh! Yes, Sir, often in disguise, in several Shapes and Forms, which did
    of old occasion so many Fabulous Tales of all the Shapes of *Jupiter*——but
    never in their proper Glory, Sir, as Emperors.[145] This is an Honour only
140   design'd to you.

Doct. And will his Grace——be here in Person, Sir?   [*Joyful.*

Char. In Person——and with him, a Man of mighty Quality, Sir,——'tis
    thought——the Prince of *Thunderland*——but that's but whisper'd, Sir, in
    the Cabal, and that he loves your Neece.

145 *Doct.* Miraculous! how this agrees with all I've seen and heard——To Night,
    say you, Sir?

Char. So 'tis conjectur'd, Sir,——some of the Caballist——are of opinion——that
    last night there was some Sally from the Moon.

Doct. About what hour, Sir?
150 *Char.* The Meridian of the Night, Sir, about the hours of twelve or one, but who
    descended, or in what Shape, is yet uncertain.

Doct. This I believe, Sir.

Char. Why, sir?

---

[145] Jupiter or Jove was the chief Roman god who frequently took on various disguises to
seduce the young women he fell in love with, becoming, for example, a cloud to visit Io.

Doct. May I communicate a Secret of that Nature?

155   *Char.* To any of the Caballist, but none else.

Doct. Then know—last night, my Daughter and my Neece were entertain'd by those illustrious Heroes.

Char. Who, Sir? The Emperor and Prince his Cousin.

Doct. Most certain, Sir. But whether they appear'd in solid Bodies, or
160   Fantomical,[146] is yet a Question, for at my unlucky approach, they all transform'd themselves into a Piece of Hangings.

Char. 'Tis frequent, Sir, their Shapes are numerous, and 'tis also in their Power to transform all they touch, by virtue of a certain Stone———they call the *Ebula*.[147]

165   *Doct.* That wondrous *Ebula*, which *Gonzales* had?

Char. The same——by Vertue of which, all weight was taken from him, and then with ease the lofty Traveller flew from *Parnassus Hill*, and from *Hymethus Mount*, and high *Gerania*, and *Acrocorinthus*, thence to *Taygetus*, so to *Olympus* Top, from whence he had but one step to the Moon. Dizzy he
170   grants he was.[148]

Doct. No wonder, Sir, Oh happy great *Gonzales!*

Char. Your Vertue, Sir, will render you as happy—but I must hast[e]——this Night prepare your Daughter and your Neece, and let your House be Dress'd, Perfum'd, and Clean.

175   *Doct.* It shall be all perform'd, Sir.

Char. Be modest, Sir, and humble in your Elevation, for nothing shews the Wit so poor, as Wonder, nor Birth so mean, as Pride.

Doct. I humbly thank your Admonition, Sir, and shall, in all I can, struggle with Humane Frailty.   [*Brings* Char. *to the Door bare.*[149] *Exit.*

Enter Scaramouch *peeping at the other Door.*

180   *Scar.* So, so, all things go gloriously forward, but my own Amour, and there is no convincing this obstinate Woman, that 'twas that Rogue *Harlequin* in Disguise, that claim'd me; so that I cannot so much as come to deliver

---

[146]   Airy substances, having no solid form.

[147]   In Godwin's tale, the Ebelus was a stone Irdonozur gave to Gonzales which allowed him to rise and descend, by weighing either more or less, depending on which side of the stone he touched to his body (pp. 110–11).

[148]   These are mountain tops: Parnassus, home of the muses and sacred to a number of gods, associated with Apollo and the Oracle of Delphi; Hymettus was near Athens and supposedly was a sanctuary for Zeus; Gerania is probably Gramos and is a mountain range on the border of Greece; Acrocorinth is a large rock overlooking the ancient city of Corinth; Taygetus is a mountain range in southern Greece; and Olympus is the highest mountain in Greece and sacred home of the Greek gods. This 'flight path' is from Lucian's *Icaromenippus* (p. 16).

[149]   Bare-headed, i.e. without a hat.

the young Ladies their Letters from their Lovers. I must get in with this damn'd Mistriss of mine, or all our Plot will be spoil'd for want of Intelligence.

———Hum,———The Devil does not use to fail me at a dead Lift.[150] I must deliver these Letters, and I must have this Wench——tho' but to be reveng'd on her for abusing me.———Let me see———she is resolv'd for the Apothecary or the Farmer. Well, say no more honest *Scaramouch*, thou shalt find a Friend at need of me———and if I do not fit you with a Spouse, say that a Woman has out-witted me.

The End of the Second Act.

---

[150] At an important moment, or in urgent need.

ACT III. SCENE I.

The Street, with the Town Gate, where an Officer *stands with a Staff like
a* London *Constable.*

Enter Harlequin *riding in a Calash, comes through the Gate towards the Stage,
dress'd like a Gentleman sitting in it. The Officer lays hold of his Horse.*[151]

Officer. Hold, hold, Sir, you, I suppose know the Customs that are due to this
City of *Naples*, from all Persons that pass the Gates in Coach, Chariot,
Calash, or *Siege Voglant.*[152]

Har. I am not ignorant of the Custom, Sir, but what's that to me?

5   *Off.* Not to you, Sir! why, what Privilege have you above the rest?

Har. Privilege, for what, Sir?

Off. Why for passing, Sir, with any of the before named Carriages.

Har. Ar't mad?——Dost not see I am a plain Baker, and this my Cart, that
comes to carry Bread for the Vice-Roy's, and the Cities Use?——ha——

10   *Off.* Are you mad, Sir, to think I cannot see a Gentleman Farmer and a Calash,
from a Baker and a Cart?

Har. Drunk by this Day——and so early too? Oh, you're a special Officer;
unhand my Horse, Sirrah, or you shall pay for all the Damage you do me.

Off. Hey day! here's a fine Cheat upon the Vice Roy; Sir, pay me, or I'll seize your

15   Horse.   [Har. *strikes him. They scuffle a little.*

——Nay, and you be so brisk, I'll call the Clerk from his Office.

Calls.— Mr. Clerk, Mr. Clerk.

> [*Goes to the Entrance to call the* Clerk, *the mean time* Har. *whips
> a Frock over himself, and puts down the hind part of the Chariot,
> and then 'tis a Cart.*

Enter Clerk.

Cler. What's the matter here?——

Off. Here's a Fellow, Sir, will perswade me, his Calash is a Cart, and refuses the

20   Customs for passing the Gate.

Cler. A Calash— Where?— I see only a Carter and his Cart.   [*The Officer
looks on him.*

Off. Ha,——What a Devil, was I blind?

Har. Mr. Clerk, I am a Baker, that come with Bread to sell, and this Fellow
here has stopt me this hour, and made me lose the Sale of my Ware—

---

[151]   Much of this scene is taken from scene five of the French *Arlequin, Empereur dans la
lune.*

[152]   A coach is a large, four-wheeled vehicle generally enclosed with a harnessed team and
a coachman; a chariot is a lightweight, four-wheeled vehicle, where the driver typically sits
high up in front apart from the passengers; a calash is a shallow, open vehicle for two people,
usually a summer vehicle; a *siège voglant* or *volant* is a lightweight, two-wheeled carriage.

5   —and being Drunk, will out-face me I am a Farmer,[153] and this Cart a
Calash.——

Cler. He's in an Errour Friend, pass on——

Har. No Sir, I'll have satisfaction first, or the Vice-Roy shall know how he's
serv'd by drunken Officers, that Nuisance to a Civil Government.

0 *Cler.* What do you demand, Friend?

Har. Demand,——I demand a Crown, Sir.

Off. This is very hard—Mr. Clerk— If ever I saw in my Life, I thought I saw a
Gentleman and a Calash.

Cler. Come, come, gratifie him, and see better hereafter.

5 *Off.* Here Sir,— If I must, I must—   *[Gives him a Crown.*

Cler. Pass on, Friend——   *[Ex. Clerk.*

        *Har. unseen, puts up the Back of his Calash, and whips off his
Frock, and goes to drive on. The* Officer *looks on him, and stops
him again.*

Off. Hum, I'll swear it is a Calash——Mr. Clerk, Mr. Clerk, come back, come
back—   *[Runs out to call him. He (Har.) changes as before.*

Enter Officer *and* Clerk.

——Come Sir, let your own Eyes convince you, Sir.——

40 *Cler.* Convince me, of what, you Sott?

Off. That this is a Gentleman, and that a——ha,—   *[Looks about on* Har.

Cler. Stark Drunk, Sirrah! if you trouble me at every Mistake of yours thus, you
shall quit your Office.——

Off. I beg your Pardon, Sir, I am a little in Drink I confess, a little Blind and

45   Mad—Sir,— This must be the Devil, that's certain.

        [The Clerk *goes out,* Har. *puts up his Calash again,
and pulls off his Frock and drives out.*

——————Well, now to my thinking, 'tis as plain a Calash again, as ever I
saw in my Life, and yet I'm satisfy'd 'tis nothing but a Cart.   *[Exit.*

SCENE [II] *changes to the Doctors House.*

The Hall

Enter Scaramouch *in a Chair, which set down and open'd, on all sides, and on
the top represents an Apothecaries Shop, the Inside being painted with Shelves
and Rows of Pots and Bottles;* Scaramouch *sitting in it dress'd in Black, with a
short black Cloak, a Ruff, and little Hat.*[154]

---

153 'Out-face' means he will deny that Harlequin is a farmer.
154 This scene has its foundation in scene seven of the French *Arlequin.*

Scar. The Devil's in't, if either the Doctor, my Master, or *Mopsophil*, know
  me in this Disguise——And thus I may not only gain my Mistriss, and
  out-wit *Harlequin*, but deliver the Ladies those Letters from their Lovers,
  which I took out of his Pocket this Morning, and who wou'd suspect an
5 Apothecary for a Pimp.——Nor can the Jade[155] *Mopsophil*, in Honour,
  refuse a Person of my Gravity, and so well set up.——

                [*Pointing to his Shop.*

  ——Hum, the Doctor here first, this is not so well, but I'm prepar'd with
  Impudence for all Encounters.

     Enter the Doctor. Scaramouch *Salutes him gravely.*

    ——Most Reverend Doctor *Baliardo*——[*Bows.*
10 *Doct.* Seignior——   [*Bows.*
 Scar. I might, through great Pusillanimity, blush—— to give you this
  Anxiety.[156] Did I not opine you were as Gracious as Communitive and
  Eminent;[157] and tho' you have no Cognisance[158] of me, your Humble
  Servant,——yet I have of you,——you being so greatly fam'd for your
15 admirable Skill, both in Gallenical and Paracelsian *Phænomena's*,[159]
  and other approv'd Felicities in Vulnerary Emericks, and purgative
  Experiences.[160]
 Doct. Seignior,——Your Opinion honours me——
  a rare Man this.   ([*Aside.*)
20 *Scar.* And though I am at present busied in writing——those few Observations
  I have accumulated in my Peregrinations,[161] Sir, yet the Ambition I aspir'd
  to, of being an Ocular and Aurial[162] Witness of your Singularity, made me
  trespass on your sublimer Affairs.
 Doct. Seignior.——
25 *Scar.* —— Besides a violent Inclination, Sir, of being initiated into the Denomination
  of your Learned Family, by the Conjugal Circumference of a Matrimonial
  Tye, with that singularly accomplish'd Person——Madam, the

---

155 A 'jade' is a female horse or mare, but also an epithet for a cheating woman.
156 Scaramouch's attempt at elevated prose with the Doctor descends into nonsensical
rhetoric.
157 Pusillanimity is faint-heartedness or lack of courage; to opine is to hold or believe, or to
express; and communitive and eminent refers to the Doctor's generosity and fame.
158 'Cognisance' here is knowledge or to be familiar with, as in 'although you don't
recognise me or know of my fame'.
159 Paracelsus was Theophrastus von Hohenheim (1493–1541), a Swiss physician, alchemist
and astrologer.
160 The terms are scatological. Emericks is probably emetics (that which produces
vomiting), which along with purgatives (laxatives) were meant to restore the body's
'humours'.
161 Travels.
162 A witness by sight and sound.

Governante of your Hostel.

Doct. Hum——A sweet-heart for *Mopsophil*!   [*Aside.*

Scar. And if I may obtain your Condescension to my Hymenæal Propositions, I doubt not my Operation with the Fair One.[163]

Doct. Seignior, she is much honour'd in the Overture, and my Abilities shall not be wanting to fix the Concord.[164]

——But have you been a Traveller,[165] Sir?

Scar. Without Circumlocutions, Sir, I have seen all the Regions beneath the Sun and Moon.

Doct. Moon, Sir! You never travell'd thither, Sir?

Scar. Not in *Propria Persona, Seignior,* but by speculation,[166] I have, and made most considerable Remarques[167] on that incomparable *Terra Firma,* of which I have the compleatest Map in Christendom——and which *Gonzales* himself omitted in his *Cosmographia* of the *Lunar Mundus.*[168]

Doct. A Map of the *Lunar Mundus,* Sir! May I crave the Honour of seeing it?

Scar. You shall, Sir, together with a Map of *Terra Incognita,*[169] a great Rarety, indeed, Sir.

Enter Bellemante.

Doct. Jewels, Sir, worth a Kings Ransome.

Bell. Ha,——What Figure of a Thing have we here——Bantering my Credulous Uncle?——This must be some Scout sent from our *Forlorn Hope,*[170] to discover the Enemy, and bring in fresh Intelligence.——Hum,——That Wink tipt me some Tidings, and she deserves not a good Look, who understands not the Language of the Eyes.   [*Aside.*

——Sir, Dinner's on the Table.

Doct. Let it wait, I am imploy'd—

[*She creeps to the other side of* Scaramouch, *who makes Signs with his Hand to her.*

---

163 A 'Hymenæal Proposition' is a marriage proposal.

164 'Concord' as in agreement, and thus the suggestion of the marriage contract.

165 A traveller was often an explorer and collector. The comic virtuoso rarely travelled himself but claimed knowledge of all parts of the world and all 'science', and prided himself on his collection of curiosities.

166 Scaramouch remarks that he has not visited the Moon in person, but rather through a telescope (speculation).

167 'Remarques' as in observations and commentary.

168 *Cosmographia* of the *Lunar Mundus* is a map of the Moon. Lunar geography or selenography, the study of the surface and physical features of the Moon, was popular in the seventeenth century.

169 *Terra incognita* is a cartographical term meaning an undocumented and/or unmapped territory.

170 'Forlorn hope' is a small band of soldiers or scouts on a military operation. Scaramouch is the scout here.

Bell. Ha,——'tis so,——This fellow has some Novel for us, some Letters or Instructions, but how to get it——

> [*As* Scar. *talks to the* Doctor, *he takes the Letters by degrees out of his Pocket, and unseen, gives 'em* Bellemante *behind him.*

55 *Doct.* But this Map, Seignior; I protest you have fill'd me with Curiosity. Has it signify'd all things so exactly say you?

Scar. Omitted nothing, Seignior, no City, Town, Village, or Villa; no Castle, River, Bridge, Lake, Spring or Mineral.

Doct. Are any, Sir, of those admirable Mineral Waters there, so frequent in our
60 World?[171]

Scar. In abundance, Sir, the Famous *Garamanteen*, a young *Italian*, Sir, lately come from thence, gives an account of an excellent *Scaturigo*,[172] that has lately made an Ebulation there, in great Reputation with the Lunary Ladies.[173]

65 *Doct.* Indeed, Sir! be pleas'd, Seignior, to 'solve me some Queries that may enode[174] some apparances of the Virtue of the Water you speak of.

Scar. Pox upon him, what Questions he asks——but I must on——([*Aside*) Why Sir, you must know,——the Tincture of this Water upon Stagnation, Ceruberates, and the *Crocus* upon Stones Flaveces; this he observes——to
70 be, Sir, the Indication of a Generous Water.[175]

Doct. Hum—— [*Gravely Nodding.*

Scar. Now, Sir, be pleas'd to observe the three Regions, if they be bright, without doubt *Mars* is powerful; if the middle Region or Camera be palled, *Filia Solis* is breeding.[176]

75 *Doct.* Hum.

Scar. And then the third Region, if the Fæces be volatil, the Birth will soon come in *Balneo*.[177] This I observed also in the Laboratory of that Ingenious

---

[171] Mineral waters, such as those at Bath and Tunbridge Wells, were popular in this period. Drinking the waters often had a purgative effect.

[172] Scaturigo as from 'scaturiginous', meaning abounding spring in the sense of flowing or gushing waters.

[173] Ebulation may be epulation, which is feasting or indulging. The lunar ladies apparently enjoy the lunar mineral waters that allow them to indulge (with a possible sexual innuendo) and then 'purge' later. Scaramouch's comments emphasise the Doctor's reputation for purgatives.

[174] 'Enode' is to make clear.

[175] Tincture here is probably colour; ceruberates may refer to the Latin *caeruleus*, meaning blue, so the water turns blue on standing. The rest of this sentence has little meaning. Todd suggests this is an attempt to use alchemical terms (Behn, *Works*, VII, p. 438 n. 119).

[176] Another attempt at alchemy. *Filia* is daughter and *Solis* Sun, so the meaning here seems to be that the Sun's daughter is breeding.

[177] Faeces are the waste discharged from the human body; volatility is the ability of a fluid to vaporise; and Balneo may be a reference to balneum, a water bath. This is alchemical jargon apparently tossed together for the benefit of the Doctor.

Chymist *Lysidono*, and with much Pleasure animadverted that Mineral of the same Zenith and Nader, of that now so famous Water in *England*, near that famous Metropolis, call'd *Islington*.[178]

Doct. Seignior——

Scar. For, Sir, upon the Infusion, the Crows Head immediately procures the Seal of *Hermes*,[179] and had not *Lac Virginis*[180] been too soon suck'd up, I believe we might have seen the Consummation of *Amalgena*.[181]

[Bellemante *having got her Letters, goes off. She makes Signs to him to stay a little. He nods.*

Doct. Most likely, Sir.

Scar. But, Sir, this *Garamanteen* relates the strangest Operation of a Mineral in the Lunar World, that ever I heard of.

Doct. As how, I pray, Sir?

Scar. Why, Sir, a Water impregnated to a Circulation with *Fema Materia*; upon my Honour, Sir, the strongest I ever drank of.[182]

Doct. How, Sir! did you drink of it?

Scar. I only speak the words of *Garamanteen*, Sir.

————Pox on him, I shall be trapt.   [*Aside.*

Doct. Cry Mercy, Sir.————   [*Bows.*

Scar. The Lunary Physicians, Sir, call it *Urinam Vulcani*, it Calibrates every ones Excrements more or less according to the Gradus of the Natural Calor.[183]

——To my Knowledge, Sir, a Smith of a very fiery Constitution, is grown very Opulent by drinking these Waters.[184]

Doct. How, Sir, grown Rich by drinking the Waters, and to your Knowledge?

Scar. The Devil's in my Tongue, to my Knowledge, Sir, for what a man of Honour relates, I may safely affirm.

Doct. Excuse me, Seignior——   [*Puts off his Hat again gravely.*

Scar. For, Sir, conceive me how he grew Rich, since he drank those Waters he never buys any Iron, but hammers it out of *Stercus Proprius*.[185]

---

[178] An area outside the City of London known for its medicinal springs.

[179] Hermes was a Greek god of mythology, a trickster and messenger of the gods, who purportedly invented fire. He is an important figure in alchemy. The Seal of Hermes refers to an airtight glass tube invented for alchemical use in the distillation process; also 'hermetic seal'.

[180] *Lac Virginis* is virgin's milk.

[181] *Amalgena* is nonsense. If the term meant is *Alchimia*, then the meaning is simply alchemy. The suggestion would be that the alchemical process is complete.

[182] Probably *Prima Materia* or first material in an alchemical action.

[183] *Urinam Vulcani* is the urine of Vulcan. Vulcan was the Roman god of fire and thus metalworking. *Calor* is Latin for heat. Scaramouch argues that the doctors on the Moon 'calibrate' or organise urine by degree or grade according to its heat.

[184] Scaramouch claims a blacksmith grew wealthy by drinking his urine.

[185] Latin for one's own dung. The smith had so much iron in his fæces that he was not required to purchase any.

Enter Bellemante *with a Billet.*[186]

105 *Bell.* Sir, 'tis three a Clock, and Dinner will be cold.———

                              [*Goes behind* Scaramouch, *and gives him the Note,
                                                         and goes out.*

     Doct. I come Sweet-heart; but this is wonderful.

     Scar. Ay, Sir, and if at any time Nature be too infirm, and he prove Costive, he
        has no more to do, but to apply a Load-stone *ad Anum.*[187]

     Doct. Is't possible?

110 *Scar.* Most true, Sir, and that facilitates the Journey *per Visera.*[188]———But
        I detain you, Sir, another time——— Sir, ——— I will now only beg the
        Honour of a Word or two with the Governante, before I go. ———

     Doct. Sir, she shall wait on you, and I shall be proud of the Honour of your
        Conversation.—   [*They bow. Exit Doctor.*

     Enter to him Harlequin, *dress'd like a Farmer, as before.*

115 *Har.* Hum———What have we here, a Taylor or a Tumbler?[189]

     Scar. Ha— Who's this?— Hum— What if it shou'd be the Farmer that the
        Doctor has promis'd *Mopsophil* to? My Heart misgives me.

                              [*They look at each other a while.*

        Who wou'd you speak with, Friend?

     Har. This is, perhaps, my Rival, the Apothecary.———Speak with, Sir, why,
120   what's that to you?

     Scar. Have you Affairs with Seignior Doctor, Sir?

     Har. It may be I have, it may be I have not. What then, Sir?———

     While they seem in angry Dispute, Enter Mopsophil.

     Mop. Seignior Doctor tells me I have a Lover waits me, sure it must be the
        Farmer or the Apothecary. No matter which, so a Lover, that welcomest
125   man alive. I am resolv'd to take the first good Offer, tho' but in Revenge
        of *Harlequin* and *Scaramouch*, for putting Tricks upon me.———Ha,———
        Two of 'em!

     Scar. My Mistriss here!

                              [*They both Bow and Advance, both putting each other by.*

     Mop. Hold Gentlemen,———do not worry me. Which of you would speak with
130   me?

     Both. I, I, I, Madam———

     Mop. Both of You?

---

[186] A billet here is a letter or note.
[187] A loadstone, or lodestone, is a magnet; thus, if constipated, he need only apply a magnet
to his anus.
[188] Latin for through the internal organs.
[189] Harlequin disparages Scaramouch here, observing that he is either a fool or a trickster.

Both. No, Madam, I, I.

Mop. If both Lovers, you are both welcome, but let's have fair Play, and take
35   your turns to speak.

Har. Ay, Seignior, 'tis most uncivil to interrupt me.

Scar. And disingenious,[190] Sir, to intrude on me.   *[Putting one another by.*

Mop. Let me then speak first.

Har. I'm Dumb.

40 *Scar.* I Acquiesce.

Mop. I was inform'd there was a Person here had Propositions of Marriage to
      make me.

Har. That's I, that's I———   *[Shoves* Scar. *away.*

Scar. And I attend to that consequential *Finis.*[191]   *[Shoves* Har. *away.*

45 *Har.* I know not what you mean by your *Finis*, Seignior, but I am come to offer
      my self this Gentlewomans Servant, her Lover, her Husband, her Dog in
      a Halter, or any thing.

Scar. Him I pronounce a Paltroon, and an Ignominious Utensil, that dares lay
      claim to the Renowned Lady of my *Primum Mobile;*[192] that is, my best
50   Affections.   *[In Rage.*

Har. I fear not your hard Words, Sir, but dare aloud pronounce, if *Donna
      Mopsophil* like me, the Farmer, as well as I like her, 'tis a Match, and my
      Chariot is ready at the Gate to bear her off, d'ye see.—

Mop. Ah, how that Chariot pleads.——   *[Aside.*

55 *Scar.* And I pronounce, that being intoxicated with the sweet Eyes of this
      refulgent Lady, I come to tender her my noblest Particulars, being already
      most advantageously set up with the circumstantial Implements of my
      Occupation.   *[Points to the Shop.*

Mop. A City Apothecary, a most Gentile Calling———Which shall I chuse?
60   ———Seignior Apothecary I'll not expostulate the Circumstantial Reasons
      that have occasion'd me this Honour.———

Scar. Incomparable Lady, the Elegancy of your Repertees most excellently
      denote the Profundity of your Capacity.[193]

Har. What the Devil's all this? Good Mr. *Conjurer* stand by———and don't
65   fright the Gentlewoman with your Elegant Profondities.   *[Puts him by.*

Scar. How, a Conjurer! I will chastise thy vulgar Ignorance, that yclips a
      Philosopher a Conjurer.[194]   *[In Rage.*

---

190   Probably disingenuous, meaning fraudulent or insincere. Not only is Scaramouch's
'occupation' fraudulent, but his apology is insincere as well.

191   *Finis* is end or task. Scaramouch claims that he is the one to propose to Mopsophil.

192   *Primum Mobile* is the prime mover (see note 116 above), so Mopsophil is the force that
moves Scaramouch's world.

193   Mopsophil's playful wit in their verbal jousts demonstrates her intelligence.

194   To 'yclip' is to call, to be named or to identify; Scaramouch claims that Harlequin's
inability to distinguish between a philosopher and a conjuror demonstrates his ignorance.

Har. Losaphers!——Prethee, if thou be'st a Man, speak like a Man——then
Scar. Why, What do I speak like? What do I speak like?

170 *Har.* What do you speak like——why you speak like a Wheel-Barrow.
Scar. How!——
Har. And how.

> [*They come up close together at half Sword Parry;*[195] *stare on each other for a while, then put up and bow to each other civilly.*

Mop. That's well Gentlemen, let's have all Peace, while I survey you both, and see which likes me best.

> [*She goes between 'em, and surveys 'em both, they making ridiculous Bows on both sides, and Grimaces the while.*

175   ——ha,——now on my Conscience, my two foolish Lovers,——*Harlequin* and *Scaramouch*; how are my Hopes defeated?— but Faith I'll fit you both.

> ([*Aside.*]
> [*She views 'em both.*

Scar. So, she's considering still, I shall be the happy Dog.   [*Aside.*
Har. She's taking aim, she cannot chuse but like me best.   [*Aside.*
Scar. Well, Madam, how does my Person propagate.[196]   [*Bowing and Smiling.*

180 *Mop.* Faith Seignior, now I look better on you, I do not like your Phisnomy so well as your Intellects;[197] you discovering some Circumstantial Symptoms that ever denote a Villainous Inconstancy.[198]
Scar. Ah, you are pleas'd Madam.————
Mop. You are mistaken, Seignior, I am displeas'd at your Gray Eyes, and

185   Black Eye-brows and Beard, I never knew a Man with those Signs, true to his Mistriss or his Friend. And I wou'd sooner wed that Scoundrel *Scaramouch*, that very civil Pimp, that meer pair of Chymical Bellows that blow the Doctors projecting Fires, that Deputy-Urinal Shaker, that very Guzman of *Salamanca*,[199] than a Fellow of your infallible *Signum*

190   *Mallis.*[200]
Har. Ha, ha, ha,————you have your Answer, Seignior Friskin[201]————and may shut up your Shop and be gone.————Ha, ha, ha.————

---

[195]   In a half-sword parry the sword blades are crossed in the middle between the two, so the opponents would be very close to each other.
[196]   To propagate means to produce or progress, as in offspring or ideas, etc.; here Scaramouch asks how well he fares in his marriage proposal.
[197]   Phisnomy is physiognomy. Mopsophil likes his personal appearance even less than his intelligence.
[198]   His looks demonstrate that he is consistently unfaithful to his lovers.
[199]   Salamanca no doubt reminded Behn's audience of Titus Oates, the 'doctor of Salamanca', who instigated the Popish Plot (1678–1681), pushing the country into dangerous political turmoil. Guzman is a derogatory term of abuse meaning a rogue, probably stemming from Mateo Alemán's novel translated by James Mabbe as *The Rogue: Or the Life of Guzman de Alfarache* (Behn, *Works*, ed. by Summers, III, p. 498 n. 446).
[200]   Bad or evil sign.
[201]   A friskin is a frisky person or a dancer of jigs; it can also refer to a hoaxer.

Scar. Hum, sure the Jade knows me——   [*Aside.*

Mop. And as for you, Seignior.

95 *Har.* Ha, Madam——   [*Bowing and Smiling.*

Mop. Those Lanthorn Jaws[202] of yours, with that most villainous Sneer and Grin, and a certain fierce Aire of your Eyes, looks altogether most Fanatically——which with your notorious Whey Beard,[203] are certain Signs of Knavery and Cowardice; therefore I'd rather wed that Spider

200 *Harlequin*, that Sceliton Buffoon,[204] that Ape of Man, that Jack of Lent,[205] that very Top, that's of no use, but when 'tis whipt and lasht, that piteous Property I'd rather wed than thee.

Har. A very fair Declaration————

Mop. [Y]ou understand me—and so adieu sweet Glister-pipe, and Seignior

205 dirty Boots,[206] Ha, ha, ha.——   [*Runs out.*

                [*They stand looking simply on each other,*
                                without speaking a while.

Scar. That I shou'd not know that Rogue *Harlequin*.   [*Aside.*

Har. That I shou'd take this Fool for a Physician.   [*Aside.*
        ——How long have you commenc'd Apothecary, Seignior?

Scar. Ever since you turn'd Farmer.——Are not you a damn'd Rogue to put

210 these Tricks upon me, and most dishonorably break all Articles between us?

Har. And are not you a damn'd Son of a——something——to break Articles with me?

Scar. No more Words, Sir, no more words, I find it must come to Action,

215 ——Draw.——   [*Draws.*

Har. Draw,——so I can draw, Sir.——   [*Draws.*

        They make a ridiculous cowardly Fight. Enter the Doctor, which
        they seeing, come on with more Courage. He runs between, and
        with his Cane beats the Swords down.

Doct. Hold—hold——What mean you Gentlemen?

Scar. Let me go, Sir, I am provok'd beyond measure, Sir.

Doct. You must excuse me, Seignior————   [*Parlies with* Harlequin.

220 *Scar.* I dare not discover the Fool for his Masters Sake, and it may spoil our Intrigue anon; besides, he'll then discover me, and I shall be discarded for bantering the Doctor.   [*Aside.*

---

202 Lantern- or square-jawed.

203 'Whey' is the milky, thin or weak substance left over in the cheese-making process. 'Whey Beard' suggests Harlequin's thin and grayish beard, a further reference to his weak stature or even his lack of a strong masculinity.

204 'Sceliton' here is skeleton.

205 'Jack of Lent'. Lent was a time of fasting, hence another reference to Harlequin's slender build. During Lent, a figure or puppet (a Jack of Lent) would be set up to be pelted.

206 A glister pipe is used to give enemas, a reference to the tools of the apothecary and thus Scaramouch; dirty boots is the farmer Harlequin.

———A Man of Honour to be so basely affronted here. ———

                             [*The* Doctor *comes to appease* Scaramouch.

Har. Shou'd I discover this Rascal, he wou'd tell the Old Gentleman I was the
225   same that attempted his House to day in Womans Cloths, and I shou'd be
     kick'd and beaten most unsatiably.   [*Aside.*

Scar. What, Seignior, for a man of Parts to be impos'd upon, — and whipt
     through the Lungs here————like a Mountebanks Zany for sham
     Cures[207]——Mr. Doctor, I must tell you 'tis not Civil.

230 *Doct.* I am extreamly sorry for it, Sir,—— and you shall see how I will have
     this Fellow handled for the Affront to a Person of your Gravity, and in my
     House——Here *Pedro*,—— [208]

                      Enter Pedro.

————Take this Intruder, or bring some of your Fellows hither, and toss
him in a Blanket——

              [*Ex.* Pedro. Har. *going to creep away,* Scar. *holds him.*
235 *Har.* Hark ye,— bring me off, or I'll discover all your Intrigue.[209]   [*Aside to*
                                                         (Scar.).

Scar. Let me alone——[210]

Doct. I'll warrant you some Rogue that has some Plot on my Neece and
     Daughter.—

Scar. No, no, Sir, he comes to impose the grossest Lye upon you, that ever was
240   heard of.

          Enter Pedro with others, with a Blanket. They put Har. *into it,*
                        and toss him.

Har. Hold, hold, ——I'll confess all, rather than indure it.

Doct. Hold,——What will you confess, Sir.

                        [(Har) *comes out. Makes sick Faces.*

Scar. —That he's the greatest Impostor in Nature. Wou'd you think it, Sir?
     he pretends to be no less than an Ambassador from the Emperor of the
245   Moon, Sir —

Doct. Ha, ——Ambassador from the Emperor of the Moon——   [*Pulls off his*
                                                     Hat.[211]

---

[207] A mountebank is a quack who sells fake cures; a zany is a jester or fool. The
mountebank typically had an accomplice to help him work the crowd.

[208] Behn changes Peter's name here to Pedro, perhaps failing to remember she named him
Peter.

[209] Harlequin demands Scaramouch save him from punishment or he will reveal the plans
for the farce the young gentlemen are planning.

[210] I.e. 'Leave it to me'.

[211] The following material here has much in common with scene six in the French *Arlequin.*

Scar. Ay, Sir, thereupon I laugh'd, thereupon he grew angry, — I laugh'd at his Resentment, and thereupon we drew——and this was the high Quarrel, Sir.

50 *Doct.* Hum,— Ambassador from the Moon.   [*Pauses.*

Scar. I have brought you off, manage him as well as you can.

Har. Brought me off, yes, out of the Frying-Pan and into the Fire. Why, how the Devil shall I act an Ambassador?   [*Aside.*

Doct. It must be so, for how shou'd either of these know I expected that Honour?
                    [*He addresses him with profound Civility to* Har.

55 Sir, if the Figure you make, approaching so near ours of this World, have made us commit any undecent Indignity to your high Character, you ought to pardon the Frailty of our Mortal Education and Ignorance, having never before been blest with the Descention of any from your World.——

60 *Har.* What the Devil shall I say now?   [*Aside.*

—I confess, I am as you see by my Garb, Sir, a little *Incognito*, because the Publick Message I bring, is very private——which is, that the mighty *Iredonozor*, Emperor of the Moon——with his most worthy Brother, the Prince of *Thunderland*, intend to Sup with you to Night — Therefore be

65 sure you get good Wine.—— Tho' by the way let me tell you, 'tis for the Sake of your Fair Daughter.

Scar. I'll leave the Rogue to his own Management.——   ([*Aside.*)

I presume, by your whispering, Sir, you wou'd be private, and humbly beging Pardon, take my Leave.   [*Ex.* Scaramouch.

70 *Har.* You have it Friend. Does your Neece and Daughter Drink, Sir?

Doct. Drink, Sir?

Har. Ay, Sir, Drink hard.

Doct. Do the Women of your World drink hard, Sir?

Har. According to their Quality, Sir, more or less; the greater the Quality, the

75 more Profuse the Quantity.

Doct. Why that's just as 'tis here; but your Men of Quality, your States-men, Sir, I presume they are Sober, Learned and Wise.

Har. Faith, no, Sir, but they are, for the most part, what's as good, very Proud, and promising, Sir, most liberal of their Word to every fauning Suiter,[212] to

80 purchase the state of long Attendance, and cringing as they pass; but the Devil of a Performance, without you get the Knack of bribing in the right Place and Time; but yet they all defy it, Sir.—

Doct. Just, just as 'tis here.——But pray Sir, How do these Great Men live with their Wives.

285 *Har.* Most Nobly, Sir, my Lord keeps his Coach, my Lady, hers; my Lord his Bed,

---

[212] 'Fauning' is fawning or groveling.

my Lady hers; and very rarely see one another, unless they chance to meet
in a Visit, in the *Park*, the *Mall*, the *Toore*,[213] or at the *Basset-Table*, where
they civilly Salute and part, he to his Mistriss, she to play.[214]

Doct. Good lack! just as 'tis here.

290 *Har.* ——Where, if she chance to lose her Money, rather than give out, she
borrows of the next Amorous Coxcomb, who, from that Minute, hopes,
and is sure to be paid again one way or other, the next kind Opportunity.

Doct. ——Just as 'tis here.

Har. As for the young Fellows that have Money, they have no Mercy upon their
295 own Persons, but wearing Nature off as fast as they can, Swear, and Whore
and Drink, and Borrow as long [as] any Rooking Citizen will lend, till
having dearly purchased the Heroick Title of a Bully or a Sharper,[215] they
live pity'd of their Friends, and despis'd by their Whores, and depart this
Transitory World, diverse and sundry ways.

300 *Doct.* Just, just, as 'tis here!

Har. As for the Citizen, Sir, the Courtier lies with his Wife, he, in revenge, cheats
him of his Estate, till Rich enough to marry his Daughter to a Courtier,
again give him all————unless his Wives Over-Gallantry break him;
and thus the World runs round.——

305 *Doct.* The very same 'tis here.————Is there no preferment, Sir, for Men of
Parts and Merit?[216]

Har. Parts and Merit! What's that? a Livery, or the handsome tying a Cravat, for
the great Men prefer none but their Foot-men and Vallets.

Doct. By my Troth, just as 'tis here.—— Sir, I find you are a Person of most
310 profound Intelligence—— under Favour, Sir,—— Are you a Native of
the Moon or this World.——

Har. The Devils in him for hard Questions.   (*[Aside.*
——I am a *Naopolitan*, Sir.

Doct. Sir, I Honour you; good luck, my Countryman! How got you to the Region
315 of the Moon, Sir?

Har. ——A plaguy inquisitive old Fool——   (*[Aside.*)
—— Why, Sir, ———
Pox on't, what shall I say? ——   (*[Aside.*)
I being——one day in a musing Melancholy, walking by the Sea-
320 side——there arose, Sir, a great Mist, by the Suns exhaling of the Vapours
of the Earth, Sir.[217]

---

213   The park is St James's Park, the Mall is Pall Mall, and the Toore or tour is the circuit
through Hyde Park. All of these were places one went to be seen.
214   Basset was a card game for gambling, a popular activity at court, where the King's
mistresses gambled thousands of pounds in an evening's play.
215   A sharper is a cheat or swindler.
216   Merit refers to being deserving of honour or esteem.
217   The story of being mistaken for a fish and fed to the Emperor of the Moon is from scene
six of Fatouville's *Arlequin, Empereur dans la lune*, although Arlequin's transportation there

Doct. Right, Sir.

Har. In this Fog or Mist, Sir, I was exhal'd.

Doct. The Exalations of the Sun, draw you to the Moon, Sir?

325 *Har.* I am condemn'd to the Blanket again.———   ([*Aside.*)
      I say, Sir, I was exhal'd up, but in my way———being too heavy, was dropt
      into the Sea.

Doct. How, Sir, into the Sea?

Har. The Sea, Sir, where the Emperors Fisher-man casting his Nets, drew
330   me up, and took me for a strange and monstrous Fish, Sir,———and
      as such, presented me to his Mightiness,———who going to have me
      Spitchcock'd[218] for his own eating.———

Doct. How, Sir, eating?———

Har. What did me I, Sir, (Life being sweet) but fall on my Knees, and besought
335   his Gloriousness not to eat me, for I was no Fish but a Man; he ask'd me
      of what Country, I told him of *Naples*; whereupon the Emperor overjoy'd
      ask'd me if I knew that most Reverend and most Learned Doctor *Baliardo*,
      and his fair Daughter. I told him I did: whereupon he made me his Bed-
      fellow, and the Confident to his Amour to Seigniora *Elaria*.

340 *Doct.* Bless me, Sir! How came the Emperor to know my Daughter?

Har. ———There he is again with his damn'd hard Questions.———([*Aside.*)
      Knew her, Sir,———Why———you were walking abroad one day.———

Doct. My Daughter never goes abroad, Sir, farther than our Garden.———

Har. Ay, there it was indeed, Sir,———and as his Highness was taking a Survey
345   of this lower World———through a long Perspective, Sir,———he saw you
      and your Daughter and Neece, and from that very moment, fell most
      desperately in Love.———But hark———the sound of Timbrils, Kettle-
      Drums and Trumpets.[219]———The Emperor, Sir, is on his Way,———
      prepare for his Reception.

            [*A strange Noise is heard of Brass Kettles, and Pans, and*
            Bells, and many tinkling things.

350 *Doct.* I'm in a Rapture———How shall I pay my Gratitude for this great
      Negotiation?———but as I may, I humbly offer, Sir.———

           [*Presents him with a Rich Ring and a Purse of Gold.*

Har. Sir, as an Honour done the Emperor, I take your Ring and Gold. I must go
      meet his Highness.———   [*Takes Leave.*

         Enter to him Scaramouch, *as himself.*

Scar. Oh, Sir! We are astonish'd with the dreadful sound of the sweetest Musick
355   that ever Mortal heard, but know not whence it comes. Have you not heard
      it, Sir?

---

is owing to vultures rather than exhalation.

[218] Split and broiled.

[219] The 'timbril' or 'timbrel' is a tambourine or similar instrument.

Doct. Heard it, yes, Fool,——— 'Tis the Musick of the Spheres, the Emperor of
the Moon World is descending.

360 *Scar.* How, Sir, no marvel then, that looking toward the South, I saw such
splendid Glories in the Air.

Doct. Ha,———saw'st thou ought descending in the Air?

Scar. Oh, yes, Sir, Wonders! haste to the old Gallery, whence, with the help of
your Telescope, you may discover all.———

Doct. I wou'd not lose a moment for the lower Universe.

Enter Elaria, Bellemante, Mopsophil, dress'd in rich Antick Habits.[220]

365 *Ela.* Sir, we are dress'd as you commanded us, What is your farther Pleasure?

Doct.———It well becomes the Honour you're design'd for, this Night to wed two
Princes———come with me and know your happy Fates.   [*Ex.* Doctor *and*
Scar.

Ela. Bless me! My Father, in all the rest of his Discourse, shows so much Sense
and Reason, I cannot think him mad, but feigns all this to try us.

370 *Bell.* Not Mad! Marry Heaven forbid, thou art always creating Fears to startle
one; why, if he be not mad, his want of Sleep this eight and forty hours, the
Noise of strange unheard of Instruments, with the Fantastick Splendor of
the unusual Sight, will so turn his Brain and dazle him, that in Grace of
Goodness, he may be Mad: If he be not;———come, let's after him to the
375 Gallery, for I long to see in what showing Equipage our Princely Lovers
will address to us.   [*Exeunt.*

SCENE [III] *The Last.*

The Gallery richly adorn'd with Scenes and Lights.
Enter Doctor, Elaria, Bellemante, *and* Mopsophil. *Soft Musick is heard.*

Bell. Ha———Heavens! what's here?———what Palace is this?———No part of our
House, I'm sure.———

Ela. 'Tis rather the Apartment of some Monarch.

Doct. I'm all amazement too, but must not show my Ignorance.   ([*Aside.*)
5   ———Yes, *Elaria*, this is prepar'd to entertain two Princes.

Bell. Are you sure on't, Sir? are we not, think you, in that World above, I often
heard you speak of? in the Moon, Sir?

---

220   If Behn did witness Fatouville's French scenes, she may have seen the young ladies in
the French *Arlequin* attired in dresses decorated with moons and other celestial images like
they appear in Gherardi's frontispiece pictured on this volume's cover. Behn's young ladies
have donned specific attire according to their lunatic father's request; their 'Antick Habits'
may, then, have been similarly adorned. B.E.'s *Dictionary* refers to antick dresses as having
'Ribbands, mismatched colours and Feathers' (p. 10).

Doct. How shall I resolve her?——For ought I know, we are.   [*Aside.*

Ela. Sure, Sir, 'tis some Inchantment.

o *Doct.* Let not thy Female Ignorance prophane the highest Mysteries of
Natural Philosophy: To Fools it seems Inchantment——but
I've a Sense can reach it,——sit and expect the Event.
——Hark——I am amaz'd, but must conceal my Wonder——that Joy of
Fools——and appear wise in Gravity.   (*[Aside.*)

5 *Bell.* Whence comes this charming Sound, sir?

Doct. From the Spheres——it is familiar to me.

> *The Scene in the Front draws off, and shews the Hill of* Parnassus;
> *a noble large Walk of Trees leading to it, with eight or ten Negroes*
> *upon Pedestals, rang'd on each side of the Walks. Next* Keplair
> *and* Gallileus[221] *descend on each side, opposite to each other,*
> *in Chariots, with Perspectives[222] in their Hands, as viewing the*
> *Machine of the Zodiack. Soft Musick plays still.*

Doct. Methought I saw the Figure of two Men descend from yonder Cloud, on
yonder Hill.

Ela. I thought so too, but they are disappear'd, and the wing'd Chariot's fled.

Enter Keplair *and* Gallileus.

20 *Bell.* See, Sir, they approach.——   [*The Doctor rises and Bows.*

Kep. Most Reverend Sir, we, from the upper World, thus low salute you,——
Keplair and *Gallileus* we are call'd, sent as Interpreters to Great *Iredonozor*
the Emperor of the Moon, who is descending.

Doct. Most Reverend Bards——profound Philosophers——thus low I bow to

25   pay my humble Gratitude.

Kep. The Emperor, Sir, salutes you, and your fair Daughter.

Gall. And, Sir, the Prince of *Thunderland* salutes you, and your fair Neece.

Doct. Thus low I fall to thank their Royal Goodness.[*Kneels. They take him up.*

Bell. Came you, most Reverend Bards, from the Moon World?

30 *Kep.* Most Lovely Maid, we did.

Doct. May I presume to ask the manner how?

Kep. By Cloud, Sir, through the Regions of the Air, down to the fam'd
Parnassus; thence by Water, along the River *Helicon*,[223] the rest by Post,

---

[221] Johannes Kepler (1571–1630), a German astronomer and mathematician; Galileo Galilei
(1564–1642), an Italian astronomer, philosopher, and mathematician.

[222] A perspective is a form of early telescope.

[223] A river in Macedonia associated with the poet Orpheus and mentioned in Greek
mythology; the river purportedly disappeared. Behn may be thinking of Mount Helicon
here which was sacred to the muses and an inspiration to poets.

upon two wing'd Eagles.[224]

35   *Doct.* Sir, are there store of our World inhabiting the Moon?

    Kep. Oh, of all Nations, Sir, that lie beneath it in the Emperors Train! Sir, you will behold abundance; look up and see the Orbal World descending; observe the Zodiack, Sir, with her twelve Signs.

        Next the Zodiack *descends, a Symphony playing all the while; when it is landed, it delivers the twelve Signs: Then the Song, the Persons of the Zodiack being the Singers. After which, the Negroes Dance and mingle in the* Chorus.

A Song for the Zodiack

      Let murmuring Lovers no longer Repine,
40   *But their Hearts and their Voices advance;*
      Let the Nimphs and the Swains in the kind Chorus joyn,
        And the Satyrs and Fauns in a Dance.
      Let nature put on her Beauty of May,
        And the Fields and the Meadows adorn;
45   *Let the Woods and the Mountains resound with the Joy,*
        And the Echoes in their Triumph return.

Chorus

      For since Love wore his Darts,
        And Virgins grew Coy;
      Since these wounded Hearts,
50   *And those cou'd destroy.*
    There ne'er was more Cause for your Triumphs and Joy.

      Hark, hark, the Musick of the Spheres,
        Some Wonder approaching declares;
      Such, such, as has not blest your Eyes and Ears
55   *This thousand, thousand, thousand years.*
      See, see what the Force of Love can make,
        Who rules in Heaven, in Earth and Sea;
      Behold how he commands the Zodiack,
        While the fixt Signs unhinging all obey.
60   *Not one of which, but represents*
          The Attributes of Love,
        Who governs all the Elements
          In Harmony above.

---

[224] Menippus in Lucian's *Icaromenippus* uses the wing of an eagle and the wing of a vulture to fly up to the palace of Zeus. The eagle is a symbol of Zeus and a messenger for the gods.

Chorus

For since Love wore his Darts,
*   And Virgins grew Coy;*
Since these wounded Hearts,
*   And those cou'd destroy.*
There ne'er was more Cause for your Triumphs and Joy.

The wanton Aries *first descends,*
*   To show the Vigor and the Play,*
Beginning Love, beginning Love attends,
When the young Passion is all-over Joy,
He bleats his soft Pain to the fair curled Throng,
And he leaps, and he bounds, and Loves all the day long.
At once Loves Courage and his Slavery
*   In* Taurus *is express'd,*
Tho' o're the Plains he Conqueror be,
*   The Generous Beast*
Does to the Yoak submit his Noble Breast,
While Gemini *smiling and twining of Arms,*
*   Shows Loves soft Indearments and Charms.*
And Cancer's *slow Motion the degrees do express,*
*   Respectful Love arrives to Happiness.*
*   Leo* his Strength and Majesty,
*   Virgo* his blushing Modesty,[225]
*   And* Libra *all his Equity.*
*   His subtility does* Scorpio *show,*
And Sagittarius *all his loose desire,*
By Capricorn *his forward Humour know,*
And Aqua. *Lovers Tears that raise his Fire,*
While Pisces, *which intwin'd do move,*
Show the soft Play, and wanton Arts of Love.

Chorus

For since Love wore his Darts,
*   And Virgins grew Coy;*
Since these wounded Hearts,
*   And those cou'd destroy.*
There ne'er was more Cause for your Triumphs and Joy.

---

[225] Virgo or the virgin is female and this should read 'her' not 'his'. This is corrected later in the text when Keplair speaks after the song.

———See how she turns, and sends her Signs to Earth.—Behold the
Ram—*Aries*— see *Taurus* next descends; then *Gemini*———see how the
100   Boys embrace ——Next *Cancer,* then *Leo,* then the *Virgin*; next to her
Libra—Scorpio, Sagittary, Capricorn, Aquarius,——*Pisces.* This eight
thousand years no Emperor has descended, but *Incognito,* but when he
does, to make his Journey more Magnificent, the Zodiack, Sir, attends
him.

105 *Doct.* 'Tis all amazing, Sir.

    Kep. Now, Sir, behold the Globick World descends two thousand Leagues below
its wonted Station, to show Obedience to its proper Monarch.

> [*After which, the Globe of the Moon appears, first, like a new
> Moon; as it moves forward it increases, till it comes to the Full.
> When it is descended, it opens, and shews the Emperor and the
> Prince. They come forth with all their Train, the Flutes playing a
> Symphony before him, which prepares the Song. Which ended, the
> Dancers mingle as before.*

A SONG

> *All Joy to Mortals, Joy and Mirth*
>   *Eternal IO'S sing;*[226]
110   *The Gods of Love descend to Earth,*
>   *Their Darts have lost the Sting.*
> *The Youth shall now complain no more*
>   *On* Silvia's *needless Scorn,*
> *But she shall love, if he adore,*
115   *And melt when he shall burn.*

> *The Nimph no longer shall be shy,*
>   *But leave the jilting Road;*
> *And* Daphne *now no more shall fly*
>   *The wounded panting God;*[227]
120   *But all shall be serene and fair,*
>   *No sad Complaints of Love*
> *Shall fill the Gentle whispering Air,*
>   *No echoing Sighs the Grove.*

> *Beneath the Shades young* Strephon *lies,*
125   *All of his wish possess'd;*

---

[226]   IO here is a classical term for an exclamation of joy or triumph.

[227]   Apollo chased the Nymph Daphne, who cried out to her father Peneus, the river god,
for help. He changed her into a laurel to protect her from ravishment.

> *Gazing on Silvia's charming Eyes,*
> *Whose Soul is there confess'd.*
> *All soft and sweet the Maid appears,*
> *With Looks that know no Art,*
30 > *And though she yields with trembling Fears,*
> *She yields with all her Heart.*

——See, Sir, the Cloud of Foreigners appears, *French, English, Spaniards, Danes, Turks, Russians, Indians,* and the nearer Climes of Christendom; and lastly, Sir, behold the mighty Emperor.——

> [*A Chariot appears, made like a Half Moon, in which is* Cinthio *for the Emperor, richly dress'd and* Charmante *for the Prince, rich, with a good many Heroes attending.* Cinthio's *Train born by four Cupids. The Song continues while they descend and land.*[228] *They address themselves to* Elaria *and* Bellemante.—— *Doctor falls on his Face, the rest bow very low as they pass. They make signs to* Keplair.

135 *Kep.* The Emperor wou'd have you rise, Sir, he will expect no Ceremony from
      the Father of his Mistress.   [*Takes him up.*

    Doct. I cannot, Sir, behold his Mightiness——the Splendor of his Majesty
      confounds me——

    Kep. You must be moderate, Sir, it is expected.

> [*The two Lovers make all the Signs of Love in a dumb show to the Ladies,*[229] *while the soft Musick plays again from the End of the Song.* ——

140 *Doct.* Shall I not have the Joy to hear their Heavenly Voices, Sir?

    Kep. They never speak to any Subject, Sir, when they appear in Royalty, but by
      Interpreters, and that by way of Stentraphon, in manner of the Delphick
      Oracles.[230]

    Doct. Any way, so I may hear the Sence of what they wou'd say.

145 *Kep.* No doubt you will—— But see the Emperor commands by signs his
      Foreigners to dance.——

                                                    [*Soft Musick changes.*

---

[228] This appears to be the second time that the two young men have 'landed', first as passengers in the Moon globe and then in the chariot. These two stage directions may refer first to the Moon machine flying across the stage as part of the spectacle, and second to when the chariot lands on stage so the characters can disembark.

[229] A 'dumb show' is to gesture without speech.

[230] The oracles always gave vague answers that were easy to misinterpret. The oracle at Delphi belonged to the temple of Apollo, god of the Sun in Roman literary discourse rather than the Moon.

[*A very Antick Dance. The Dance ended, the Front Scene draws off, and shows a Temple, with an Altar, one speaking thorugh a Stentraphon from behind it.*[231] *Soft Musick plays the while.*]

Kep. Most Learned Sir, the Emperor now is going to declare himself, according
    to his Custom, to his Subjects. Listen.———
Sten. Most Reverend Sir, whose Vertue did incite us,
150   Whose Daughters Charms did more invite us;
    We come to grace her with that Honour,
    That never Mortal yet had done her,
    Once only, *Jove* was known in Story,
    To visit *Semele* in Glory.[232]
155   But fatal 'twas, he so enjoy'd her,
    Her own ambitious Flame destroy'd her.
    His Charms too fierce for Flesh and Blood,
    She dy'd embracing of her God.
    We gentler marks of Passion give,
160   The Maid we love, shall love and live;
    Whom visibly we thus will grace,
    Above the rest of human Race.
    Say, is't your Will that we shou'd Wed her,
    And nightly in Disguises Bed her.
165 *Doct.* The Glory is too great for Mortal Wife.   [*Kneels with Transport.*
Sten. What then remains, but that we consummate
    This happy Marriage in our splendid State?
Doct. Thus low I kneel, in thanks for this great Blessing.

[*Cinthio* takes *Elaria* by the Hand; Charmante, Bellemante; *two of the Singers in white being Priests, they lead 'em to the Altar, the whole Company dividing on either side. Where, while a Hymeneal Song is sung,*[233] *the Priest joyns their Hands. The Song ended, and they Marry'd, they come forth; but before they come forward, ——two Chariots descend, one on one side above, and the other on the other side; in which, is* Harlequin *dress'd like a Mock Hero, with others, and* Scaramouch *in the other, dress'd so in Helmets.*[234]

---

[231]   The character Stentraphon here is a personification of an early device resembling a speaking tube such as a trumpet or form of megaphone. Behn redevelops the 'character' Stentor, the talking head of the prologue, as the person standing behind the temple, projecting the voice of the Emperor of the Moon.
[232]   Semele was one of Jove's (Zeus in Greek mythology) lovers. Juno coerced her to ask Jove to appear in his divine image. As soon as Jove did so, Semele was incinerated.
[233]   A hymeneal song is a marriage song.
[234]   This battle scene has much in common with scene eight in the French *Arlequin.*

Scar. Stay mighty Emperor, and vouchsafe to be the Umpire of our Difference.

[Cinthio *signs to* Keplair.

70 *Kep.* What are you?

Scar. Two neighbouring Princes to your vast Dominion.

Har. Knights of the Sun, our Honourable Titles. And fight for that fair Mortal,
   Mopsophil.

Mop. Bless us!——my two precious Lovers, I'll warrant; well, I had better take
75   up with one of them, than lye alone to Night.

Scar. Long as two Rivals we have Lov'd and Hop'd,
   Both equally endeavour'd, and both fail'd.
   At last by Joynt Consent, we both agreed
   To try our Titles by the Dint of Lance,
80   And chose your Mightiness for Arbitrator.

Kep. The Emperor gives Consent.————

> [*They both, all arm'd with gilded Lances and Shields of Black,
> with Golden Suns painted. The Musick plays a fighting Tune. They
> fight at Barriers, to the Tune.——*[235] Harlequin *is often Foil'd, but
> advances still; at last* Scaramouch *throws him, and is Conqueror;
> all give Judgment for him.*

Kep. The Emperor pronounces you are Victor.——   [*To* Scar.

Doct. Receive your Mistriss, Sir, as the Reward of your undoubted Valour——

[*Presents* Mopsophil.

Scar. Your humble Servant, Sir, and *Scaramouch*, returns you humble Thanks.
185   ——   [*Puts off his Helmet.*

Doct. Ha,——Scaramouch—— [*Bawls out, and falls in a Chair. They all go to
                                                              him.*

   My Heart misgives me—Oh, I am undone and cheated in every way.—

[*Bawling out.*

Kep. Be patient, Sir, and call up all your Vertue,
   You're only cur'd, Sir, of a Disease
190   That long has raign'd over your Nobler Faculties.
   Sir, I am your Physician, Friend and Counsellor;
   It was not in the Power of Herbs or Minerals,
   Of Reason, common Sense, and right Religion,
   To draw you from an Error that unman'd you.

195 *Doct.* I will be Patient, Gentlemen, and hear you.
   ——Are not you *Ferdinand*?

Kep. I am,——and these are Gentlemen of Quality,

---

[235] Barriers or obstruction between the knights, such as a partition, like that used in a
jousting tournament.

That long have lov'd your Daughter and your Neece.
Don Cinthio this, and this *Don Charmante*,
200   The *Vice-Roys* Nephews, both.———
Who found as men———'twas impossible to enjoy 'em,
And therefore try'd this Stratagem.—
Cin. Sir, I beseech you, mitigate your Grief,
Altho' indeed we are but mortal men,
205   Yet we shall Love you,——Serve you, and obey you———
Doct. Are not you then the Emperor of the Moon?
And you the Prince of *Thunderland*?
Cin. There's no such Person, Sir.
These Stories are the Fantoms of mad Brains,
210   To puzzle Fools withal——the Wise laugh at 'em,——
——Come Sir, you shall no longer be impos'd upon.
Doct. No Emperor of the Moon,——and no Moon World!
Char. Rediculous Inventions.
If we'd not love'd you, you'd been still impos'd on;
215   We had brought a Scandal on your Learned Name,
And all succeeding Ages had despis'd it.
Doct. Burn all my Books, and let my Study Blaze,   *[He leaps up.*[236]
Burn all to Ashes, and be sure the Wind
Scatter the vile Contagious Monstrous Leys.
220   ——Most Noble Youths——you've honour'd me with your Alliance,
and you, and all your Friends, Assistances in this Glorious Miracle, I invite
to Night to revel with me.—Come all and see my happy Recantation of all
the Follies Fables have inspir'd till now. Be pleasant to repeat your Story, to
tell me by what kind degrees you Cozen'd me—
225   I see there's nothing in Philosophy——   *[Gravely to himself.*
Of all that writ, he was the wisest Bard, who spoke this mighty Truth.——
    "He that knew all that ever Learning writ,
    "Knew only this——that he knew nothing yet.[237]

---

[236]   This action was misattributed in Behn's play to Charmante. The Doctor is clearly the one to 'leap up' here.

[237]   This idea is attributed to Socrates. See Diogenes Laertius' *Lives of the Eminent Greek Philosophers*, Book 2, 32, where the author claims Socrates admitted that the only thing he knew was his own ignorance. In Milton's *Paradise Regained*, Christ says, 'The first and wisest of them all profess'd | To know this only, that he nothing knew' (4.293–94).

EPILOGUE.

To be spoken by Mrs. *Cooke.*

With our old Plays, as with dull Wife it fares,
To whom you have been marry'd tedious years.
You Cry ————*She's wondrous good, it is confess'd,*
But still 'tis Chapon Boüillé *at the best;*[238]
That constant Dish can never make a Feast:
Yet the pall'd Pleasure you must still pursue,
You give so small incouragement for new;
And who wou'd drudge for such a wretched Age?
Who want the Bravery, to support one Stage.
The wiser Wits have now new Measures set,
And taken up new Trades, that they may hate,
No more your nice fantastick pleasures serve,
Your Pimps you pay, but let your Poets starve.
They long in vain, for better Usage hop'd,
Till quite undone and tir'd, they dropt and dropt;
Not one is left will write for thin third day,
Like desperate Pickeroons,[239] *no Prize no Pay;*
And when they've done their best, the Recompence,
Is, Dam the Sot, his Play wants common Sense.
Ill natur'd wits, who can so ill requite
The Drudging Slaves, who for your Pleasure write.
    Look back on flourishing Rome, *ye proud Ingrates,*
And see how she her thriving Poets treats:
Wisely she priz'd 'em at the noblest Rate,
As necessary Ministers of State,
And contributions rais'd to make 'em great.
They from the publick Bank she did maintain,
And freed from want, they only writ for Fame;[240]
And were as useful in a City held,
As formidable Armies in the Field.
They but a Conquest over Men pursu'd,

---

[238]   French for boiled capon.
[239]   A pickeroon is a thief or outlaw; a pirate or privateer, as well as the name of a small pirate ship. In the prologue to her play *The Forc'd Marriage, or The Jealous Bridegroom,* Behn humorously claims that the vizarded prostitutes in the theatre are simply 'Pickeroons that scour for prey' (Behn, 'Prologue' in *Forc'd Marriage* (London, 1671), unpaginated ([p. 2]).
[240]   Behn argues that in Rome, poets were useful to the state and thus financed and supported by the state.

While these by gentler force the Soul subdu'd.
Not Rome *in all her happiest Pomp cou'd show*
A greater Cæsar *than we boast of now;*
35   Augustus *Reigns, but Poets still are low.*[241]
    May Cæsar *live, and while his Mighty Hand*
Is Scattering Plenty over all the Land;
With God-like Bounty recompencing all,
Some fruitful drops may on the Muses fall;
40   *Since honest Pens do his just cause afford*
Equal Advantage with the useful Sword.

FINIS.

---

[241]   While a 'Ceasar' (a Stuart) may indeed rule, poets are still little valued.

ARLEQUIN
EMPEREUR
DANS
LA LUNE.
COMÉDIE.

Par Monsieur D***.

A TROYES,

Chez GARNIER, Imprimeur
Libraire, rue du Temple.

PLAYERS

ARLEQUIN Emperor in the Moon.

THE DOCTOR.

SCARAMOUCHE.

THE AGENT.

THE CONSTABLE.

THE KNIGHT of the Sun.

ISABELLE, Daughter of the Doctor.

EULARIA, Niece of the Doctor.

COLOMBINE, Servant of the Doctor.

PIERROT, the Valet of the Doctor.

Arlequin, Emperor in the Moon

FIRST SCENE

The Stage represents a Garden, at the far end of which a great Telescope is upright on a stand.

THE DOCTOR, PIERROT.

DOCTOR *Is it possible, Pierrot, that you don't want to shut up?*[1] Shut up, if you please!

PIERROT But, Sir, how do you expect me to shut up? I don't get a moment of peace. All day long, I have to work looking after your Daughter, your Niece and your Servant woman; and just as soon as night comes, I have to look after you. The very moment I get to bed, you start chiming on: Pierrot, Pierrot, get up right away, light your candles and get me my long-range Telescope, I want to observe the stars; and you try to get me to believe that the Moon is a world like our own. The Moon? Good Heavens, I'm furious.

DOCTOR *Pierrot, once again, shut it. I'll beat you with a stick.*

PIERROT By Heaven, Sir, even if you're going to kill me, I've got to get something off my chest. I won't be such a fool as to believe that the Moon is a world; the Moon, the Moon, goddammit, it's not any bigger than an eight-egg Omelette.

DOCTOR *Impertinent fool!* If you had even the tiniest amount of good sense, I'd argue with you rationally. *But you're a brute, an ignorant animal with its head unhinged, shut your mouth* and shut up, once again, and you'll be better off.

PIERROT (*getting irritated*) By God, I'll get myself chopped into pieces.

DOCTOR *My patience is miraculous.* Let's see, nonetheless, if it's possible to pull him out of this stubbornness. *Dimwit servant.* Have you ever noticed certain Clouds that we see around the Moon? These...

PIERROT I understand completely; those make the fringe around the Omelette.

DOCTOR The fringes of the Devil take you! Shut up, *damn it*, and stop thinking about the Omelette. So then, these clouds that we see around the Moon are called Crepuscules. And here is how I argue my case.

PIERROT Let's have it.

DOCTOR If there are two Crepuscules in the Moon, *then there must be a generation, and a corruption, and if a corruption and a generation take*

---

[1] Throughout the lines of dialogue in these scenes, italics indicate Italian text in the Garnier edition and roman letters indicate French text. This corresponds to the typeface in the source edition.

place, then it must be that we are seeing animals and vegetables being born, and if animals and vegetables are being born, ergo the Moon is an inhabitable World like our own.

PIERROT Ergo as much as you like. As far as I'm concerned, Nego; and here's
35   how I prove it. You say that in the Moon the three... crep... pus, the three Crap-pushes.

DOCTOR *Crepuscules,* and not Crap-pushes, you nitwit.

PIERROT In any case, the three... well you know what I mean, and if there are indeed three Crap-push-stools, then there must be a generation and a
40   corruption.

DOCTOR *Most certainly.*

PIERROT Oh yeah? Well here's what Pierrot says.

DOCTOR *Let's see.*

PIERROT If there is a generation and a corruption in the Moon, then it must be
45   that worms are being born there. Now how could it be true that the Moon is full of worms? Eh? What do you think? There's just nothing, by Jesus, to say to that.

DOCTOR *(laughing)* Oh, surely not. Hey! Tell me, Pierrot, *in this World of ours, are worms being born?*

50   PIERROT Yes, Sir.

DOCTOR And does it follow from there *that our world is full of worms?*

PIERROT *(after thinking it over for a moment)* There's some truth in that.

DOCTOR *To be sure. Well then, Pierrot, let's leave the Moon alone and talk about something else.*

55   PIERROT That's well played, because with your devil of a Moon, it strikes me that at some point you didn't move along a Quarter at a time like it does.

DOCTOR *Silence, insolent fool.* My Daughter, my Niece and my Servants are quite a handful. Isabelle is only interested in poetry, and my house is always full of Poets. Elarias [*sic*] my Niece always has some young Pansy-
60   boy following her around, and the Maids have become as foolish as their Mistresses to better suit their madness. But I'll soon marry off all four of them, and I'll be pleased to clear out the house. I have a number of interested Parties who've showed interest in my Daughter and my Niece, and in my Servants as well. A Hog Butcher is asking for Olivette, and as
65   for Colombine...

ARLEQUIN *(appearing at the back of the stage, having heard Colombine's name)* Colombia [*sic*], my Mistress!

PIERROT *(to the Doctor, thinking that he is the one speaking)* You're mistaken, Sir, Colombine is your Servant, and not your Mistress.

70   DOCTOR Yes indeed, Colombine my Servant.

ARLEQUIN *(still in the back)* Well then, Colombine your Servant, what's she done?

DOCTOR (*to Pierrot*) She hasn't done anything; do be patient. She has been asked
   for in marriage by an Apothecary, an…

5   ARLEQUIN (*still in the back*) Ahem!

PIERROT (*looking at the Doctor*) What's wrong, Sir, do you have colic?

DOCTOR *Pierrot, I swear I'll beat you with a stick, let me speak.*

PIERROT You're the one, Sir, who's talking just like an echo.

DOCTOR I've been asked for Colombine's hand by an Apothecary, a Farmer, and

30   a Baker.

ARLEQUIN (*still in the back*) And a Cavalry Regiment.

DOCTOR (*slapping Pierrot and knocking him to the ground*) I hope a cancer eats
   you alive, by the Devil, curse you!

PIERROT (*after getting back up*) Effects of the Moon! Effects of the Moon! [*Exit.*

35   DOCTOR (*pretending to chase him*) Wait! Wait! Has anybody ever seen a more
   insolent jerk! I can't even say twenty words in a row with him. He's always
   itching to speak for reasons impossible to understand, and he doesn't even
   have an ounce of common sense… But let's come back to Colombine for a
   moment. I'm not sure which of the three Parties I should give her to. The

90   Apothecary, they say…

ARLEQUIN (*in the back*) Is a crook.

DOCTOR (*looks all around himself and Arlequin starts to hide*) The Apothecary
   is fairly well-off, so are you.[2]

ARLEQUIN (*still in the back*) The Baker is a criminal, and so are you!

95   DOCTOR[3] Oh yeah! What is all this? (*He looks around in every direction.*) The
   Baker, I was saying, is richer. Still, I'm more inclined to go with the
   Farmer, and I'll give her to him.

ARLEQUIN Ah! I'm dead.

DOCTOR (*tired of hearing a voice but not seeing anyone, shakes out his Robe,*

100   *Coat, and Hat, and then says*) Aha! I know what it is; it's Pierrot's words
   that got stuck in place.

[*Exit.*

---

[2]   The last words of this line appear to be a printer error. The words 'vous aussi' are
repeated at the end of Arlequin's next line and make sense there, but not here.
[3]   An apparent printer error led to 'LE DOCTEUR' being placed immediately before
Arlequin's line. We have corrected the text by placing 'DOCTOR' here.

SCENE II

ARLEQUIN, alone.

[ARLEQUIN] Ah! I'm so unhappy! The Doctor wants to marry off Colombine to a Farmer, and I'll live without Colombine? No, I want to die. Ah! Ignorant Doctor! Ah! Colombine, so unfaithful! Ah! Farmer very crook! Ah! Arlequin extremely depressed.[4] Let us charge forth unto death! It
5   shall be written in History both ancient and modern: Arlequin died for Colombine. I'll go into my room, I'll tie a rope to the ceiling, I'll climb up on a chair, I'll put the rope around my neck, I'll kick out the chair, and look there, I'm hanged. (*He takes the posture of a hanged man.*) It's all settled, nothing can stop me, it's off to the Gallows. To the Gallows? But
10   suppose, Sir, that you don't think about that. Kill yourself for a girl! How stupid would that be… Yes, Sir, but a girl betraying a good man, it's such a crime… True. But after you've hung yourself, will you be fatter? No, I'll be thinner. I want to have a nice physique, you know, what do you have to say to that? If you want to attend the event, you're welcome to come along…
15   Whoa! No to that! But you won't go anyway… Oh I will go… Oh no you won't go… Oh, yes I will so… (*He draws a Dagger, stabs himself, then says*) Whew! I'm finally free from that creep. Now there's nobody around; let's go hang ourselves. (*He starts to leave, then stops suddenly.*) Wait, no. Hanging oneself is an ordinary death, a death we see every day. That
20   wouldn't be honourable. Let's think of some extraordinary death, some heroic death, some Arlequinian death. (*He ponders this.*) I've got it. I'll cover up my mouth and nose, the wind won't be able to get out, and that way I'll die. Just like that, it's done. (*He covers up his nose and mouth with both hands, and after staying in that position for a while, he says*) No, the
25   wind just comes out the other end; this isn't worth the Devil. Alas! what a pain it is to die. (*Speaking to the audience below the stage.*) Gentlemen, if any of you would like to die to show me how it's done, I would be very grateful… Oh! By Heaven, I've got it. We read in the Histories, that some people have died from laughing. If I could die laughing, that would sure
30   be a funny death. I'm quite ticklish, and if people tickled me for a long time, they'd surely make me die laughing. I'm going to go tickle myself, and that's how I'll die.

> (*He tickles himself, laughs, and falls down. Pasquariel [sic] enters, finds him on the ground, concludes that he's drunk, calls to him, revives him, consoles him and leads him away.*)

---

4   In his extreme emotional state, Arlequin speaks in rapid-fire sentence fragments.

(*Note. Every time that there are ellipses*[5] *following a sentence in this scene, this indicates that at those moments, Arlequin changes his voice or his gestures, moving off one way or the other. The meaning of the words makes this fairly clear; that's why it isn't spelled out each time. People who saw this scene will agree that it's one of the most amusing ones that has ever been performed on the Italian Stage.*)[6]

SCENE III.

PIERROT, *as the Doctor's wife [and]* ARLEQUIN, *as a Chambermaid.*

PIERROT Good morning, Sweetheart.

ARLEQUIN I was told, Ma'am, that you needed a Chambermaid. I've come to offer you my services, and to find out if I'd be agreeable to you.

PIERROT And where are you coming from, Sweetheart?

ARLEQUIN At present, Ma'am, I've just come from a position with the Wife of a Partisan, and she was the most difficult Mistress to serve in the whole world. I think that during the three years I worked with her, I only saw her go in her closet one single time.

PIERROT She didn't go in her closet? You must be joking, Sweetheart.

ARLEQUIN It's as true as anything, ma'am. She used to do it in her bedroom. She's the one that started the trend.

PIERROT Started the trend!

ARLEQUIN Oh, oh, I'd shock you a lot more if I told you that she went to the Bathhouse every week, and that her Husband never got her to trust him enough for her to take off her gloves when she went to bed. She's an extremely clean woman. For a whole Empire, she wouldn't have allowed her Husband to kiss her cheek for fear of smudging her makeup. I'm telling you, she is a marvellously clean woman.

PIERROT And you call that cleanliness, Sweetheart!

ARLEQUIN I truly believe it's cleanliness.

---

[5] We have used the modern term 'ellipses' here for clarity, but in the Garnier edition the expression used is 'petits points', which we could translate instead as 'little dots'. In some cases in the monologue above, there are several such dots (as many as seven at a time) separating Arlequin's remarks, instead of the conventional three used in a modern ellipsis. The absence of the term 'ellipses' in the French is no doubt owing to the fact that the practices of seventeenth-century punctuation were not as fixed as they are today. In fact, in Antoine Furetière's dictionary, the entry 'ELLYPSE' presents the geometrical sense of the term but makes no reference to punctuation or grammar. This suggests either that the convention of using three dots as a stable sign in punctuation and calling it an ellipsis (by metonymy to the rhetorical figure) had not yet been established at this time, or that the author or editors of the edition ignored it.

[6] This note is written within the text itself, presumably by the author, and is not the translator's note.

PIERROT How did you work up the nerve to leave such a clean woman?

ARLEQUIN To tell you the truth, I have a fair amount of regret about it. But since they were trying to force me clean up after three big Jerk Agents staying in the house, and they kept doing their horseplay all around me... You know, Ma'am, nothing is more important than honour. Lately, those sleazes said some things to me... Well anyway, there were plenty of reasons that I wanted to get out of there.

PIERROT Didn't those Agents try to recruit you for their purposes as well?

ARLEQUIN Agents, Ma'am! Agents! You can say whatever you like, but a young girl like me is no prey for Agents. If I'd wanted to lend an ear to such silliness, there were as many fancy folk coming through our place as in any house in Paris. But, thank Heaven, the men never tempted me.

PIERROT But tell me, my dear, have you never served gentry of quality?

ARLEQUIN Could there be people of greater quality than bourgeois politicians?

PIERROT I'm not telling you otherwise. But I'm asking if you haven't ever served people at Court?

ARLEQUIN What do you mean, Ma'am, by people at Court?

PIERROT I mean Countesses, Marquises, and Duchesses.

ARLEQUIN Oh, that's exactly it, I've never done any other work in my entire life. I also served a Commander, I was his chambermaid. That was a great position while it lasted.

PIERROT Chambermaid for a Commander! That's something else entirely.

ARLEQUIN Hey, why not, Ma'am? Ladies certainly have their private Valets.

PIERROT She's right. I really like this girl. Tell me, Sweetheart, do you do whitening?

ARLEQUIN Yes, ma'am, I do hair, I do whitening, I do a little embroidering, I can make hand ointment, I can have Skirts made, I can spiff up Coats, I do a great job of giving remedies, and finally I am proud to say that I am very skilled and I know how to do anything at all that a pretty lady like you might need, Ma'am.

PIERROT But, don't you also do the... mix up a little bit of skin cream for the face?

ARLEQUIN Why, that's where I triumph, and the Countess that I used to serve can tell you all about it. Three months after I quit working for her, she had aged eighty years. I had used up more than two-hundred jars of special Cream all over her body, and I had made all of her skin just as smooth as a mirror. If I had the honour of treating you for just two weeks, your Husband wouldn't recognise you anymore. Truly, truly, I've fixed up complexions a great deal more bedevilled up than yours. To do some good, we'll need to tighten up that face of yours from top to bottom. After that, you'll be charming all of Paris.

PIERROT Crazy girl! Fine, you're going to work for me.

ARLEQUIN Regarding the wages, Ma'am, I believe you're reasonable.

PIERROT It's fine, fine, you won't have any complaints about me.

ARLEQUIN You offer wine, I take it?

PIERROT Wine! But girls don't drink that.

ARLEQUIN That's true, Ma'am: it's that I'm very delicate. I barely eat anything, but I drink a lot.

PIERROT Well then, I'll make you happy.

ARLEQUIN What is that, Ma'am? What horrible arms do you have there? They're all hairy. We'll have to pull out all of that awful hair, there.

PIERROT (*yelling*) Ouch! Ouch!

DOCTOR (*enters, sees his wife, and says*) Good day, my Wife.

PIERROT Good day, my little man.

ARLEQUIN (*to Pierrot*) Who is that man? (*He points to the Doctor.*)

PIERROT That's my Husband.

ARLEQUIN He's just so cute!   (*He gulps hard, bites his lip, makes faces and hyperventilates.*)

DOCTOR (*who has watched Arlequin's antics, says to Pierrot*) My Wife, who is that girl with us?

PIERROT (*to the Doctor*) She's a chambermaid whom I'm taking into my service.

DOCTOR That girl in your service? Don't even think about it. She's a streetwalker who prances around every day with thirty Soldiers in front of the bronze Horse.

PIERROT (*to Arlequin, in an angry tone*) What!? Floozy! You have the nerve to ask me to hire you? A streetwalker who prances around with thirty Soldiers on the Pont-neuf? Get out of my house right this minute!

ARLEQUIN (*putting both hands on his hips*) Who told you that, Ma'am?

PIERROT My Husband did.

ARLEQUIN Your Husband's an idiot.

PIERROT And you are a disgrace.

ARLEQUIN I'm begging you to believe you've lied about this.[7]

PIERROT A denial of the sort with a Woman like me!

(*He slaps Arlequin across the face, who pounces in turn on Pierrot's wig and pulls it off. They grab each other by the hair, fall to the ground, fight, and finish the scene.*)

---

[7]   This odd expression may be a printer error but could also be a nonsensical joke made by Arlequin. In fact, who is telling the lie? They are both false here.

SCENE IV

ISABELLE and COLOMBINE.

ISABELLE Is there an unhappier person anywhere under Heaven? I have my tablets in my hand. I put them on the table, and quicker than I could get my imagination to put together a few rhyming words, a Demon, yes, Colombine, an invisible Demon, wrote some verses with these very same
5   words on my tablets! And right then, Cinthio, who is still in my room, he catches sight of my tablets and absolutely insists that these verses must have been given to me by a Rival, and the more I try to convince him otherwise, the more he digs in and refuses to believe anything else. Curse that visit I paid to Angélique yesterday! Curse even more that man who
10   put the idea in my head to come up with rhyming words!

COLOMBINE Wow! You regret speaking with great minds? And since when have you been upset about it? Oh, you've changed your tune a bit late about that one. For six months you've been going without food and drink so that you could afford to go into that cursed house twice a day and restock
15   your provisions of fashionable words. By Heaven, I believe you've been bewitched with foolishness, and that somebody has addled your good sense. If your Uncle knew about all of this, he'd certainly forbid you from seeing...[8]

ISABELLE Oh don't be so hard on me, Colombine. Angélique's behaviour isn't so
20   bad, and there's no risk in saying that she's a good, respectable girl.

COLOMBINE The marvel of it! Ugly as she is, and she's still a good, respectable girl at forty-six. But that's not even what I'm thinking of. It's her gatherings full of silliness that she holds night and day in her house, where two or three goofy Clerics pretend to be Academicians and spew out all the bad
25   Verses they've collected in the City in front of the *Précieuses* from our neighbourhood.[9]

ISABELLE You sure think like a servant, Colombine, and I'm sad to see that you don't like the language of the Gods!

COLOMBINE Why don't you say the language of the losers? Because Poets'
30   carriages don't exactly impress people in the streets these days. For example, that one Jailer's son is pretty lucky; he steals Riddles, Sonnets, Elegies, and a thousand other drugs of that nature right out of printed books, and you peddle them to me every evening! I could fill up my trunk with your silly trifles! And what do you think would happen if people sued

---

[8]   The Doctor is actually Isabelle's father, not her uncle. This may again be a printer error.
[9]   We have left '*Précieuses*' in French. It was a term that Molière made famous in his comedy *Les Précieuses ridicules* (1659), which caricatured women who composed and recited poetry in salons. The *OED* defines this term as referring to a woman who is absurdly over-refined in language and taste.

fake Poets like they do coin Counterfeiters?

ISABELLE Your simple-mindedness is such a bore! You must not know, Colombine, that Prose is the very excrement of the mind and that a Madrigal moves the heart with more tenderness than thirty of the best-turned prosaic quips? You'd have to be from the most vulgar Commoner stock to not be madly in love with Poets.

COLOMBINE Hey, you've already gone a fair way on that route.

ISABELLE As for me, I'm so taken with Verses that a Poet could easily lead me to the very edge of tenderness.

COLOMBINE My goodness, you're losing your mind.

ISABELLE Ah! Colombine, how charming a man is when we make promises that have been filtered through the colander of the Muses! How might one defend against a declaration that strikes the ear with its rhythm, and whose figural expression casts sensibility into the most rebellious and wild of souls! What pleasure, Colombine, to thrill one's heart with such ingenious novelties, that bind up so much passion in so few Verses! Ah, the wondrous talent that lets us bind our emotions and thoughts to the feet and measures prescribed by Poetry!

COLOMBINE Are you aware, Miss, that those very feet are likely to lead you straight to the Asylum? Hey, by my very death, why must a girl your age spend all her time gobbling up verses by three or four numbskulls that laziness has raised up as poets, but who wouldn't have dared look at you in Prose?

ISABELLE But what did those people do you to make you hate them so much?

COLOMBINE To me? Nothing. But I'm furious to see you duped by a pile of little Poet-nincompoops thinking that they need only stoop and grab, and that you're a girl who'd marry a Rondeau or an Elegy. To be perfectly frank, they're not a proper crowd for a Doctor's Daughter.

ISABELLE Am I not already mortified enough to be a Doctor's Daughter without you reminding me of it out of turn when you criticise me? Don't you see that I'm trying to lighten the darkness of the spoon and laxative by frequenting better people, and that I'm wiping off the filth as best I can among people of the highest merit? A Doctor's Daughter! How brutal your words are!

COLOMBINE Brutal? You're already going there. Well, that won't prevent me from getting this off my chest, and from calling you out on your association with these Lowlifes who infect your mind with plagues of invented phrases that clash with all good sense. Good Heavens! Since Molière celebrated the *Précieuses*, we've seen them sprout up everywhere, standing around, waiting to be admired. Look at that busy crowd of marriage-eager men gathering around your Angélique! Nonetheless, to

hear you talk, she's the sharpest wit in Paris. Miss, it's a good thing to have an intellect, but you need something else entirely in a marriage. As much of a Servant as I may be, I wouldn't want a Poet either for a Husband or a Lover. What good is it to be the Wife of a miserable Rhymer? Can you
80 furnish a room with Epigrams? Can you cover a table with Madrigals and pay a Butcher in Sonnets? Good Heavens, if I were in your shoes I would throw myself at some good, fat Financier who would roll my merit around in a carriage, and who'd...

ISABELLE A Financier! Oh, the horror!

85 COLOMBINE Oh, don't be such a sugar puff. That wouldn't exactly be your choice, I'm sure.

ISABELLE But, Colombine, do you really think that I could stifle myself and settle down with a man with no gift for conversation, and who'd count out money from morning till night?

90 COLOMBINE Oh, not at all. Fine then. You'd be much better off taking the devil by the tail with some dimwit Poet who'd make ends meet Quatrain by Quatrain.

ISABELLE And how could I make up my mind to love an intolerable man?

COLOMBINE What a sweet little thing you are! Does a girl really marry a rich
95 man so she can love him? We only marry to get comfortable; and when the kitchen is up and running, we easily figure out ways of consoling ourselves about everything else.

ISABELLE But Colombine, how could you live with a man like that?

COLOMBINE You'll live like Parisian Women live. For the first four or five
100 years, you'll eat well and stay warm by the fire, and then when you've used up most of your Husband's wealth paying for furniture, clothes, accessories, and jewellery, you'll get a separation in body and means, your marriage will done for, and you'll live ever after as a fat Matron. What I'm describing here is the great Cows path. You know, only dupes would go
105 about it otherwise.

ISABELLE But Colombine, is that really how you resist the Marriage bond? And do you really think it's that easy to get a separation?

COLOMBINE Well then, Lady, for that, you do have to take some extraordinary measures, and to get to that point, first of all, you work to get a legal
110 Expert on your side. And then, little by little, you irritate the husband, you belittle him, you insult him, and finally he'll lose his patience. He'll slap you around, give you a few kicks in the arse. Then you lodge a complaint. The legal Expert does his job. And there you have it, that's how you earn yourself reliable peace and quiet for the rest of your life.

115 ISABELLE Truly, Colombine, you seem like a very precocious girl to me, and I see more wisdom in you than one generally expects at your age.

COLOMBINE That's because I don't fool around with trifles like you do. I plan

early and think about how to get settled, and as young as I may be, I'd
stare down any man who would dare write to me, unless it was to get
married. Oh, my heaven, there's no reason to bother me for anything else.

20   I like to laugh, but...   *[The Doctor calls her inside.*

ISABELLE. That's my Father calling us. We're in deep trouble if he was
listening.

COLOMBINE. You're insane! Does a Doctor understand French?

SCENE V

THE FARMER FROM DOMFRONT

ARLEQUIN ALONE AND THE AGENT.

ARLEQUIN (*in a soufflet*)[10] Hey! Ho!

AGENT (*aside*) Here's the man with the soufflet. Let's see if he paid the fees at the
office. (*To Arlequin*) Where did the soufflet come from?

ARLEQUIN A slap?[11] I didn't touch you.

5   AGENT I'm asking you by what right you have a soufflet?

ARLEQUIN (*in an angry tone*) I never got a slap, Sir, and take care with what you
say to me.

AGENT It's a Carriage that...

ARLEQUIN You're the nag![12] I find you very insolent indeed to treat me that

10   way.

AGENT Ha, ha, you're trying to talk your way out of this! We'll teach you to talk
your way out right now. Here's a Constable who's coming at the perfect
time.

CONSTABLE There's a lot of commotion here. What's going on?

15   AGENT Not much, Sir. There is a soufflet...

CONSTABLE Someone slapped you! Let me take your statement.

AGENT Uh, no Sir. There is this man with a carriage that is called a 'soufflet'.
He hasn't paid the fees at the office, and Sir, I'm asking for the Carriage
to be impounded.

---

[10]   This French word refers ambiguously to either a two-wheeled carriage or an insulting
slap in the face. Much of the comic effect of the scene rests on this double-meaning.

[11]   Arlequin intentionally misinterprets this as meaning to slap, a different sense of the
word *soufflet*.

[12]   In the French, the Agent says, 'C'est un Carosse qui...', which we have translated literally
here. However, Arlequin hears or pretends to understand 'C'est un rosse qui', which could
mean 'This is a nag', referring to the poor condition of the horse pulling the carriage. In
his *Dictionaire universel* of 1690, Antoine Furetière defines a 'rosse' as a 'Mean, worn-out
and sway-backed horse who does not react to the spur or the whip' (translation our own).
Furetière makes no mention of the use of the term attested later as an insult for people, like
'nag'. See <http://www.cnrtl.fr/definition/rosse>. In any case, Arlequin responds as if the
Agent were insulting him or his animal with this epithet.

ARLEQUIN, *during this time, changes his Jumpsuit and Hat, and is now dressed as a Baker, in a red shirt and a wool cap, and his Carriage has now transformed into a baker's cart.*

20 CONSTABLE Let's see where it is. (*He turns around,*[13] *and sees a Cart instead of a convertible Carriage, and starts laughing.*)

ARLEQUIN (*to the Constable*) Mister Constable, that fellow is crazy, at least a little bit.

CONSTABLE. Thinking a Baker's cart is a convertible Carriage! Ha! Ha! Ha!

(*He laughs.*)

AGENT (*bewildered*) Mister Constable, I beg your pardon, I was mistaken.

25 CONSTABLE That's not good enough. You owe me a fine.

ARLEQUIN Yes, you owe me too!

AGENT (*to the Constable*) That's quite fair, Sir, how much do I owe?

CONSTABLE One gold louis.[14]

ARLEQUIN And fifteen francs for me!

30 AGENT (*to the Constable*) Here you go, Sir, one gold louis, but please do consider that this man right here is asking me for fifteen francs because he got delayed a moment here.

ARLEQUIN There have been more than fifty moments!

CONSTABLE (*to Arlequin*) Shut up. Why did you ask for fifteen francs?

35 ARLEQUIN Because I lost some time, and now my bread will burn in the oven in Gonesse.

CONSTABLE Look at this crook! Asking for fifteen francs for the instant that he's spent here!

ARLEQUIN (*to the Constable*) In truth, Sir, that's the normal price. You can go
40   compare elsewhere, I'm just asking for your business.

CONSTABLE Shut up, I'm telling you, you're a cheat. It's not right to harass people. (*to the Agent*) Sir, give him six écus.   [*Begins to Exit.*

ARLEQUIN (*to the Constable*) Psst, psst, Mister Constable. (*The constable turns around.*) Come on, come, there's bread in it for you.

45 CONSTABLE (*putting his finger to his mouth*) Morus.[15]

---

[13] The Constable had his back to Arlequin while the latter transformed the carriage.

[14] Characters in this scene mention three denominations of currency circulating in early modern France: the *franc*, the *écu*, and the gold *louis*. Antoine Furetière's *Dictionaire universel* notes that the *Sols* or *sous* were a small denomination in seventeenth-century France and offers equivalents of other coinages (see 'Sol'). According to Furetière, twenty *sols* were equivalent to 100 *francs*, while a silver *écu* was worth sixty *sols*, and three (French) pounds. In theory, a gold *écu* equated to 114 *sols* and approximately six pounds (*livres*). He writes that the value of a gold *louis* was eleven pounds in 1690. Thus, if we assume that the characters are talking about silver *écus* instead of gold ones, these coins are each probably worth about 300 *francs*, while the gold *louis* are likely worth three or four *écus* (and between 900 and 1200 *francs*) each.

[15] This word is poorly printed in italics in the Garnier edition, but appears to read 'Morus', a Latin word for 'madman'. It is difficult to interpret here since we cannot exclude the

AGENT (*to Arlequin*) Here are six écus; but you'll pay for this.

ARLEQUIN (*taking the money*) Let it be a lesson to you not to defame Gonesse bread.

AGENT (*aside*) I can't take it anymore. I see a man in a 'soufflet', don't take my
50   eyes off him, I come right here, and then I find that instead of a 'soufflet' there's a Baker's Cart. No, you must be a devil to be able to...

(*He turns back toward the cart and sees Arlequin dressed as a farmer in the same carriage that he had seen before.*)

I knew it, I knew I hadn't been wrong. Mister Constable, Mister Constable.

(*He runs after the constable, and at just the same time, Arlequin disguises himself as a Baker again and his Carriage turns back into a cart.*)

CONSTABLE (*Coming back*) What? What's changed?

AGENT (*to the Constable*) I definitely told you Sir, that I'd seen a man in a
55   'soufflet'.

CONSTABLE Where is he?

AGENT Right here, look!

(*They turn toward Arlequin, see the Cart and the Baker, and they disappear; the Constable bursts out laughing, and the Agent is stunned and confused. Afterward, Arlequin takes on the Farmer disguise again, and the Doctor arrives.*)

DOCTOR I haven't had any news of the Farmer from Domfront. But he should have arrived by now. I'm worried that something may have happened to
60   him. (*Noticing Arlequin in a Carriage*) What kind of a vehicle is this?

ARLEQUIN (*looking at the Doctor*) Good day, my friend.

DOCTOR That's an awfully familiar tone.

ARLEQUIN Speak! Are you from this Town? Or does the Town belong to you?

DOCTOR [*aside*] He's some madman. (*To Arlequin*) No Sir, I am not from this
65   Town, and the Town doesn't belong to me.

ARLEQUIN Swear to it.

DOCTOR That's a funny thing to say! I never swear, Sir. I am a Foreigner, and I have lived in this Town for a long time indeed.

ARLEQUIN Could you inform me about whom I'm looking for?

70 DOCTOR And who are you looking for?

ARLEQUIN You're awfully curious!

DOCTOR You sure are a funny one. I'd need to know who you are looking for if

possibility of a printer error. The 1700 Gherardi edition reads 'Motus', a Latin word for movement, gesture or emotion, without italics and followed by an exclamation point. It may be that the Constable is trying to communicate cryptically to Arlequin that the Agent is insane without further disturbing the man, who is becoming increasingly upset.

you want me to give you news about the matter.

ARLEQUIN He's right. Since that's the case, Sir, I'll inform you that I'm looking
for a certain em... em... embroiderer. Cate... Bay... bacon caterer, yes
that's it. Sir, you wouldn't happen to know a bacon Caterer, would you?

DOCTOR No, I know several Caterers, but none of them are bacon Caterers.

ARLEQUIN He's a learned man, a very well-educated man, who knows how to
read and write.

DOCTOR An educated Caterer! Aren't you more likely asking for a Doctor?

ARLEQUIN You said it. I'm looking for a Doctor of bacon. You don't happen to
know anyone, do you, Sir?

DOCTOR I know every Doctor in the City, but I don't know one by that name.

ARLEQUIN Yet there certainly must be one.

DOCTOR Doctor Bacon! You might be mean Doctor Balouard.

ARLEQUIN You've got it; Doctor Balouard, yes, my Heavens, that's exactly the
one I'm asking around for. I knew it was something about lard.

DOCTOR Balouard, lard. And what do you want from him, Sir? I am he.

ARLEQUIN You yourself are in fact the Doctor Balouard!

DOCTOR Yes, Sir, at your service.

ARLEQUIN Don't you know me? I'm Domfront's son, the one coming to marry
you.[16]

DOCTOR Ah! Ah! you are Colin's Son, the Farmer from Domfront who's coming
to finalise Colombine's marriage!

ARLEQUIN Yes, indeed. I'm the son of Colin Tampon, and I've come to wed
Colobine's [sic] marriage.

DOCTOR I'm delighted to see you. I've been waiting for you for a long time. Why
is it that you took so long getting here?

ARLEQUIN It's that I couldn't move forward, Sir, because of a headwind.

DOCTOR A headwind in a carriage! (*He laughs*) Colombine will be pleased to see
you. Step down and come into my home.

> *A Peasant from Domfront arrives during all of this, and says that he is
> looking for Doctor Balouard. The Doctor identifies himself, the Peasant
> hands him a letter from Colin, the Farmer from Domfront. Arlequin
> sees this.*

ARLEQUIN Doctor, Sir, hurry me up, the marriage is getting away.[17]

> *The Doctor reads the letter, learns that Colin's son is ill, and that he*

---

[16]   Both here and in Arlequin's subsequent line, it is unclear whether his nonsensical use of
the words 'épouser' (to marry) and 'mariage' (wedding) is intended for comic effect or rather
results from printer error. We have translated these lines literally. It may be that Arlequin's
excitement leads him to fumble his wording, allowing for further humour.

[17]   Here Arlequin strangely refers to a wedding as though it were an animal or person
capable of fleeing on foot, and he irrationally inverts his imperative, asking the Doctor to
hurry him. The odd wording may be part of the humour or printer error.

won't be able to travel right away. At the same time, he glances over at Arlequin, who shamelessly insists that he is the Son of the Farmer from Domfront, and that he is quite well. The Doctor asks the Peasant if he knows him. The Peasant replies that no, that's not his master's son. Arlequin, taken by surprise, turns toward the Doctor.

ARLEQUIN Sir, I beg your pardon. I thought that's who I was.

The Doctor and the Peasant threaten him and leave. Arlequin stays, in despair. Pasquariel [sic] arrives, consoles him, and dresses him up as Ambassador of the Emperor of the World of the Moon, and they leave as they see the Doctor coming back.

SCENE VI

WITH THE ENVOY AND ARLEQUIN'S TRAVELS IN THE EMPIRE OF THE MOON

DOCTOR, ARLEQUIN.

ARLEQUIN (*pretending to be out of breath, and running from one end of the Stage to another*) Hey! For charity, somebody please tell me where Doctor Grazian Balouard lives! (*He puts his hand to his mouth and imitates a Trumpet.*) Toot! Toot! For fifteen sols, Doctor Grazian Balouard?

DOCTOR What does all this mean? (*To Arlequin*) Doctor Grazian Balouard. Here he is. What do you want with him?

ARLEQUIN Ah! Sir, congratulations on being found. Pay me plenty of compliments and bow down to me aplenty. I am the special Ambassador, sent by the Emperor of the World of the Moon, to ask for Isabelle's hand in marriage.

DOCTOR Somebody else. Tell it to somebody else, buddy. I'm not so easily taken in. An Emperor in the Moon!

ARLEQUIN Yes, by Heaven, an Emperor, and an illustrious Emperor, a noble like the King.

DOCTOR (*aside*) That might well be the case, since the Moon is a world like our own; there likely could be someone governing it. (*To Arlequin*) But, my friend, are you from that Land yourself?

ARLEQUIN No Sir, I am neither from that Land, nor from this Land. I am an Italian from Italy, at your service, born a native of the City of Prato, one of the most charming towns in all of Tuscany.

DOCTOR But, how did you manage to get all the way up to the Empire of the Moon?

ARLEQUIN Well, here goes, I'll tell you how. I had met up with three friends of mine to go out and eat a Goose in Vaugirard. The group tasked me with going off to buy the Goose. I took a ride to Poverty Valley. I made the purchase there, and then I headed back toward our meeting place. When I arrived at the Vaugirard plain, suddenly six starving Vultures pounce down on my Goose and carry it upward. I was afraid of losing it, so I hung on dearly to its neck, such that the higher the Vultures lifted up my Goose, the higher they took me up with it. When we got really high up indeed, a new Regiment of Vultures came to assist the first ones, and threw themselves onto my Goose, and right then we both lost sight of the highest mountains and the highest bell towers. I was as intent as a Demon not to let go, at least until my Goose's neck gave way, and I fell into Lake. Luckily, some Fishermen had put their nets out, and I fell into them. The Fishermen drew me out of the water, and thinking I was a pretty impressive Fish, they hoisted me up onto their shoulders and delivered me as a gift to my lord the Emperor. They put me right down on the floor, and the Emperor and his whole court gathered around. Somebody asked, 'What kind of a fish is that?'

The Emperor answered, 'I believe it's an anchovy'.

'I beg your pardon, my lord', asked a fat aristocrat who was trying to be witty, 'it's more of a toad.'

'In any case', said my lord the Emperor, 'We want this fish fried, whatever kind it is'. When I heard that they were going to fry me up, I started to scream, 'But my lord!'

'What?' he said, 'Do fish speak?'

'Anytime people want to fry us up, we are allowed to complain, my lord.' I explained that I wasn't a Fish, and how I had come to the Empire of the Moon. He immediately asked: 'Do you know Doctor Grazian Balouard?'

'Yes, my lord.'

'Do you know his Daughter Isabelle?'

'Yes, my lord.'

'Well then, I want you to serve as my Ambassador, and to go ask for her hand in marriage on my behalf.'

I answered, 'But my lord, I'd never be able to find the way back, because I don't know which way I came up here.'

'Don't let that worry you', he added, 'I'll send you to Paris in an influence I'm sending there, loaded with rheumatisms, runny noses, chest congestions, and other little trifles of that nature.'

'But my lord, what will you do to Doctor Grazian Balouard? He's a great man, a learned man, who studies Rhetoric, Philosophy, Spelling.'

'Ho! Ho!' he replied, 'the Doctor! I've reserved one of the best posts in the Empire for him.'

65 DOCTOR Could it be possible? Did he tell you what it is?

ARLEQUIN He certainly did. He said that about two weeks ago, among the twelve
     signs of the Zodiac, Scorpio died, and he wants you to replace him, Sir.

DOCTOR Me, replacing Scorpio! My lord the Emperor must be joking.

ARLEQUIN No, I swear, may the plague take me! How in the devil! You'll become
70   one of the twelve most important men in that land.

DOCTOR I'm not concerned with such honours. But tell me, is the City where the
     Emperor lives beautiful?

ARLEQUIN She's one of the prettiest Cities in the world, pretty, well put-together,
     a nice figure, a beautiful complexion…[18]

75 DOCTOR The City has a beautiful complexion! And the houses, Sir, how are they
     built? Are they like ours?

ARLEQUIN No, the houses of that land are furnished on the outside, and they
     don't have anything inside. The roofs of every house are made out of
     Licorice, and when it rains, it rains Herbal Tea on the whole Town.

80 DOCTOR That sure is practical for sick people.

ARLEQUIN The Emperor's Palace is made of mineral crystals, the Gate columns
     are made of tobacco ropes, the Roof of a great, thick Flemish Wool, the
     Windows are made of the finest French Needlework anybody's ever seen.

DOCTOR That sure is odd. And how do people live in that Land? Do they eat
85   like we do here?

ARLEQUIN Yes and no.

DOCTOR What does that mean, 'Yes and no'?

ARLEQUIN Yes, about the food. They eat everything that we eat here, but no
     about the way they eat it, which is very different from how we do it.

90 DOCTOR How do they do it then?

ARLEQUIN You'll see. For example, when my lord the Emperor wishes to eat,
     he sits down at an empty table, on which nobody serves anything during
     mealtime.

DOCTOR (laughing) That's one way to have a good meal.

95 ARLEQUIN Which is why he does so.

DOCTOR So he does it away from the table, then?

ARLEQUIN Pardon me, at the table.

DOCTOR And you just told me that the table is empty when he sits down and at
     it, and that nobody serves anything on it as long as he stays there.

100 ARLEQUIN That's true. But it doesn't mean that he doesn't have a great meal, and
     that he doesn't eat all of the most delicious meat and Fish.[19]

---

[18] Arlequin uses the words 'taille' (figure) and 'teint' (complexion) which evoke a woman's
body and face, not a city. This eroticisation of the vocabulary is intended no doubt to suggest
Arlequin's lust for Isabelle to comic effect.
[19] Here, as elsewhere, we have retained the capitalisation appearing in the Garnier edition.
In this case 'chair' (meat) is not capitalised but 'Poisson' (fish) is.

DOCTOR I don't understand any of this.

ARLEQUIN I'll help you to understand. While my lord the Emperor is at the table, at his right he has twenty people, each of whom holds a huge golden Crossbow loaded with a Woodcock, a Sausage, a little pâté, and other things. On his left, there are twenty other people with silver Syringes, just as huge, and one of them is filled with Spanish wine, another with wine from the Canary Islands, with Muscadet wine, with Champagne wine, *et sic de cœteris*.[20] When my lord the Emperor wishes to eat, he turns to the right, opens his mouth, and right then, crack! the Crossbowman shoots a little Pâté, a Sausage, an Ox... And when he wants to drink, he turns to the left, and the man holding the wine Syringe squirts Saint Laurence wine, Canary Island wine, Normandy wine or what have you, depending on what he wants to drink.

DOCTOR I understand that marvellously well now, and I find that to be the most wonderful way of dining in the whole world, just as long as the Crossbowmen shoot straight.

ARLEQUIN Damn! They don't hire any who aren't very experienced since the unfortunate incident that one time.

DOCTOR What incident? Do tell.

ARLEQUIN My lord the Emperor wanted eggs fried in black butter, and a clumsy Crossbowman shot him one, but instead of aiming for his mouth, he aimed at his eye, and that caused a great deal of discomfort. His Doctors thought he would go blind, but by a stroke of luck there was no permanent harm done, and he was fine after he wore a bandage over his eye for a few days. Since then, people have always called those eggs, poached eggs.

DOCTOR Now there's a historical episode that I wasn't aware of, and I never would have imagined that the term 'poached eggs' had come out of an accident that happened to the Emperor of the world of the Moon.

ARLEQUIN It's just as I told you.

DOCTOR Say, tell me something. Does my lord the Emperor have a Symphony at his table?

ARLEQUIN Excuse me, he sure does. It's the best Symphony in the world. His Orchestra is far better than the one at the Opera.

DOCTOR Oh! When it comes to that, Sir, pardon me if I don't believe a word of it. There is no Orchestra in the world better than the one at the Paris Opera, that's what all the connoisseurs say. But what instruments are there? Violins? Flutes? Bass viols? Theorbos? Harpsichords? Bassoons? Oboes? Trumpets? Timpani? Drums? Fifes? Harps? Kettle drums? Psalteries? Carillons? Guitars?

(Arlequin answers 'No' every time the Doctor names an instrument.)

---

[20]   Arlequin uses this Latin expression meaning 'and so forth'.

DOCTOR Well what the devil kinds of instruments do they play there then?

ARLEQUIN Here goes, I'll tell you. The people of that Country have extremely long noses. They tie a gut string from one end of their nose to the other, then they put their left hand on the small end of their nose, and with a

145   Bow that they hold in their right hand, they play their nose like we play the violin here.

DOCTOR That sure must make a funny harmony.

ARLEQUIN By Heaven, I sure think so. It makes an enchanting nasalisation. Ovid would play perfectly. That's why they call him Ovid Nazon.

150 DOCTOR But tell me, what language does the Emperor speak? How did you manage to understand him?

ARLEQUIN My lord the Emperor speaks French like you and I, and better in fact.

DOCTOR Ha! There you go, you're pulling my leg! My lord the Emperor speaking

155   French! How could he have learned it?

ARLEQUIN He learned it thanks to a speaking Trumpet that a language Teacher uses every night at midnight, giving him his lessons from the Pont-neuf.

DOCTOR And a speaking Trumpet would suffice to make oneself heard that far up?

160 ARLEQUIN Who would doubt it? It's done thanks to the repercussion of the air that directly strikes the concave shape of the column that pushes down on the hole at the base, and then it's pushed onward by vocal impulsion so as to create the sharp sound that cuts through the Clouds and is heard by... That's what we call sophisticated Physics. You'll understand it later.

165   I'll head off to get a speaking Trumpet of the same kind that the Emperor gave me as a gift, and I'll speak with him right in front of you.

DOCTOR If you do that, I won't have anything more to say, and I'll consent to whatever you want.

ARLEQUIN Wait for me here. I'll be right with you in a moment.   [*Exit*

170 DOCTOR If what this man says is true, then what a joy for my daughter! And what a coup against the ignoramuses trying to claim that the Moon isn't a world like ours!

ARLEQUIN (*returning with a Trumpet*) Look here, Sir, you'll be an eyewitness to the truth. Take off your hat.

175 DOCTOR Why would I take off my hat?

ARLEQUIN To show respect for my lord the Emperor. For a Doctor, you sure are ignorant. (*The Doctor takes off his hat and takes a bow. Arlequin is in front of him, bows as well, turns around and says to the Doctor:* Lower, Sir, lower down.

The Doctor lowers himself further, and at the same time Arlequin raises his own behind so that the Doctor gets his nose in it. After this

*Italian lazzo, Arlequin raises the Trumpet into the air, and while
pretending to speak into it.)*

180   My lord the Emperor, I spoke to the Doctor about the wedding. He's
delighted with the idea, my lord. And if you could order him to pay me six
gold Louis for my trouble, and be much obliged to you, my lord.

A voice can be heard that says Doctor, give six gold Louis to Arlequin. This is
the Emperor of the Moon, ordering you to do so.

185   DOCTOR *(stunned)* Is that my lord the Emperor?

ARLEQUIN Yes, Sir, that's him, I recognize his voice.

DOCTOR He ordered me to give you six gold Louis, and I'm happy to do it.
You've brought me news that's too wonderful not to reward you as you
deserve. Here you are.

*(He produces a coin purse, takes out six Louis, and gives them to Arlequin.
Arlequin takes them, puts them in his pocket, then, after he notices a
Diamond ring on the Doctor's finger, he takes his hand and asks him what
it is. The Doctor answers that it's a Diamond that had belonged to his late
wife, and that it is worth at least 60 Louis. Arlequin thinks for a moment,
then raises his Trumpet in the air.)*

190   ARLEQUIN My lord the Emperor, the Doctor gave me six gold Louis, and I offer
you my humblest thanks. But if you might be so kind as to order him to
give me a Diamond worth sixty Louis that he's wearing on the ring finger
of his left hand, I'd be doubly obliged to you, my lord.

THE VOICE Doctor, give your Diamond to Arlequin. The Emperor of the Moon
195   commands it.

DOCTOR Hey! He gives more orders than all the Doctors in Paris.

ARLEQUIN Oh, Sir, he's a very generous Prince.

DOCTOR Generous with others' wealth. Listen here, I gladly gave you the six
Louis as he ordered, but as for the Ring, I won't give it to you. It belonged
200   to my late wife, and I want to keep it because I loved her.

ARLEQUIN *(in an angry tone)* You don't want to give it to me? Well then Sir, keep
it. I'll tell my lord the Emperor about it, and the wedding will be called
off.

(He tries to speak into his Trumpet.)

DOCTOR *(stopping him)* What? If I don't give you the ring, the Emperor will get
205   angry and he won't marry my Daughter?

ARLEQUIN Excellent question! Of course; and you'll lose Scorpio's position in
the Zodiac.

DOCTOR *(aside)* Losing my Daughter's fortune over a Ring worth sixty *Pistoles?*[21]

---

[21]   Furetière defines a *pistole* as a coin minted in Spain or in certain Italian states,
equivalent in value to a gold *louis.*

No, my dear Wife wouldn't approve. (*To Arlequin*) Here. Sir, there's my
10　Ring, I'm giving it to you.

ARLEQUIN You're giving it to me, and I'm taking it. (*After he puts in on his finger,
he stares attentively at something that hanging out of the Doctor's pocket.*)
What do I see there?

DOCTOR Those are the laces to my coin purse.

15　ARLEQUIN And what is there in your coin purse?

DOCTOR There were fifty Louis, but I gave you six of them, and now there are
forty-four left.

ARLEQUIN Forty-four gold Louis! (*After daydreaming for a moment*) I'm going
to have another word with the Emperor.

20　DOCTOR (*stopping him*) Whoa, no, please don't.
(*He pushes him to make him go away, and Arlequin moves away laughing.*)

DOCTOR (*alone*) And where is Pierrot right now, anyway? I would have liked to
have him there for the conversation with the Ambassador. He wouldn't
be so sceptical about that Moon business anymore. But let's go give my
Daughter the good news.

SCENE VII

WITH THE APOTHECARY

ARLEQUIN, as an apothecary [and] THE DOCTOR.

ARLEQUIN (*coming out of a Sedan, which opens up to reveal an Apothecary's
Shop*) I'm convinced, Sir, that a Seat with a hole in it would be a better sign
for an apothecary than a Sedan with porters. But since that type of Seat
wouldn't smell very nice to a Mistress, and this vehicle would be great in
5　a Wedding, I'm having myself carried to your home, Sir, with elegance,
so that I can offer you all the respects that Pharmacy owes Medicine. I
wouldn't come for a consultation with you, Sir, if this was regarding an
ordinary illness, but I'm coming to you now in desperation with an issue
that simple folk can do nothing about, and finding the cure would do great
10　honour to your Institution. It is I, Sir, who am both the stricken and the
illness; It is I who am spoiled down to the very marrow of my bones, with
that horrendous sickness that can only be healed through ceremonies, and
for which the remedy is often more dangerous than the disease; it is I who
am infected with the gangrene of Colombine's perfection; It is I who wish
15　to marry her. And it is I, finally, begging you to prescribe her for me like
a delicious Purgative that I will take with delight. The Doctor will have all
the honour, and the Apothecary all the pleasure.

DOCTOR Words don't stink; you are indeed an Apothecary, then?

ARLEQUIN Yes, Sir, I am, by the grace of Heaven, up close and personal; and
20   on any given day at my shop we prepare concoctions for thirty dozen
enemas. It is I, Sir, who purge the thirteen Villages on May Day every
year, and I can declare, without vanity, that there is no Foreign Country
where people do not know Mister Arsewhistle.[22] This is the name of your
humble servant.

25   DOCTOR Mister Arsewhistle!

ARLEQUIN Alas, Sir, if it weren't for the Lawsuit from the Perfumers, we would
be beyond rich.

DOCTOR What?

ARLEQUIN It's a deplorable thing, Sir, to witness the decline of our Professions;
30   and I'll wager to assure you that the Perfumers' actions concern Doctors
just as much as Apothecaries.

DOCTOR You must be joking, Mister Arsewhistle, what would Doctors have to
do with it?

ARLEQUIN What do Doctors have to do with it? Well does Pharmacy not go
35   hand in hand with Medicine? If we didn't carefully blend the ingredients
every day for you to use with the Sick, then what would become of careers
in Medicine? Because as for checking a pulse, you know that there is no
Maidservant or Midwife these days who doesn't try this right under your
nose in every house in Paris. Believe me, Sir, this is a serious issue both for
40   you and for us all; and if we lose out, then there'll be nothing left to do but
hang up our Syringes for good.

DOCTOR But these Perfumers, Mister Arsewhistle.

ARLEQUIN What? It's a strict Grammar rule, that the sentence is out of whack if
the adjective doesn't fit with the noun. In the same way, Medicine might
45   have to go to the Hospital when the Apothecaries don't take action.

DOCTOR Hey! Let's talk about the Perfumers, Mister Arsewhistle, without a long
prologue.

ARLEQUIN I'm getting there, Sir, I'm getting there. The conservation of beauty
has been Women's main activity since the beginning of time, and you
50   have wisely imagined that the beneficial properties of certain ingredients
might greatly aid the freshness of their complexion. The question has been
how to apply such a remedy, and thanks to our sly disposition, (which we
have them to thank for), we have discovered how to beautify them without
touching them, to freshen them up without them seeing anything, and to
55   shoot them up with beauty from behind. Yet despite the well-established
state of our Profession, Perfumers are seeking to prevent us from giving
enemas to women in good health, claiming that beauty aids should come

---

[22]   The term in the scene is 'Cusiffle', which evokes both the word 'cul' (arse) and 'siffler'
(to whistle).

from their Boutiques, and that it's not our business to mess with faces.

DOCTOR What's wrong with those fools? So they would abolish the Enema Syringe?

ARLEQUIN Truly, Sir, they're stuck right on the idea, and if we let them get away with it, they'll stymie both Doctors and Apothecaries with some horrible Ointment made of eggshells, Sheep hooves and other ingredients that they'll market to Women under the pretext of making them look more beautiful. You know well, Sir, that a Woman can't stay fourteen years old forever, and there's nothing truer than the notion that no price is too high if she imagines she can buy youth and beauty. Those Dimwit perfumers go after their weakest point, leading them to believe that their Ointment is a mask that counters the years and that a little white and red spread onto their face will call Baptism Records into question. Would you believe, Sir, that one of them had the insolence to promise a seventy-five-year-old woman to make her into a Girl again, with nothing but an ounce of Ointment?

DOCTOR Ah! What lies you've told, you Perfumers! We'll whip you back into shape. The University will defend the Enema down to the very last drop. Why the Devil would a woman pay four Pistoles for a jar of Ointment when two sols pay for an Enema?

ARLEQUIN How delighted I am, Sir, to see you get so hot and bothered about the Syringe! Between you and me, it's the prettiest rose in our bonnet, and if we lost it, we'd be in bad shape. Because the more Enemas there are, the more Chamberpots, and the more Apothecaries, the more Doctors.

Enter Colombine.

COLOMBINE Sir, it's a Woman who's ninety-three years old, crying about her Husband's death, and she's complaining about vapours.

DOCTOR A ninety-three-year-old Woman is complaining about vapours!

COLOMBINE Goodness, Sir, she's crying out for mercy and she's asking for your Balm.

DOCTOR Colombine, tell her that I'm coming down.

ARLEQUIN (*noticing Colombine*) What? Sir, is this Colombine, the one I love and that I aim to marry? Ah! Please allow me to pay her a compliment with that in mind.

DOCTOR Colombine, do a curtsy for Mister Arsewhistle.

COLOMBINE What did you just say, Sir?

DOCTOR I told you to do a curtsy for Mister Arsewhistle.

COLOMBINE Ha! Mister Arsewhistle! Ha, ha, what a funny name!

DOCTOR Shut up, impertinent girl. Don't you know that he's the best man in the world at giving an Enema? Come closer, Sir.

ARLEQUIN (*after bowing to Colombine*) My lady, my mind is so constipated in

the bowels of my ignorance that I shall need the Syrup of your insights to
liquefy the substance of my thinking.

100 COLOMBINE Ha! Liquefy your thinking! What a gallant turn of phrase! What a
handsome Apothecary man Mister Arsewhistle is!

ARLEQUIN Ah! My lady you are squirting praises into me that you rather
deserve yourself. Your mouth is an Alembic in which the subtlest notions
find their quintessence. All of the senna and rhubarb in my Boutique do
105   not purge illness as well as your bright eyes calm the acrid and stinging
humors of burning love, against which you will be the laxative pill, since
your effervescent mood is a potent Antidote[23] against the melancholic
sufferings of a heart with blockages due to your rare virtues and your
eminent qualities.

110 COLOMBINE I didn't think, Mister Arsewhistle, that I was such a potent remedy
against insanity. If you keep going on that way, you're going to make me
into a cure for all ailments.

ARLEQUIN How happy is the wound upon which such a bandage will be placed!
Farewell, oh Catholicon of my soul.[24] Farewell oh beautiful Peach flower. I
115   shall infuse into the flask of my memory the gracious features that Nature
bestowed upon you.

COLOMBINE Farewell, Mister Arsewhistle.

ARLEQUIN Farewell, sweet Antimony for my worries. Farewell, dear Analgesic
for my thoughts. (*He turns back toward the Doctor.*) I'm much obliged
120   to you, Sir, for the joy you have just given me in allowing me to speak
with Colombine! I would be pleased if, as a reward for this gift, you got
Haemorrhoids; I'd then cure them for you in twenty-four hours.

SCENE VIII

ARLEQUIN Emperor of the Moon, THE DOCTOR, EULARIA, ISABELLE,
COLOMBINE, SCARAMOUCHE.

ARLEQUIN Since it must be the case, Doctor, that through the ages, the Moon
and Love have been the main forces moving in the heads of Women, and
sometimes those of men too, whereupon it happens that love often leads
to marriage, and marriage almost always leads to a waxing crescent; this
5   is the reason that I have come down to this place from my Empire to ask
for Isabelle's hand in marriage, while hoping you'll enjoy having me use it

---

[23] Arlequin uses the word 'Orvietan', referring to an effective counter-poison which,
according to Antoine Furetière, had been brought to Paris by someone from Orvieto and
was widely used.
[24] Furetière notes that the 'Catholicon' was a powerful mixed purgative made of many
ingredients.

to make a Full Moon right away, and no doubt thereafter to make a whole clutch of little crescents. What good fortune for a Doctor to have sired the Sultana of my Empire!

DOCTOR My lord, your Highness is very kind to have come from so far away to infuse Emperors into my Family. I joyfully accept this honour. Yet since my old age won't allow me to follow my Daughter to the Empire of the Moon, might I dare ask your Highness what your Subjects are like?

ARLEQUIN My Subjects. They're practically without faults, because nothing but greed and ambition governs them.

COLOMBINE That's just as it is here.

ARLEQUIN Each one tries to get settled as best he can at everyone else's expense, and the greatest virtue in my Empire is to have a lot of wealth.

DOCTOR That's just as it is here.

ARLEQUIN Would you believe that there aren't any Executioners in my States?

COLOMBINE What! My lord, you don't punish guilty people?

ARLEQUIN By the plague! We punish them severely. But instead of getting rid of them in fifteen minutes in a Public Square, I hand them over to Doctors to be killed, and they put them to death just as cruelly as their patients.

COLOMBINE What?! My Lord, up there, Doctors kill people! Sir, that's just as it is here.

ISABELLE And in your Empire, my lord, are there great Minds?

ARLEQUIN It's the very source of them. It's been more than seventy years that they've been working on a Dictionary that still won't be complete two centuries from now.

COLOMBINE That's just as it is here. And in your Empire, my Lord, is true Justice done?

ARLEQUIN We do it perfectly enough for paintings.

ISABELLE And the Judges, my lord, don't they give in a bit to corruption?

ARLEQUIN Women bribe them, as is done elsewhere. They give them gifts from time to time. But otherwise, everything goes along by the rules.

DOCTOR That's just as it is here. My lord, in your Empire, are Husbands tolerant?

ARLEQUIN That vogue came to us as soon as it got to France. At first, we had a hard time getting used to it, but now everyone considers it a point of honour.

COLOMBINE That's just as it is here. And do Usurers make a good profit, my lord?

ARLEQUIN Fie! By the Devil, I don't tolerate those creeps. They're pests that we won't allow a foothold. But in my big Cities, there are decent people, quite well-off, who loan money to children in families, take silver dishes as collateral, and charge twenty-five per cent interest, if they can't invest at thirty per cent.

ISABELLE That's just as it is here. And are the Wives in your Empire happy, my
50   lord?

ARLEQUIN That's something that's impossible to understand. They're the ones
who handle all the money and spend it all. The Husbands' only task is to
pay out profits and have houses repaired.

COLOMBINE That's just as it is here.

55   ARLEQUIN Our Wives only ever get out of bed in the afternoon. They usually
spend three hours primping, then they get into a carriage and have
somebody take them to the Theatre, to the Opera, or out for a stroll. After
that, they have dinner with some chosen beau. After dinner, they gamble
or go to the Ball, depending on the Season, then four or five hours after
60   midnight, the Wives come back and go to bed in a separate Apartment
from their Husbands. This means that a poor devil of a man goes as long
as six weeks without ever seeing his Wife in his own house, and you see
him running around in the street on foot while Madame uses the carriage
to have fun.

65   EVERYONE TOGETHER That's just as it is here.

DOCTOR (*seeing a man come in and walk right up to Arlequin, says to him*) My
lord, what does that man want?

ARLEQUIN (*turning around, looks at the grotesquely-dressed man, and says to the
Doctor*) Doctor, Sir, isn't this the Window-washer?

DOCTOR He's dressed like him. (*The man gives a piece of paper to Arlequin
without saying anything, then exits.*)

ARLEQUIN (*unfolds the piece of paper, looks at it, turns it this way and that, then
70   says to the Doctor*) Doctor, Sir, do you know how to read?

DOCTOR Yes, my lord.

ARLEQUIN (*giving the paper to the Doctor*) Read that then, because we Emperors
don't bother with reading, it's far too Bourgeois for us.

DOCTOR (*after having read it quietly to himself*) My lord, somebody's challenging
75   you to a duel.

ARLEQUIN A duel! A duel! To challenge me, the Prince of the Fog, the King of
the Dusk, and the *Imperativo modo tempore præsenti!*[25] And who are these
audacious fools who dare challenge me?

DOCTOR The three Knights of the Sun.

80   ARLEQUIN Let them show themselves then.

(*The three Knights of the Sun enter to the sound of Trumpets and Drums,
and after they circle around the Stage, one of them approaches Arlequin,
and says to him:*) 'Cowardly and false Emperor of the Moon, three Knights

---

[25]   Latin for 'Imperative mood, present tense!'

of the Sun, armed with the symbol of justice, do hereby challenge you, and contend that it was madness to seek to marry Eularia, Isabelle, and Colombine. Renounce your love for them, or prepare to defend yourself!'

ARLEQUIN (*with a proud and resolute voice*) Gentlemen, I see you're acting like Gascons,[26] coming in a group of three like this, while I'm all by myself. But right here are the Doctor and Scaramouche who'll second me, and then if you like it will be three against three.

85 KNIGHT *What will you do?*

ARLEQUIN We'll play a round of bocce.[27]

KNIGHT *Drop your buffoonery and let's see if you have as much strength in your arm as your tongue has insolence!*

(*The drums and trumpets start to sound again, Arlequin, the Doctor, and Scaramouche take up their weapons, fight, and are defeated.*)

A KNIGHT (*to Arlequin who is on the ground*) *Surrender or die.*

ARLEQUIN Ah! Discourteous knight! Thou hast slain me.

THE KNIGHT *Renounce your love for Eularia, Isabelle, and Colombine.*

90 ARLEQUIN *I renounce* Eularia, Isabelle, Colombine, the dog, the cat, the fleas, the bedbugs. and the whole Family.

ANOTHER KNIGHT (*comes up and says to Arlequin*) *Cowardly knight, take Colombina freely; it's enough for me to have won her.*

(And the Comedy ends.)

ARLEQUIN'S SONG (To the tune of *Green Youth*)

A Captain says to ARLEQUIN.

95
> Put us, I beg you
> In a secret place,
> No cheating
> Don't pry into my business:
> Without fear, I do love her,
> And am cherished by her;
100
> Leave us alone,
>
> I am her Husband.
> We need a soup,

---

[26] Gascons were soldiers or courtiers from the region of Gascony. The term 'Gascon' evoked the brutish manners and horseplay that purportedly held sway at the court of King Henry IV, who surrounded himself with allies from that region during his reign. Arlequin suggests ironically that these knights do not respect honour and refinement in ritual combat.

[27] An Italian game somewhat like lawn bowling.

With a Capon on it,
And in the cup
105   Wine of the best vintage,
And this rack
of Calf, well-roasted,
Which, in your kitchen,
I chose.

110   With great riches
This bag is filled
Haphazardly
Do you see? Look here:
Take a handful
115   All that you need;
I'm the Captain,
Lets climb up there quickly.

Boys of Guingustet[28],
Take care of us,
120   In perfect joy,
You'll all be happy:
May your Service
To us be given here;
Your reward
125   Will be a great one.

ARLEQUIN *answers the Captain*

Ah! the good Apostle!
Go for it, what a Husband!
Go ask somebody else
about your Rendezvous:
130   With your fancy talk
You only got a Rat;
This is a Wedding
Drawn up without a Contract.

THE END

ANOTHER SONG
From the Italian Stage
They say that young Iris

---

[28]   This appears to be the name of a fictional location.

135
Loves her Thrycis far too much,
It's just a cruel rumour:
But they say that in her demeanour
She affects pride
That reaches madness, I think
140
That is the pure truth.

They say that at every moment,
She chases after her Lover,
It's just a cruel rumour;
They say that her impatience
145
To get his affection back,
Drives her to make advances;
That is the pure truth.

They say that her Lover
Is what she thinks about all the time;
150
It's just a cruel rumour:
They say that in his absence
She looks really grumpy,
But not in his presence:
That is the pure truth.

155
They say that to speak to him
She always seems to be in hurry;
It's just a cruel rumour:
Rather, this Beauty gets ahead of herself
And steps on his foot,
160
To get in his good graces:
That's the pure truth.

They say that her rush
To see her Lover
Is beyond belief:
165
But they say that in return,
Her Lover also
Is just as impatient
That's the pure truth.

THE END.

APPENDIX A

Biography of Aphra Behn

Although in the second half of the seventeenth century Aphra Behn was a prolific writer of plays, poems, and fiction, as well as translations and adaptations, few verifiable facts about Behn's personal life are extant. One of the earliest biographies is entitled 'Memoirs on the Life of Mrs. Behn. Written by a Gentlewoman of her Acquaintance', published in 1696 in *The Histories And Novels of the Late Ingenious Mrs Behn*; the collection was reissued and expanded in a third edition in 1698 as *All the Histories and Novels Written by the Late Ingenious Mrs. Behn,* and the memoir retitled 'The History of the Life and Memoirs of Mrs. Behn. Written by one of the Fair Sex'.[1] This biography was probably composed by Charles Gildon, who claimed to have been acquainted with Behn in her lifetime, but how close this association, how much he knew for certain, and whether he enhanced what he did know raises questions for scholars today. Biographers of Behn have noted that Gildon was 'a capable literary hoaxer' and thus it is not unreasonable to assume that he may be the 'one of the fair sex' who wrote the memoir.[2] As Germaine Greer has pointed out, Gildon was a 'ventriloquist and [...] very capable of writing in the imitation of a style [...] The problem of an editor is to decide what is Behn and what is Gildon'.[3]

What seventeenth-century information about Behn that is available, particularly her birth and early life, is minimal, confused, often contested, and generally unreliable. For example, an early note by Anne Finch, Countess of Winchilsea, in a manuscript collection of her poems, claims that Behn was born

---

[1]   *All the Histories and Novels Written by the Late Ingenious M^{rs}. Behn, Entire in One Volume,* 3rd edn (London: for Samuel Briscoe, 1698), pp. 1–60. Unless otherwise noted, we have used this expanded version here.
[2]   George Woodcock, *Aphra Behn, The English Sappho* (1948. Montreal: Black Rose Books, 1989), pp. 11–12. See also Maureen Duffy, *The Passionate Shepherdess: Aphra Behn 1640–1689* (1977. London: Phoenix Press, 1989), pp. 25–26. Janet Todd argues that the expanded biography and the accompanying letters in the third edition of *All the Histories and Novels* may have been by anyone, including Gildon, Samuel Briscoe, or any of Behn's female friends; Todd, *Secret Life,* p. 12.
[3]   Germaine Greer, 'Roundtable Discussion', in *Aphra Behn (1640–1689) Identity, Alterity, Ambiguity,* ed. by Mary Ann O'Donnell, Bernard Dhuicq, and Guyonne Leduc (Paris: L'Harmattan, 2000), pp. 277–93 (p. 292).

in Kent and was the daughter of a barber who lived in Wye.[4] But this note has been called into question. Vita [Victoria] Sackville-West, George Woodcock, and more recently Maureen Duffy suggest that the Countess of Winchilsea wrote the note, but Angeline Goreau disputes this, claiming the note was written by the English poet and literary critic Edmund Gosse.[5] Janet Todd suggests that the note is in Finch's handwriting, but since, as Finch admits, the information came to her second hand, it may not be reliable.[6]

According to the 'History of the Life and Memoirs', Behn was

> a Gentlewoman, by Birth, of a good Family in the City of *Canterbury*, in *Kent*; her paternal Name was *Johnson*, whose Relation to the Lord *Willoughby*, drew him [her father] for the advantageous Post of Lieutenant-General of many Isles, besides the Continent of *Surinam*, from his quiet Retreat at *Canterbury*, to run the hazardous Voyage of the *West-Indies*. (2)

A note by Thomas Culpepper, son of Sir Thomas Culpepper and Dame Barbara [Sydney], written in his manuscript *Adversaria*, observes that Behn's family name was Johnson, that the family came from the Canterbury area, and that Behn's mother was Culpepper's wet nurse.[7] Duffy suggests that if these early assumptions are correct, Behn's father was probably Bartholomew Johnson, a member of the local gentry.[8] Todd objects to the notion that Johnson was of the gentry, claiming he was a barber.[9]

Goreau posits that Aphra Behn may have been an illegitimate child, perhaps of the Willoughby family, and given to the Johnsons to raise as their own; her father's connection to the Willoughby family may have been why he was appointed Lieutenant General of Surinam.[10] Both Woodcock and Goreau find support for such a connection from a note in a nineteenth-century text which states that Lord Willoughby 'deputed a relation of his named Johnson' to be governor of the colony (of Surinam), and that Johnson took with him his wife and family and 'an adopted daughter' whose name was given as Afra or Aphra Johnson.[11] And, finally, in a brief account of Behn that prefaces her play *The Younger Brother*, Charles Gildon notes that 'Her Maiden Name was *Johnson*, her

---

[4] Todd notes that this manuscript collection is in the Folger Shakespeare Library in Washington, DC; Todd, *Secret Life*, p. 437 n. 10.

[5] V. Sackville-West, *Aphra Behn: The Incomparable Astrea* (1927. New York: Viking Press, 1928), pp. 19–20; Woodcock, p. 13; Duffy, pp. 24–25; Angeline Goreau, *Reconstructing Aphra: A Social Biography of Aphra Behn* (Oxford: Oxford University Press, 1980), p. 9.

[6] Todd, *Secret Life*, pp. 12–13.

[7] Duffy, p. 27. Duffy refers to British Library Harley MS 7587–605, vol. 2.B; Todd, *Secret Life*, pp. 13–14.

[8] Duffy, p. 29. In the introduction to his revised biography on Behn, Woodcock suggests that Duffy was correct in assigning Behn's family name as Johnson, p. xiii.

[9] Todd, *Secret Life*, p. 15.

[10] Goreau, pp. 12–13.

[11] Woodcock, pp. 20–22; Goreau, pp. 12–13; see also Duffy on Behn's origins, pp. 23–31.

father was a Gentleman of a good Family in *Canterbury* in *Kent*'.[12]

Behn's birth and early history, then, can only be conjectured. General consensus gives her a birthdate around 1640, and most of her biographers put her shipboard and bound for Surinam in August of 1663. However, if Gildon's 'Account' is to be believed, that Behn went there when 'she was very Young [...] with her Father, Mother, Brother and Sisters',[13] and if she had been born in 1640, then she would have been twenty-three years old when she left for Surinam and therefore not so 'very young' as Gildon claims. Todd offers a number of solutions to this disparity, including, for example, that Behn's travels in Surinam may have begun much earlier and that Behn was there on a Royal assignment; that she may have travelled there as an 'indentured servant like the Widdow Ranter'; or that she travelled to Surinam as someone's mistress and the comment about her being very young was a cover to hide her disgrace; or, perhaps that she travelled there with a number of more 'socially elevated ladies than herself'.[14] For Behn's father to have been appointed to such a high position in Surinam, her family must have had some connection to a family of privilege. Duffy suggests that it is more likely that Behn's father went to Surinam as a planter, since Willoughby had put forward a call for planters for his new plantations in Surinam, and that Behn's father was more likely appointed captain general.[15]

Todd proposes that the story of Behn's father's appointment and his death on the journey to Surinam is fiction and simply drawn from Behn's own novel, *Oroonoko: Or, The Royal Slave* (1688).[16] Behn does record in *Oroonoko* that her father was appointed 'Lieutenant-General of Six and thirty Islands, besides the Continent of *Surinam*'; however, she adds, 'My stay was to be short in that Country, because my Father dy'd at Sea [...], so that though we were oblig'd to continue on our Voyage, we did not intend to stay upon the Place', but to live in Surinam until return passage could be arranged.[17] While it remains unclear, then, under what circumstances Behn may have travelled to Surinam, what did apparently occur there was a brief flirtation with William Scot, a conclusion drawn from a note about 'Astrea' in a letter from William Byam to Sir Robert Harley. Byam notes that 'Celedon', possibly a clandestine name for Scot, had been courting 'Astrea', a code name later used by Behn in her espionage mission for Charles II. Byam records having put the fair shepherdess on a ship bound for England, much to her discontent.[18]

[12]   Charles Gildon, 'An Account of the Life of the Incomparable Mrs. BEHN', in *The Younger Brother: Or, The Amorous Jilt* (London: for J. Harris, 1696), unpaginated [pp. 1–3], ([p. 1]).
[13]   Gildon, 'Account of the Life', [p. 1].
[14]   See Todd, 'General Introduction', *Works*, ed. by Todd, I, pp. ix–xxxv (p. xvi).
[15]   Duffy, p. 40.
[16]   Todd, *Secret Life*, pp. 39–40.
[17]   Behn, *Oroonoko: Or, The Royal Slave. A True History* (London: for William Canning, 1688), pp. 148–49.
[18]   Duffy, pp. 51–52; Goreau, pp. 68–69; Todd, *Secret Life*, p. 66.

Behn's Surinam association with Scot is an important one, because the next piece of information about Behn comes from her espionage mission during the Second Dutch War (1665–1667). Using the code name Astrea, she was sent to Antwerp in 1666 to contact William Scot, the man she had met in Surinam, who claimed to have information about the Dutch, including pro-Dutch sympathisers in England who were plotting rebellion. Scot had indicated his interest in divulging his knowledge about the Dutch in return for a pardon. How or why she was chosen for the mission is unclear, but she must have been in communication at least initially with men like Henry Bennet, Earl of Arlington (1618–1685), who was Secretary of State, or Thomas Killigrew (1612–1683), Groom of the King's Bedchamber, to whom she wrote letters while abroad. Goreau claims it was Thomas Killigrew 'who introduced her [Behn] to the spying network'.[19]

Behn was indeed on a mission of espionage and she did contact Scot, as nineteen documents are extant in the *State Papers* in regard to this period of her life.[20] In her correspondence with the court, she frequently notes her expenses and requests further financial support to continue her mission, even pawning her jewellery when necessary to ease financial constraints. When she finally received the order to return to England, it came without fare for her passage. Desperate to return, she borrowed funds from one Edward Butler, a debt she could not repay when she returned, nor one the court was apparently eager to undertake. When Butler did not receive repayment of the loan, he had her prosecuted for the debt. Document Ninety in the *Calendar of State Papers* for 1668 is a petition from A. Behn asking for an order to either William Chiffinch (1602–1691), Closet-Keeper to Charles II, or Baptist May (1628–1698), Keeper of the Privy Purse, for payment of the loan to Butler. A second petition, Document Ninety-One in the *Calendar of State Papers* is a petition to the King asking for payment to Butler in the amount of £150.[21] Attached to this second petition is a personal letter addressed to Thomas Killigrew, in which Behn writes that she will send her mother to the King to seek the funds:

> *I must go to prison to-morrow if I have not the money to-night [...] I will send my mother to the King with a petition, and not perish in a prison, whence he [Butler] swears I shall not stir till I have paid the uttermost farthing. If I have not the money to-night you must send me something to keep me in prison, for I will not starve.* (127)

Document Ninety-Two notes that Lord Arlington claimed he had neither the

---

[19]   Goreau, pp. 93–94; Todd, 'General Introduction', *Works*, I, p. xvii.
[20]   William James Cameron lists these documents in *New Light on Aphra Behn* (Auckland: University of Auckland, 1961), pp. 34–86.
[21]   For these documents, see the *Calendar of State Papers, Domestic Series, of the Reign of Charles II*, 1668–1669, IX, 127. These documents are listed under undated petitions.

money nor orders regarding Behn's petition, so Butler purportedly 'threw her into prison' (127).

There is no record as to whether Behn was in fact incarcerated, but given the slow process for official accounting and payment, it is not unlikely that Behn found herself behind bars, at least for a short time. Someone eventually paid the debt, however, and some biographers give Thomas Killigrew credit for this.[22] Janet Todd offers the possibility that Killigrew paid the debt on condition Behn return to espionage, this time in Italy.[23] No evidence exists, although much has been conjectured, as to how Behn survived between her release from prison — if she was released in 1668 — and the next two years.[24] What is certain, however, is that Behn was out of prison at least by 1670, when her play *The Forc'd Marriage, or The Jealous Bridegroom* was on the boards at the Duke's Company, and her life as a professional writer commenced.

How or why Behn chose to write for the theatre is as much a question as how or why she engaged in espionage or how she obtained a release from Butler's prosecution. If she did have a relationship of some kind with Thomas Killigrew, who was manager of the King's Company, as some biographers have conjectured, then he may have assisted her with getting her first play on the boards, although the play was produced by William Davenant's Duke's Company. Killigrew would have had difficulty producing Behn's play in his own theatre company since the play satirised Arlington, and Killigrew was married to Arlington's aunt. Perhaps Mary Davenant, Davenant's widow and a female manager in what was clearly a male-dominated sphere, took a sympathetic view of Behn's desire to write for the theatre and supported her work.[25] Whatever the case, Behn's plays largely continued to be produced by the Duke's Company.

If the information about Behn's early years is largely a collection of bits and pieces gleaned from notes, letters, and documents, which in themselves are sometimes vague or incomplete, her life for the following 19 years, from her first produced play in 1670 until her death in 1689, is just as obscure. Biographers have largely assembled their views of the life of this indefatigable woman through the plays, poems, novels, and translations that have been attributed to her, where Behn comments on a number of issues, such as the reception of her work, her audience's general interest in the theatre, and her male colleagues. In the prologue to her first play, *The Forc'd Marriage, or The Jealous Bridegroom* (1671), for example, she acknowledges — albeit playfully — the challenge to male playwrights of a woman writing for the theatre:

---

[22]   Sackville-West, p. 81; Woodcock, p. 44; Duffy, p. 100; Frederick M. Link, *Aphra Behn* (New York: Twayne Publishers, 1968), p. 21.

[23]   Todd, *Secret Life*, p. 119.

[24]   Woodcock, pp. 45–48.

[25]   Hayden, *Of Love and War*, pp. 9–12.

> To day one of their party ventures out,
> [...]
> Discourage but this first attempt, and then,
> They'le hardly dare to sally out again.[26]

Behn on occasion remarks on her personal life — although what and how much Behn offers there should be weighed cautiously, as the projection of a professional persona, particularly a woman's, had to be carefully constructed. She does reveal on occasion more personal fragments of her life, although whether these are genuine snippets or simply the persona of the textual speaker/ narrator is questionable. For example, in The History of the Nun: or, The Fair Vow-Breaker (1689), she confides that she, too, at one point was

> design'd an humble Votary in the House of Devotion, but fancying my self not endu'd with an obstinacy of Mind, great enough to secure me from the Efforts and Vanities of the World, I rather chose to deny my self that Content [...] I have sufficiently bewailed that mistaken and inconsiderate Approbation and Preference of the false ungrateful World.[27]

That her gender was an issue for a number of her male colleagues — as well as some of her female audiences — and that it continued to be an issue throughout her career, Behn observes in her preface to The Dutch Lover. This play, which failed dismally, was sabotaged, she claims, not only by the actors intentionally failing to repeat their lines correctly, but also by the critics, particularly the 'long, lither, phlegmatick, white, ill-favour'd, wretched Fop' who announced that the audience should 'expect a woful Play' because 'it was a womans'.[28] In the epilogue to Sir Patient Fancy (1678), Behn points out 'I Here, and there, o'reheard a Coxcomb Cry | Ah, Rott it — 'tis a Womans Comedy'.[29] But why, she asks, must gender determine intellect? Why should these be mutually exclusive? '[P]ray tell me then | Why Women should not write as well as Men' (ll. 43–44).

Behn reveals a serious decline in her health toward the end of her life in her elegy to Edmund Waller, writing 'I, who by Toils of Sickness, am become | Almost as near as thou art to a Tomb'.[30] In her translation of Bernard le Bovier de Fontenelle's Entretiens sur la pluralité des mondes, Behn notes that she had difficulty deciding whether simply to translate Fontenelle's text into English or to revise it completely. Although she declares that she had the intellectual

---

[26]   Behn, 'Prologue', The Forc'd Marriage, or The Jealous Bridegroom (London: for James Magnus, 1671), unpaginated [pp. 1–2], ([p. 1]).
[27]   Behn, The History of the Nun: or, The Fair Vow-Breaker (London: for A. Baskerville, 1689), p. 6.
[28]   Behn, 'Preface', The Dutch Lover, [p. 6].
[29]   Behn, 'Epilogue', Sir Patient Fancy, [p. 92].
[30]   Behn, 'On the Death of E. Waller, Esq;', in Poems To The Memory Of that Incomparable Poet Edmond Waller Esquire (London: for Joseph Knight and Francis Saunders, 1688), pp. 17–20 (p. 17, ll. 3–4).

understanding to provide a book *'made my own'*, she points out candidly that she had *'neither health nor leisure'* and so provided the 'French *Book into English'*.[31] And in the dedication to George Greenviel of her story *The Lucky Mistake* (1689), Behn observes that she dedicates this work to him because her *'increasing Indisposition makes me fear I shall not have many opportunities of this Kind, and shou'd be loath to leave this ungrateful World, without acknowledging my Gratitude more signally then [sic] barely by word of Mouth'*.[32]

In the last years of her life, Behn began to write fewer plays and turned to prose and translations. This may have had much to do with the state of the theatre. In a letter to her publisher Jacob Tonson (1655–1736) of 1684, Behn writes that she could no longer support herself with plays as audience interest had greatly declined.[33] The amalgamation of the two main acting companies as the one United Company in 1682 meant there was less opportunity for the production of new plays, and this remained the case from 1682 until after Behn's death.

A further arrest and possible imprisonment may also have discouraged Behn's playwriting. In August 1682, a warrant was issued for the arrest of Behn and Mary Lee, Lady Slingsby.[34] Behn had written both the prologue and epilogue to the play *Romulus and Hersilia* (1683), and the lines spoken in the epilogue by Lady Slingsby proved troublesome.

> And of all Treasons, mine was most accurst;
> Rebelling 'gainst a King and Father first.
> A Sin, which Heav'n nor Man can e're forgive.[35]

This was perceived as an attack on James Scott, Duke of Monmouth, the illegitimate son of Charles II, whose ambition it was to replace the Catholic heir, James, Duke of York, in the line of succession. There is no proof that Behn was actually imprisoned on this occasion, and the play and the offending lines were subsequently published, but certainly such an arrest may have caused her some hesitation about further dramatic production.

Behn's intimate friendships are also obscure. That she may have married has often been conjectured, but no records have been found to substantiate this.

---

[31] Behn, 'The Translator's Preface', in *A Discovery of New Worlds*, unpaginated [pp. 1–26], ([p. 26]).

[32] Behn, 'To George Greenviel, *Esq*;', in *The Lucky Mistake: A New Novel* (London: for R. Bentley, 1689), unpaginated [pp. 1–6], ([p. 5]). This was probably George Granville, Lord Lansdowne (1666–1735).

[33] *The Literary Correspondence of the Tonsons*, ed. by Stephen Bernard (Oxford: Oxford University Press, 2015), p. 86.

[34] The notice of the order is printed in *The True Protestant Mercury, or Occurrences Foreign and Domestic*. See Mary Ann O'Donnell, *Aphra Behn: An Annotated Bibliography of Primary and Secondary Sources*, 2nd edn (1986. Burlington, VT: Ashgate, 2004), p. 299 n. 11.

[35] Aphra Behn, 'Epilogue', *Romulus and Hersilia; or, The Sabine War* (London: for D. Brown and T. Benskin, 1683), unpaginated [pp. 63–64], ([p. 63], ll. 7–9).

Many biographers, including Gildon, have concluded that on Behn's return to England from Surinam she married a Dutch merchant, one Mr Behn, who probably died during the plague which ravaged London between 1664 and 1666.[36] No records of such a marriage nor the death of Mr Behn have surfaced, nor should the intimate love letters included in the *Histories and Novels* be assumed to have been composed by Behn, particularly given the nature of the editor. While there are suggestions of romantic dalliances with William Scot in Surinam and possibly two young London lawyers, Jeffrey Boys and John Hoyle, we are given hints rather than proofs.

On the other hand, if we allow the speaker of Behn's poems to speak for the poet herself, which is always a tenuous practice at best, then her poems do present an interesting account of her personal, romantic life. She did, for example, write poems to one J.H., including, 'A Ballad *on Mr. J.H. to* Amoret', in which the speaker claims she fought to guard her heart from Amyntas but was 'intirely won and lost', and in her poem 'On Mr. J.H. *In a Fit of Sickness*', the speaker begs Amyntas 'In Pity to *Astrea* live'.[37] In a poem to 'Lysander', however, the speaker claims she was overwhelmed by both music and the lover's charms, for 'When from so many ways Loves Arrows storm, | Who can the heedless Heart defend from harm?'[38] To create a tangled relationship between the poet, the speaker of poems, and a character *in* the poems, however, can be problematic since the speaker is often a persona adopted by the poet and does not necessarily reveal the true poet him- or herself. Certainly suggestions can be found from contemporaries who link her with 'a Gray's Inn lawyer'. There is little doubt that there was indeed some relationship between Behn and a lawyer, ostensibly John Hoyle, but if she did have an intimate relationship with Hoyle, it evidently came to little since the relationship deteriorated and Hoyle chose to recognise his homosexual desires over his heterosexual ones.[39]

Toward the end of her life, Behn witnessed tremendous political turmoil brought about by the death of her beloved Charles II in February 1685, followed by the ascendancy of the Catholic James II, and finally the change in monarchy with the Glorious Revolution in 1688, which saw the invasion of William of Orange and the departure of James II for France. Always a staunch champion of the Stuart monarchy, Behn had to have been distraught with this sudden turn

[36] Gildon, 'Account of the Life', [p.1]; Sackville-West, pp. 54–55; Woodcock, pp. 28–29; Link, p. 21; Duffy, pp. 56–59; Goreau, pp. 84–86; Todd, *Secret Life*, pp. 67–71.

[37] 'A Ballad *on Mr.* J.H. *to* Amoret, *asking why I was so sad*', in *Poems Upon Several Occasions* (London: for R. Tonson and J. Tonson, 1684), pp. 29–32 (p. 32); and 'On Mr. J.H. *In a Fit of Sickness*', pp. 106–09, (p. 108).

[38] 'To Lysander *at the* Musick-Meeting', in *Poems Upon Several Occasions*, pp. 118–20 (p. 119).

[39] Sackville-West, pp. 96–97; Woodcock, pp. 113–15; Duffy, pp. 191–94; Goreau, pp. 189–206; Todd, *Secret Life*, p. 342.

of political events. Although Gilbert Burnet, one of those who invited William to intervene in England's political affairs and take the throne of England, had asked Behn to write a congratulatory poem on the new monarchy, Behn did not. Instead, she penned a Pindaric to Burnet, explaining her refusal:

> What must I suffer when I cannot pay
> Your Goodness, your own generous way?
> And make my stubborn Muse your Just Commands obey.
> [...]
> But Loyalty Commands with Pious Force,
> That stops me in the thriving Course.[40]

Behn remained loyal to the ousted James II, demonstrating her loyalty in the poem she wrote for the new queen — praise of Mary as the *daughter* of James II.[41]

> Yet if with Sighs we View that Lovely Face,
> And all the Lines of your great Father's Trace,
> [...]
> But if the *Monarch* in your Looks we find,
> Behold him yet more glorious in your Mind.

Behn spent the last years of her life ill, in pain, and mostly in debt. In a 1684 letter to Jacob Tonson, Behn requests an additional payment of five pounds for her collection of poems, *Poems upon Several Occasions*, noting that she had been 'without getting so long that I am just on the poynt of breaking'.[42] She ends her letter with 'I want extreamly or I wo'd not urge this'. As Charles Gildon observes in his account of Behn, 'she was too great a favourite of Nature, to have many obligations to fortune; at least the latter part of her Life found her Circumstances much below her Desert', and thus she succumbed in 1689, 'after a tedious Sickness'.[43] She was buried in the cloisters of Westminster Abbey. The epitaph on her grave, which reads in part 'Here lies a Proof that Wit can never be | Defence enough against Mortality', has been attributed to John Hoyle.[44]

Behn endured tremendous difficulty in becoming a female professional writer at a time when women writers were often vilified as whores, for to publish — and certainly to write plays for the public theatre — was to become

---

[40] Behn, *A Pindaric Poem to the* Reverend Doctor Burnet *On The Honour he did me of Enquiring after me and my MUSE* (London: for R. Bentley to be sold by Richard Baldwin, 1689), sigs A3–A3v, stanza 4.

[41] Behn, *A Congratulatory Poem to Her Sacred Majesty Queen Mary, Upon Her Arrival in England* (London: for R. Bentley and W. Canning, 1689), p. 5.

[42] *Literary Correspondence of the Tonsons*, p. 86.

[43] Gildon, 'Account of the Life', [p. 3].

[44] Sackville-West, pp. 127–28; Woodcock, pp. 212–13; Duffy, p. 294; Goreau, p. 292; Todd, *Secret Life*, p. 435.

a 'public' woman, a prostitute.[45] Furthermore, women's public speaking, and/ or writing was viewed as usurping masculine authority and privilege, so that women writers often endured resentment, if not open hostility.

For centuries, Behn's legacy was the subject of intense and negative criticism, as critics disparaged her work for its indecency; for example, an entry for Behn in *Biographia Britannica* asserted that her comedies contained lewd scenes and expressions,[46] while an anonymous writer in *Blackwood's Edinburgh Magazine* claimed that her 'Plays [...] rushed down from that polluted pen like the contents of a sewer after rain'.[47] On occasion, however, such negativity was countered by those few who recognized Behn's skill and talent. 'Mrs Behn suffered enough at the hands of supercilious prudes, who had the barbarity to construe her sprightliness into lewdness; and because she had wit and beauty, she must likewise be charged with prostitution and irreligion.'[48]

Behn was also frequently charged with plagiarism. The author of a review of a reprint of Behn's *Plays, Histories and Novels* in *The Athenaeum* claimed that 'Mrs. Behn's plays are stolen [...] she carries off what suits her purpose'.[49] The outcome of such accusations led to Behn's works being neither read nor studied. Eventually, as Sackville-West noted, 'She ceased to arouse either an exaggerated partisanship or a jealous hostility; she took her place finally among those effigies of literature, known to all, and read by none'.[50] Fortunately, this is today no longer the case. Aphra Behn's writing is read and studied with enthusiasm, and while she was not the first female writer in England to have a play produced on the public stage, she was (to the best of scholarly knowledge) the first professional female writer in England.

For a woman in seventeenth-century England to engage in a career as a professional writer was not only unconventional, but an extraordinary feat, inconceivable and certainly shocking. Behn achieved a remarkable literary

---

[45] A few examples to explore are Maura Smyth, *Women Writing Fancy: Authorship and Autonomy from 1611–1812* (New York: Palgrave, 2017); *The History of British Women's Writing 1610–1690*, ed. by Mihoko Suzuki (New York: Palgrave Macmillan, 2011); Hayden, *Of Love and War* (2010), particularly pp. 194–201; Pamela Allen Brown, *Better a Shrew than a Sheep: Women, Drama and the Culture of Jest in Early Modern England* (New York: Cornell, 2003); *Women, Texts, and Histories 1575–1750*, ed. by Clare Brant and Diane Purkiss (New York: Routledge, 1992); and Janet Todd, *Sign of Angellica: Women, Writing and Fiction, 1660–1800* (London: Virago, 1987).

[46] *Biographia Britannica: Or, The Lives Of The Most Eminent Persons Who Have Flourished In Great Britain and Ireland*, ed. by Andrew Kippis and others, 5 vols, 2nd edn (London: W. and A. Strahan,1778–1793), II, ed. by Kippis (1780), pp. 141–46 (p. 146).

[47] 'Biographia Dramatica', in *Blackwood's Edinburgh Magazine*, 89 (Feb. 1861), pp. 218–35 (p. 230).

[48] Robert Shiells [with additions and revisions by Theophilus Cibber], *The Lives of the Poets of Great Britain and Ireland*, 5 vols (London: for R. Griffiths, 1753), III, pp. 17–29 (p. 27).

[49] *The Athenaeum* (9 March 1872), pp. 201–303 (p. 302).

[50] Sackville-West, p. 135.

output for any writer of her historical period, be it male or female. As Samuel Briscoe noted in Behn's posthumously printed story *The Unfortunate Bride: or, The Blind Lady a Beauty*, 'all the Men of Wit, that were her Contemporaries, look'd on [Behn] as the Wonder of her Sex'.[51]

[51] S. Briscoe, 'To Richard Norton, of *Southwick* in *Hantshire*, Esquire', in Aphra Behn, *The Unfortunate Bride: or, The Blind Lady a Beauty* (London: for Samuel Briscoe, 1698), p. 2.

APPENDIX B

Biography of Anne Mauduit de Fatouville

Little is known about Anne Mauduit de Fatouville, the likely author of the French scenes in *Arlequin, Empereur dans la lune*. His date of birth is unknown, although he is thought to have died on 2 September 1715.[1] The majority of the biographical information on Fatouville is based on archival research carried out by Giacomo Cavallucci, whose findings were published in an influential article in 1936. Cavallucci concluded that Anne Mauduit, who held the titles of Lord of Fatouville and La Bataille, was both a magistrate and an author of French scenes for the Italian actors, the *comédiens italiens*. He also served as counsellor at the *Cour des Aides* in the city of Rouen. As Cavallucci discovered, previous mentions of the author had mistakenly referred to him as 'Nollent de Fatouville', confusing him with a someone else from a different Norman family.[2]

Fatouville is best known for the French scenes he wrote for the Italian theatre, the *Hôtel de Bourgogne*, in Paris between 1681 and 1692. He was the first major French collaborator with the Italian troupe, and the only French author working with them during the period between 1681 and 1687.[3] When 'the Locatelli-Fiorilli troupe began to play in Paris in 1653', they were very popular in what was an 'Italianate court'.[4] Although this group of actors was successful and became a permanent fixture in Paris by 1660, their material was less accessible to a French-speaking audience. After the troupe took over the *Hôtel de Bourgogne* in 1680, they began to experiment with performances in French, as they aspired to increase audience attendance and 'to support a full production schedule'.[5]

Why Fatouville was the person they chose is unclear; however, in addition to providing scenes in French for the *comédiens italiens*, Fatouville also

[1] *Théâtre du XVIIe siècle*, ed. by Jacques Sherer and others (Paris: Gallimard, 1975–1992), vol. 3, ed. by Jacques Truchet and André Blanc (1992), pp. 1113–14.
[2] Giacomo Cavallucci, 'Fatouville, auteur dramatique', *Revue d'Histoire littéraire de la France*, 43e.4 (1936), 481–512 (p. 512).
[3] Charles Mazouer, *Le Théâtre d'Arlequin: Comédies et comédiens en France au XVIIe siècle* (Fasano et Paris: Schena editore et Presses de l'Université de Paris-Sorbonne, 2002), p. 163.
[4] Virginia Scott, 'The *Jeu* and the *Rôle*: Analysis of the Appeals of the Italian Comedy in France in the Time of Arlequin-Dominique', in *Western Popular Theatre*, ed. by David Mayer and Kenneth Richards (London: Methuen, 1977), pp. 1–27 (p. 3).
[5] Scott, 'The *Jeu* and the *Rôle*', p. 5.

wrote three comedies and scenes for a fourth between 1688 and 1692.[6] In Évariste Gherardi's six-volume collection of scenes, a short, ambiguous note of attribution precedes those scenes ascribed to Fatouville: 'mise au théâtre par Monsieur D***' [Staged by Monsieur D***]. Although the name 'Fatouville' does not appear in association with the published versions of the French scenes in Gherardi's collection, he may nevertheless have contributed scenes to more than a dozen performances. According to Cavallucci, the use of the letter D indicates attribution to Fatouville because he likely used the pseudonym Darennes for his theatrical writing.[7]

In his *Mémoires*, the Abbé Louis Le Gendre, a canon of Notre Dame (1655–1733), offers a description of Fatouville:

M. de Fantouville [*sic*] [...] a voluptuary who was overwhelmed with property and came to squander it in Paris [...] he and his patron with others of their society made the French scenes for the Comédie-Italienne.[8]

Scott observes that while this piece from Le Gendre confirms that Fatouville wrote for the *Comédie-Italienne*, it does not connect him to the Monsieur D***, who Gherardi notes authored so many of the French scenes and plays in his collection. Scott lists several people who could have been in some way connected to Monsieur D***, either as collaborator, co-author, or even author. On the other hand, the French theatre historian Jean-Nicolas de Tralage (*c*. 1640–*c*. 1720) observed in 1690 that the author of the French scenes in *Arlequin Jason* was Fatouville, a text Gherardi attributes to Monsieur D***.[9]

In May 1697, Louis XIV closed the *Comédie Italienne* and banned the players from Paris, purportedly based on a claim by Françoise d'Aubigné, Marquise de Maintenon (1635–1719) that one of their plays, *La Fausse Prude*, presented her in a derogatory light.[10] A number of scholars, however, have suggested that there was more behind the banning of the *comédiens italiens* of the *Hôtel de Bourgogne* than this. William Brooks claims that there were internal disputes among the troupe, which created a 'disruptive influence' within the Paris theatre scene in general, that the troupe's plays had become more indecent and offensive, and that the players were being sued by the *Comédie-Française* for infringement of their monopoly.[11] It is unlikely that the King would have dismissed the Italian players for a 'single misdemeanor'.[12] Bent Holm suggests that the expulsion came at a time when the King was becoming more devout

---

6 Mazouer, p. 163.
7 Cavallucci, p. 512.
8 Scott, *The Commedia dell'Arte in Paris*, pp. 280–81.
9 Truchet and Blanc, *Théâtre du XVII* siècle*, III, p. 1114
10 Scott, *The Commedia Dell'Arte in Paris*, p. 281.
11 William Brooks, 'Louis XIV's Dismissal of the Italian Actors: The Episode of *La Fausse Prude*', *Modern Language Review*, 91 (1996), 840–47 (p. 842).
12 Brooks, p. 841.

and 'prohibition of theatre was being hotly debated', not least owing to Bishop Jacques-Bénigne Lignel Bossuet (1627–1704), who had the King's favour and who preached at court; Bossuet, who argued against all theatre, claiming theatre performances were repugnant, had 'a zealous advocate' in the King, but 'in the end, only the Italians were sacrificed'.[13]

Fatouville appears to have quit writing for the theatre in 1692, but the reasons are unclear. It may have been owing to turmoil within the troupe, or that the King's symbolic identity was shifting toward 'a divine figure [...] where his only model is the Christian God'.[14] Certainly, once the *Comédie-Italienne* was banned from Paris, Fatouville would have found himself in much the same situation as Behn when the two public theatres in London united — without an active and vibrant market for his work. He would not have been welcomed by the French theatre since he was apparently so integral to the Italian one and since the French had spent so much effort in trying to discredit, if not destroy, the Italian theatre.

Whatever the reason, in 1692 Monsieur D*** appears to have ended his playwrighting career.

[13] Bent Holm, 'Picture and Counter-Picture: An Attempt to Involve Context in the Interpretation of Théâtre Italien Iconography', *Theatre Research International*, 22.3 (1997), 219–33 (p. 226).
[14] Holm, p. 226.

BIBLIOGRAPHY

Primary Texts

All the Histories and Novels Written by the Late Ingenious Mrs. Behn, Entire in One Volume, 3rd edn (London: for Samuel Briscoe, 1698)

BEHN, APHRA, *The Dutch Lover: A Comedy* (London: for Thomas Dring, 1673)

—— *Sir Patient Fancy: A Comedy* (London: for Richard Tonson and Jacob Tonson, 1678)

—— *The Feign'd Curtizans, or, A Night's Intrigue* (London: for Jacob Tonson, 1679)

—— *The Second Part of The Rover* (London: for Jacob Tonson, 1681)

—— 'Epilogue', *Romulus and Hersilia; Or, the Sabine War* (London: for D. Brown and T. Benskin, 1683)

—— *Love-Letters Between a Noble-Man And his Sister* (London: for Randal Taylor, 1684)

—— *Poems Upon Several Occasions: With A Voyage To The Island of Love* (London: for R. Tonson and J. Tonson, 1684)

—— *The Emperor of the Moon: A Farce. As it is acted by Their Majesty's Servants in the Queens Theatre* (London: for Joseph Knight and Francis Saunders, 1687)

—— *The Luckey Chance, Or An Alderman's Bargain* (London: for W. Canning, 1687)

—— *Agnes de Castro: or, The Force of Generous Love* (London: for William Canning, 1688)

—— *A Discovery of New Worlds. From the French. Made English by Mrs. A. Behn* (London: for William Canning, 1688)

—— *On the Death of* E. Waller, Esq;', in *Poems To The Memory Of that Incomparable Poet Edmond Waller Esquire* (London: for Joseph Knight and Francis Saunders, 1688)

—— *Oroonoko: Or, The Royal Slave. A True History* (London: for William Canning, 1688)

—— *A Congratulatory Poem to Her Sacred Majesty Queen Mary, Upon Her Arrival in England* (London: for R. Bentley and W. Canning, 1689

—— *The History of the Nun: Or, the Fair Vow-Breaker* (London: for A. Baskerville, 1689)

—— *The Lucky Mistake: A New Novel* (London: for R. Bentley, 1689)

—— *A Pindaric Poem to the* Reverend Doctor *Burnet On The Honour he did me of Enquiring after me and my Muse* (London: for R. Bentley, 1689)

—— *The Younger Brother: Or, The Amorous Jilt* (London: for J. Harris, 1696)

—— *The Unfortunate Bride; Or, The Blind Lady a Beauty* (London: for Samuel Briscoe, 1698)

—— *The Works of Aphra Behn*, ed. by Janet Todd, 7 vols (Columbus: Ohio State University Press, 1992–1996)

BERGERAC, SAVINIEN CYRANO DE, *Histoire comique des états et empires de la lune et du soleil* (Paris, 1657), trans. by A. Lovell as *The Comical History of the States and Empires of the Worlds of the Moon and Sun* (London: for Henry Rhodes, 1687)

BULSTRODE, RICHARD, *The Bulstrode Papers*, formed by Alfred Morrison, 1667–1675 (Printed for Private Circulation, 1897)

Calendar of State Papers, Domestic Series, in the Reign of Charles II

CAWDREY, ROBERT, *A Table Alphabeticall* (1604), rpr. as *The First English Dictionary*, intro. by John Simpson (Oxford: Bodleian Library, 2007)

COLES, ELISHA, *A Dictionary, English-Latin and Latin-English* (London: for Peter Parker, 1677)

CROWNE, JOHN, *The Dramatic Works of John Crowne*, ed. by James Maidment and William Hugh Logan, 4 vols (Edinburgh: William Paterson, 1873–1874)

DAY, JOHN and OTHERS, *The Travails of the three English Brothers* (London: for John Wright, 1607)

DRYDEN, JOHN, *The Works of John Dryden*, gen. eds Edward Niles Hooker and H. T. Swedenberg Jr, and Vinton A. Dearing, 20 vols (Berkeley: University of California Press, 1956–2000)

ERASMUS, DESIDERIUS, *In Praise of Folly* (1511), trans. by Betty Radice, with an introduction and notes by A. H. T. Levi (London: Penguin, 1993)

EVELYN, JOHN, *Diary of John Evelyn*, ed. by E. S. De Beer, 6 vols (Oxford: Clarendon, 1955)

FATOUVILLE, ANNE MAUDUIT DE, *Arlequin, Empereur dans la lune. Comédie* (A Troyes: Chez Garnier Imprimeur Libraire, rue du Temple, n.d.)

GALILEI, GALILEO, *Sidereus Nuncius, or The Sidereal Messenger*, trans. with introduction, conclusion, and notes by Albert Van Helden (Chicago: University of Chicago Press, 1989)

GODWIN, FRANCIS, *The Man in the Moone*, ed. by William Poole (Peterborough, Ontario: Broadview Press, 2009)

HOOKE, JACOB, *Pinacotheca Bettertonœana: Or, A Catalogue of the Books, Drawings, Prints, and Paintings of Mr. Thomas Betterton, that Celebrated Comedian, lately Deceased* (1710), ed. by David Roberts (rpr. London: Society for Theatre Research, 2013)

The Literary Correspondence of the Tonsons, ed. by Stephen Bernard (Oxford: Oxford University Press, 2015)

LUCIAN OF SAMOSATA, *Certain Select Dialogues of Lucian: Together with his True History*, trans. by Francis Hickes (London: for Richard Davis, 1663)

MARVELL, ANDREW, *The Poems and Letters of Andrew Marvell*, ed. by H. M. Margoliouth, 2 vols, 3rd edn (Oxford: Clarendon, 1971)

MOLIÈRE [JEAN-BAPTISTE POQUELIN], *Le Tartuffe*, ed. by Jean Serroy (1664. Paris: Gallimard, 1997)

NASHE, THOMAS, *Pierce Penilesse his Supplication to the* Diuell (London: by Richard Jhones, 1592)

OTWAY, THOMAS, *The Works of Thomas Otway*, ed. by Montague Summers, 3 vols (Bloomsbury: The Nonesuch Press, 1926)

PEPYS, SAMUEL, *The Diary of Samuel Pepys*, ed. by William Matthews and Robert Lathan, 11 vols (Berkeley: University of California Press, 1970–1983)

PHILLIPS, EDWARD, *The New World of Words: or, A Universal English Dictionary* (London, 1696)

RABELAIS, FRANÇOIS, *Gargantua*, in *Œuvres completes*. Texte établi et annoté par Jacques Boulenger (Paris: Gallimard, 1951), pp. 23–186

SHADWELL, THOMAS, *The Complete Works of Thomas Shadwell*, ed by Montague Summers, 5 vols (London: Fortune Press, 1927)

SPRAT, THOMAS, *History of the Royal Society of London, for the Improving of Natural Knowledge* (London: for J. Martyn and J. Allestry, Printers to the Royal Society, 1667)

Le Théâtre Italien, ou Le Recueil de Toutes les Scènes Françoises, ed. by Evaristo Gherardi (Paris: Chez Guillaume de Luyne, Libraire Juré, au Palais, dans la Salle des Merciers, à la Justice, 1694)

Le Théâtre Italien de Gherardi, ou le Recueil Général de toutes les Comédies et Scènes Françoises jouées par les Comédiens Italiens du Roi, pendant tout le temps qu'ils ont été au Service, ed. by Evaristo Gherardi, 6 vols (Paris: Jean-Bapt. Cusson et Pierre Witte, 1700)

VILLARS, ABBÉ NICOLAS-PIERRE-HENRI DE MONTFAUCON DE, *Le Comte de Gabalis, ou Entretiens sur les sciences secrètes* (Paris 1670), trans. by Philip Ayers as *The Count of Gabalis: Or, The Extravagant Mysteries Of The Cabalists Exposed in Five Pleasant Discourses On The Secret Sciences* (London: for B. M., 1680)

WILKINS, JOHN, *A Discovery Of A New World, Or, A Discourse Tending to prove, that 'tis Probably there may be another Habitable World in the Moon* (London: for John Gillibrand, 1684)

Secondary Texts

ASMUSSEN, SUSAN DWYER, *An Ordered Society: Gender and Class in Early Modern England* (Oxford: Blackwell, 1988)

Aphra Behn (1640–1689): Identity, Alterity, Ambiguity, ed. by Mary Ann O'Donnell and others (Paris: L'Haarmattan, 2000)

BAKHTIN, MIKHAIL, *Rabelais and His World*, trans. by Hélène Iswolsky (Bloomington: Indiana University Press, 1984)

BEHRMANN, ALFRED, 'Aphra Behn's *The Emperor of the Moon*: Anatomy of a "European" Comic Play', *Yearbook of Research in English and American Literature*, 2 (1984), 229–74

A Biographical Dictionary of Actors, Actresses, Musicians, Dancers, Managers & Other Stage Personnel in London, 1660–1800, ed by Philip H. Highfill Jr and others, 16 vols (Carbondale: Southern Illinois University Press, 1973–1993)

BOQUET, GUY, 'Les comédiens italiens à Paris au temps de Louis XIV', *Revue d'histoire moderne et contemporaine*, 26.3 (1979), 422–38

BRAVERMAN, RICHARD, *Plots & Counterplots: Sexual Politics and the Body Politic in English Literature* (Cambridge: Cambridge University Press, 1993)

BROOKS, WILLIAM, 'Louis XIV's Dismissal of the Italian Actors: The Episode of "La Fausse Prude"', *The Modern Language Review*, 91.4 (1996), 840–47

BUCKNELL, PETER A., *Commedia Dell'Arte at the Court of Louis XIV: A Soft Sculpture Representation* (London: Stainer & Bell, 1980)

The Cambridge Companion to Aphra Behn, ed. by Derek Hughes and Janet Todd (Cambridge: Cambridge University Press, 2004)

CAVALLUCCI, GIACOMO, 'Fatouville, auteur dramatique', *Revue d'Histoire littéraire de la France*, 43e.4 (1936), 481–512

CHILTON, MEREDITH, *Harlequin Unmasked: The Commedia dell'Arte and Porcelain Sculpture* (New Haven: Yale University Press, 2002)

COPPOLA, AL, 'Retraining the Virtuoso's Gaze: Behn's *Emperor of the Moon*, The Royal Society, and the Spectacles of Science and Politics', *Eighteenth-Century Studies*, 41.4 (2008), 481–506

COTTIGNIES, LINE, 'Aphra Behn's French Translations', in *The Cambridge Companion to Aphra Behn*, ed. by Derek Hughes and Janet Todd (Cambridge: Cambridge University Press, 2004), 221-34.

DUCHARTE, PIERRE LOUIS, *The Italian Comedy: The Improvisation Scenarios, Lives, Attributes, Portraits and Masks of the Illustrious Characters of the Commedia dell'Arte*, trans. by Randolph T. Weaver (London: George G. Harrap, 1929)

DUFFY, MAUREEN, *The Passionate Shepherdess: Aphra Behn 1640-1689* (1977. London: Phoenix Press, 1989)

FINDLEN, PAULA, 'Between Carnival and Lent: The Scientific Revolution at the Margins of Culture', *Configurations*, 6.2 (1998), 243–67

French Theatre in the Neo-Classical Era, 1550-1789, ed. by William D. Howarth and others (Cambridge: Cambridge University Press, 1997)

GIBSON, WILLIAM, *James II and the Trial of the Seven Bishops* (Basingstoke Hampshire: Palgrave Macmillan, 2009)

GLASSEY, LIONEL K. J., 'Shaftesbury and the Exclusion Crisis', in *Anthony Ashley Cooper, First Earl of Shaftesbury 1621-1683*, ed. by John Spurr (New York: Routledge, 2011), pp. 207-31

GOREAU, ANGELINE, *Reconstructing Aphra: A Social Biography of Aphra Behn* (Oxford: Oxford University Press, 1980)

GRIFFITHS, BRUCE, 'Sunset: From *Commedia dell'Arte* to *Comédie Italienne*', in *Studies in the Commedia dell'Arte*, ed. by David George and Christopher J. Gossip (Cardiff: University of Wales Press, 1993), pp. 91–105

HARRIS, TIM, *Politics Under the Later Stuarts: Party Conflict in a Divided Society 1660-1715* (London: Longman, 1993)

—— *Restoration: Charles II and his Kingdoms 1660-1685* (London: Allen Lane, 2005)

HAYDEN, JUDY A., 'Intersections and Cross-Fertilization', in *Travel Narratives, the New Science, and Literary Discourse 1569-1750*, ed. by Judy A. Hayden (Burlington, VT: Ashgate, 2012)

—— *Of Love and War: The Political Voice in the Early Plays of Aphra Behn* (Amsterdam: Rodopi, 2010)

HENDERSON, KATHERINE USHER, and BARBARA F. MCMANUS, *Half Humankind: Contexts and Texts of the Controversy about Women in England, 1540-1640* (Urbana-Champaign: University of Illinois Press, 1985)

HOLLAND, PETER, 'Farce', in *The Cambridge Companion to English Restoration Literature*, ed. by Deborah Payne Fisk (Cambridge: Cambridge University Press, 2000), pp. 107-26

HOLM, BENT, 'Picture and Counter-Picture: An Attempt to Involve Context in the Interpretation of Théâtre Italien Iconography', *Theatre Research International*, 22.3 (1997), 219-33

HOLMES, GEOFFREY, *The Making of a Great Power: Late Stuart and Early Georgian Britain 1660-1722* (London: Longman, 1993)

HUFF, TOBY E., *Intellectual Curiosity and the Scientific Revolution: A Global Perspective* (Cambridge: Cambridge University Press, 2011)

HUGHES, DEREK, *English Drama 1660-1700* (Oxford: Clarendon Press, 1996)

HUME, ROBERT, 'The Dorset Garden Theatre', *Theatre Notebook*, 36.3 (1982), 99-109

JARDINE, NICHOLAS, 'The Place of Astronomy in Early Modern Culture', *Journal for the History of Astronomy*, 29.1 (1998), 49–62

JORDAN, PETER, *The Venetian Origins of the Commedia dell'Arte* (New York: Routledge, 2014)

KEIL, INGE, 'Johann Wiesel's Telescopes and His Clientele', in *From Earth-Bound to Satellite: Telescopes, Skills, and Networks*, ed. by Alison D. Morrison-Low and others (Leiden and Boston: Brill, 2012), pp. 21–39

KISHLANSKY, MARK, *A Monarchy Transformed, Britain 1603-1714* (London: Allen Lane, 1996)

KNUTSON, HAROLD C., *The Triumph of Wit: Molière and Restoration Comedy* (Columbus: Ohio State University Press, 1988)

KUHN, THOMAS S., *The Copernican Revolution: Planetary Astronomy in the Development of Western Thought* (Cambridge, MA: Harvard University Press, 1957)

LACEY, ROBERT, *Robert, Earl of Essex* (New York: Atheneum, 1971)

LAWNER, LYNNE, *Harlequin on the Moon: Commedia dell'Arte and the Visual Arts* (New York: Harry N. Abrahams, 1998)

LEVIN, CAROLE, *The Heart and Stomach of a King: Elizabeth I and the Politics of Sex and Power* (Philadelphia: University of Pennsylvania Press, 1994)

LINK, FREDERICK M., *Aphra Behn* (New York: Twayne Publishers, 1968)

The London Stage, 1660-1800, ed. by William Van Lennep, Emmett L. Avery, and others, 5 vols in 11 (Carbondale: Southern Illinois University Press, 1960–1968)

MAZOUER, CHARLES, *Le Théâtre d'Arlequin: Comédies et comédiens en France au XVIIᵉ siècle* (Fasano et Paris: Schena editore et Presses de l'Université Paris-Sorbonne, 2002)

MAZZIO, CARLO, 'Shakespeare and Science, c. 1600', *South Central Review*, 26.1/2 (2009), 1–23

McCOLLEY, GRANT, 'The Third Edition of Francis Godwin's *The Man in the Moon*', *The Library*, s4, 17.4 (1937), 472-75

McKEON, MICHAEL, 'Historicizing Patriarchy: The Emergence of Gender Difference in England, 1660-1760', *Eighteenth-Century Studies*, 28.3 (1995), 295-322

McLEOD, JANE, *Licensing Loyalty: Printers, Patrons, and the State in Early Modern France* (University Park: Pennsylvania State University Press, 2011)

McCLURE, ELLEN, *Sunspots and the Sun King: Sovereignty and Mediation in Seventeenth-Century France* (Urbana: University of Illinois Press, 2006)

MILLER, JOHN, *Charles II* (London: Weidenfeld and Nicolson, 1991)

——*James II* (1978. New Haven: Yale University Press 2000)

——*Popery and Politics in England 1660-1688* (Cambridge: Cambridge University Press, 1973)

MULLER, FRANS, 'Flying Dragons and Dancing Chairs at the Dorset Garden: Staging *Dioclesian*', *Theatre Notebook*, 47.2 (1993), 80–95

Musical Theatre at the Court of Louis XIV: Le Mariage de la Grosse Cathos, trans. and ed. by Rebecca Harris-Warrick and Carol G. Marsh (Cambridge: Cambridge University Press, 2005)

O'BRIEN, JOHN, *Harlequin Britain: Pantomime and Entertainment 1690-1760*

(Baltimore: Johns Hopkins University Press, 2004)

O'DONNELL, MARY ANN, *Aphra Behn: An Annotated Bibliography of Primary and Secondary Sources*, 2nd edn (Burlington, VT: Ashgate, 2004)

OWEN, SUSAN J., *Restoration Theatre and Crisis* (Oxford: Clarendon Press, 1996)

RAVEL, JEFFREY S., *The Contested Parterre: Public Theatre and French Political Culture 1680–1791* (New York: Cornell University Press, 1999)

ROBERTS, DAVID, *Thomas Betterton: The Greatest Actor of the Restoration Stage* (Cambridge: Cambridge University Press, 2010)

The Routledge Companion to Commedia dell'Arte, ed. by Judith Chaffee and Olly Crick (New York: Routledge, 2015)

SACKVILLE-WEST, V., *Aphra Behn: The Incomparable Astrea* (1927. New York: Viking Press, 1928)

SCHMITT, NATALIE CROHN, '*Commedia dell'Arte*: Characters, Scenarios, and Rhetoric', *Text and Performance Quarterly*, 24.1 (2004), 55–73

SCHOCHET, GORDON J., 'Partriarchalism, Politics and Mass Attitudes in Stuart England', *Historical Journal*, 12.3 (1969), 413-41

SCOTT, VIRGINIA, *The Commedia dell'Arte in Paris: 1644-1697* (Charlottesville: University Press of Virginia, 1990)

—— 'The *Jeu* and the *Rôle*: Analysis of the Appeals of the Italian Comedy in France in the Time of Arlequin-Dominique', in *Western Popular Theatre*, ed. by David Mayer and Kenneth Richards (London: Methuen, 1977), 1–27

—— '"My Lord, the Parterre": Space, Society, and Symbol in the Seventeenth-Century French Theatre', *Theatre Symposium. A Journal of the Southeastern Theatre Conference*, 4 (1996), 62–75

SPRING, JOHN R., 'Dorset Garden Theatre: Playhouse or Opera House', *Theatre Notebook*, 34.2 (1980), 60-69

Théâtre du XVIIe siècle, gen. ed. Jacques Sherer and others (Paris: Gallimard, 1975–1992), vol. 3, ed. by Jacques Truchet and André Blanc (1992)

TODD, JANET, *The Secret Life of Aphra Behn* (London: André Deutsch, 1996)

TURNER, HENRY S., *The English Renaissance Stage: Geometry, Poetics, and the Practical and Spatial Arts 1580–1630* (Oxford: Oxford University Press, 2006)

VAN HELDEN, ALBERT, 'The Telescope in the Seventeenth Century', *Isis*, 65.1 (1974), 38–58

WESTMAN, ROBERT S., *The Copernican Question: Prognostication, Skepticism, and Celestial Order* (Berkeley: University of California Press, 2011)

WILSON, JOHN HAROLD, 'Theatre Notes from the Newdigate Newsletters', *Theatre Notebook*, 15.3 (1961), 79–84

WOODCOCK, GEORGE, *Aphra Behn: The English Sappho* (1948. Montréal: Black Rose Books, 1989)

Lightning Source UK Ltd.
Milton Keynes UK
UKHW020009191219
355627UK00003B/143/P